CONTEMPORARY TOTALITARIANISM

A SYSTEMS APPROACH

BY
ALEXANDER KORCHAK

EAST EUROPEAN MONOGRAPHS, BOULDER
DISTRIBUTED BY COLUMBIA UNIVERSITY PRESS, NEW YORK

1994

EAST EUROPEAN MONOGRAPHS, NO. CDII

Dedicated to the memory of Andrei Sakharov

ACKNOWLEDGMENTS

I owe a debt of gratitude to my daughter Vera, who patiently translated the manuscript, and without whose continuous encouragement this book would never have been completed. Also, I would like to express my deepest thanks to Professor Fisher-Galati, whose effort made this book possible. I am also grateful to Kathy Perez for proofreading and typesetting the material.

ALEXANDER KORCHAK

July 11, 1994

PREFACE

This investigation originated from the attempts to explain the reasons of Stalin's tyranny and, in particular, its connection with the Russian statehood. It was completed before the disintegration of the communist empire. The disintegration itself revealed many aspects of the mechanism of totalitarian power, however, few changes in the text were necessary. The reason was that general functional regularities of the contemporary totalitarianism were accentuated, rather than its individual varieties represented by individual ideologies. This circumstance, together with chances of the recurrence of any variety of totalitarianism, justifies this publication.

Even a cursory acquaintance with Russian history reveals that Russian autocracy bears some very specific features, among which the most noticeable are: a continuous centuries-long expansion of the state, a permanent warfare of the apparatus of power against its own people up to their complete enslavement followed by partial liberation, enigmatic vacillations of domestic policy (reform - anti-reform), and many others which do not lend themselves to an easy explanation of Russia's intermediate position between the West and the East alone. This is why Russian autocracy should probably be considered an exclusive rather than an intermediate form of autocracy.

The simplest model of autocracy contains three major elements, separated by isolating barriers: a supreme leader (tsar, emperor, chief, tyrant), an apparatus of rule, and a population under control. The distinctive character of Russian history and history of Russian statehood is usually associated with the third element: serfdom, legacy of the Mongol Yoke, poor development of civil society, ignorance of the population, and so on. The distinctive character of the centralized apparatus of power as an independent element is usually not taken into account, or it is considered of a secondary, or even third-rate, importance, still associated with the ignorance and submissiveness of the masses ("Every people is worth its rulers"). This attitude was demonstrated by Westernizers and Slavophiles, Soilists and Eurasists.

The cornerstone in the foundation of this apparatus of power was laid by Peter the Great in his "Table on Ranks" which established a single hierarchical (fourteen levels!) order of service in military and civil departments. Such a two-hierarchical system of state administration, which is subjugated to the autocrat and in which the civil and military hierarchies are inter-connected at the upper levels and even integrated into one another, creates a more stable and conservative apparatus of power. Together with semi-military terminology (e.g., general-governor, captain-executive), such features as semi-military discipline, subordination, and rank worship were incorporated into civil administration for the very reason that the army is the most universal and simple, polished-over-centuries, system of subjugation and centralization of power. However, the most important property of such two-hierarchical semi-Eastern autocratic systems of power is the creation of more perfect mechanisms of hierarchical selection, which forwards an "industrial" reproduction of bureaucracy and gradually increases the isolation of the apparatus of power and the autocrat from the population.

Preserving autocracy after the October Communist Revolution, and even its strengthening (conversion into totalitarian tyranny), is usually explained by Russia's intermediacy, or its serfdom, or the specific mentality of Russian people, and so on. All these explanations ignore the fact that it was the isolated bureaucratic apparatus of power that turned out to be the most conservative and viable element of tsarist autocracy. Almost all classes and strata of pre-revolutionary Russia, including the most numerous one - peasantry, were exterminated almost completely. As for the apparatus of autocratic rule, it not only survived, but even strengthened and perfected itself, transforming into the totalitarian one. Its restructuring was carried out very gradually, carefully, in direct opposition to how all strata and classes were treated. Lenin himself testifies to it: "We call ours an apparatus which is still alien to us, which is still a bourgeois and tsarist jumble..." He said it two years after the ending of the Civil War! It took almost twenty years (it was finished by the time of the Second World War) to complete the transformation of the tsarist apparatus into a soviet, new one. And was it really "new"? Because replacing old functionaries ("old specialists") with new ones (party - soviet ones) does not imply that the system of centralized bureaucratic power changes, because it is universal in its main features.

Transition from tsarist autocracy to communist totalitarianism meant, first of all, an unprecedented reproduction of bureaucracy and its expansion into all spheres and "cracks" of society. In this process, its inner structure and inner social and economic mechanism was simplified rather than made more complex. This was achieved partially by replacing the Orthodox Church with Marxist-Leninist ideology, primitive in its essence. However, the main tool used was regular selective repressions - not only against certain individuals, outstanding in this or that respect, but also against whole layers of society, and even against whole nations. Bureaucratization of the whole society made it more uniform and simple. This is why it seemed possible that methods of exact sciences can be successfully used for its study. The author could not resist the temptation to make such an attempt. In this connection, the book is provided with a special Appendix, which contains popularized explanations of the main concepts of the systems theory. In particular, much attention is given to self-organized systems usually studied in biology. Much space is given to the analysis of the Marxist-Leninist ideology. One may ask whether it is justified now, after the ideology's universal collapse? As an excuse, the author can put forward the consideration that its decline is undoubtedly temporary and it is caused by the collapse of the corresponding organizations. The latter are already starting to resuscitate under new names and new slogans. Besides, it is unavoidable that any totalitarian system of power has to lean upon some totalitarian ideology. The author is attempting to show the connection between the two in general form.

CONTENTS

CONTENTS

INTRODUCTION

One of the unexpected results of a seven-year *perestroika* is the ease and rapidity with which ruling communist parties - in an effort to retain vanishing power - denied, and are still denying, all communist attributes and programs. It confirms, however, the evident truth that power is the communists' end in itself. As for ideology, it is only a means of capturing and holding this power.

Another unexpected lesson is the dramatic drop in the number of ideologized citizens, and the influence of ideology in general, after the fall of communist regimes. As soon as power was lost and elements of coercion disappeared, the number of "voluntarily convinced" communists dropped down to the regular social fluctuations.

Defeated ruling communist parties almost everywhere went underground, having reserved their most reliable cadres (incorporating them into new democratic structures and businesses) and even considerable material possessions. The present situation reminds one of the time before the 1917 October coup in Russia: economic ruin, universal dissatisfaction of the population, and hidden Bolshevism (now with the prefix "neo", and touched with brown) aimed at again capturing power. One needs to be a great optimist to maintain hope that whatever democratic changes take place, they will be able to eliminate, or at least neutralize, this menacing, skillfully camouflaged (as Social-Democratic, Socialist, Islamist, for example) opposition. Bolshevism engulfed many more countries, and took deeper roots in their social and political structure, than fascism before the Second World War, and to neutralize the latter the Nuremberg process was needed.

The main difference between neo-Bolshevism and orthodox Bolshevism is that the former does not include an international dimension. But even for orthodox Bolshevism, this dimension serves only to justify outward expansion and to control centrifugal nationalistic forces. Having got rid of this dimension, neo-Bolshevism can rapidly transform (and is already doing so) into national-Bolshevism, which is even more dangerous for society. This is the third lesson of *perestroika*.

The developments in the Soviet system beginning in 1956 - the Twentieth Party Congress, the dismissal of Khruschev, the Soviet occupation of Czechoslovakia - made me turn my attention from science to questions of world view. I wanted to review my own perceptions towards the obligatory Marxist-Leninist ideology, and to understand its role in twentieth-century history. Little

1

by little, I arrived at a simple truth. Ideology is only one of many effective means used by various totalitarian organizations to achieve their goals. The secret of the unlimited power of such dictators as Stalin, Hitler, Mao, Hussein, Castro and Kadaffi is in the specific organizations that supported (and support) their power. The ideologies can be very different. The organizational principles are, on the contrary, very similar and, in fact, extremely simple. What are they?

In this work, I investigate an intrinsic structure of ruling apparatuses (bureaucracies) in a totalitarian state. Using a systems approach together with the modeling method, I study the evolution of totalitarian regimes. I am using Bolshevism as an example.

The strength of Bolshevism is in its specific organization, combining elements of both mafia and bureaucracy. Lenin recognized the importance of this combination long ago, disguising his "invention" as an innocent-appearing principle, combining both legal and illegal activity (*What is To Be Done?*, 1902). The principle of "democratic centralism" (1906) is nothing but an organizational form for this utterly successful camouflage: democracy for legal, open activity and centralism for illegal, conspiratory acts. Using this "organic synthesis" of a small conspiratory nucleus of professional revolutionists with broad labor organization, it was very simple to capture power in Russia. This organizational principle defined the whole evolution of the Bolshevik party. When power was captured, this principle was embodied in the whole system of state power; it penetrated its whole structure and all spheres of its activity. On this organizational structure, as on a matrix, all totalitarian regimes of our century were reproduced, with minor differences due to varying national and territorial features.

To understand this organizational and functional structure, it is important to digress from these national and territorial features, and ideological variations, and to consider the phenomenon of totalitarianism as a system of power rigidly connected with the social structure of society. Although notions of "systems" and a "systems approach" are currently permeating all natural sciences and many social ones as well, considerable effort and practice are needed to operate them correctly.

A systems approach (described briefly) is a consideration of complex objects as systems, concentrating attention on their fragmentation into parts (sub-systems), studying intrinsic ties between these parts, and disclosing the wholeness of the object in its interaction with its environment. Thus, a totalitarian (and any other) bureaucracy can be considered a system and subjected to a systems approach if, by some uniform method, we can distinguish within it certain sub-systems, as well as define a boundary separating it from society (its environment). Again, it should be analyzed using some uniform method, independent of any individual bureaucratic apparatus' specific features. As for the modeling method, in essence its idea is to simplify reality - to distinguish some specific facets or processes within the studied object, which can be described by a finite number of parameters - and therefore, to formalize the study - to simplify and abridge it. Such formalization can be omitted at first reading, without detriment to the understanding of main conclusions.

The family is an example of the simplest and most common system. A systems approach to its study would be to investigate the relationships between a grandfather and a grandson, a mother-in-law and a daughter-in-law, and/or a husband and a wife, rather than those of John and Peter, Margaret and Susan, Peter and Jane, as is the case in fictional literature. Great effort and a special approach are needed to be able to ignore all the infinite varieties of personalities, and to study in an abstract manner these basic relations that go deep into the biological nature of humans.

The key and most stable structural element of any totalitarian regime of our time is an autonomous bureaucratic department. Here the abstract relationships would be those of a higher-level and a lower-level functionary, of a boss and his subordinates. The abstract relations depend on the character of the official hierarchy, the hierarchical level, administrative tasks, national and local traditions and many other factors, and their roots also go deep into the biological nature of man. In this case, we would study both these relationships and also their influence on the structure of the departments, as well as their interrelations in the totalitarian structure.

The major shortcoming of all studies of bureaucracies is that they do not account for the dynamics of the phenomenon. I am making an attempt to trace the evolution of bureaucratic systems in a totalitarian state. I distinguish three stages in this evolution: 1) partocracy (the term was first introduced by Avtorkhanov) - a young totalitarianism characterized by inward expansion into the society (outward expansion is also starting); 2) commandocracy - a command administrative system, mature totalitarianism (in Russia it is the Brezhnev era) characterized by outward expansion (inward expansion continues); 3) gangocracy - degenerating totalitarianism in which inward expansion is exhausted and outward expansion slows down due to inner and outer reasons.

It is shown that in its evolution, bureaucracy acquires some features of so-called self-organizing systems. Such systems are studies mainly in biology. In them, the relationship between sub-systems has a probability character rather than a rigid one. Hence, such systems are characterized by the utmost dynamism in their interaction with the environment, by the utmost adjustability and stability. The major difficulty with the systems approach to the bureaucracy study is determining the links of the sub-systems to the environment. In biology, this problem is overcome by considering the hierarchy of self-organizing structures as a whole: a molecule, a cell, an organism, population, biocenosis, biosphere. It is not very probable that such a distinct chain can be defined in a human socium, however. Still, it is shown below that when the dynamics of bureaucracy are studied we can, using analogy, distinguish two interrelated factors: a universally human (external) one, and a structural one. In a totalitarian society, the basic structure consists of an autonomous hierarchically centralized department. It is characterized by the vertical three-layer structure typical of all mafia-type organizations: a command element ("dome"), an apparatus, and executors ("buttons"). This structure can restore itself through the mechanism of self-organization. Commandocracy is a hierarchy of such departments. It combines a stable conservatism of the party bureaucracy with the dynamism and conspiracy of a mafia. Such systems are extremely stable and are not reformable from the inside. They only oscillate about some equilibrium state, adjusting to changes in the environment. Therefore, all restructurings of the system of power, including the latest one, are caused by a change of outer conditions. In responding to them, a shift in the "backbone" of power takes place. Let us consider two examples: Stalinism and the Brezhnev era.

First, Stalin's single-handed dictatorship was based on the relative independence of two autonomous departments: the Party apparatus and the Security. In order to preserve his power, he needed to sustain the independence of these two departments, which he achieved by periodically setting them against each other. At such an approach, Stalin is nothing more than a talented (maybe even a genius) functionary of the system, who best fit the task and used ideological cover in a very masterly manner to conceal it. The way it was incarnated in the organizational and functional structure of these departments and the whole Stalinist system - this is the key question to be studied at the systems approach.

During the Brezhnev era, the system of state power was based on a stable equilibrium among three departments: the Party, State Security and the Army (including the military-industrial complex). It was the system's super-stability that gave rise to its stagnation. By the mid-1970s, a fast augmentation of State Security (KGB) began, comparable in its scale with the tremendous growth of the years 1920-24 and of the 1930s. As in these two previous cases, sooner or later the growth of the KGB had to cause a shift of power in the system's "backbone", leading to the subsequent restructuring of the whole system. It was this "tectonic" shift that is responsible for the latest *perestroika*, in spite of the particular reasons that caused this growth: the degradation of the Brezhnev party apparatus, the eradication of dissidence, or the necessity to steal industrial secrets from the West. So, this *perestroika* could be predicted a decade before it began. But its character and direction - could they be predicted too?

If one assumes that *perestroika* means radical change in the system of power, as, for example, was the case after Lenin's death (rather than just economic reforms, or shifts in domestic and foreign policy, or the reformulation of economic dogmas), then some predictions were possible and they are discussed below. Such radical *perestroika* did not start until mid-1988 and only lasted for about one year. From the offset, it was clear that its aim was to restore an elastic two-hierarchical system of power such as Lenin envisioned, with the addition that the two main posts (those of Secretary General and the head of the parallel hierarchy of the soviets) were combined into one. It did not happen, however, since the ruling party began to disintegrate and fall apart before the hierarchy of the soviets was reanimated and gained any real power.

CHAPTER ONE
SCIENTIFIC TOTALITARIANISM

Totalitarian states can be found throughout history. But what is so special about contemporary totalitarianism? How does the present epoch of scientific and technological revolution affect it?

Before we try to answer these questions, let us distinguish the most characteristic feature of a totalitarian state, common to all its varieties: the unification, co-subordination, and even amalgamation of three major hierarchies - those of power, money (property) and knowledge (science). These hierarchies are distinct in any society since the origination of states. When they amalgamate, the personal sphere narrows to its limit, and the ability of civil society to oppose, restrict, and control state power gradually decreases. (This results in the well-known features of a totalitarian state: "absolute control over all aspects of life,...complete regulation by the state of all legal organizations, discretionary power in the hands of the rulers, prohibition of all democratic organizations, and liquidation of constitutional rights and freedoms" - *Big Soviet Encyclopedia*). The degree to which the sphere, in which citizens are allowed (and are able) to exercise free choice[1], is reduced characterizes the degree of "totalitariazation" of a society.

To illustrate this point, let us look at some totalitarian systems of the past. In Ancient Egypt, power was constituted by two parallel hierarchies: religious (priests) and governmental (functionaries). Their relative independence from each other created good conditions for the authoritarian rule of the idolized Pharaoh. To strengthen and stabilize this power, a third, military hierarchy (army) was used. As for the origins of Chinese totalitarianism (Zin Empire, 221-206 B.C.), the power of the Emperor was based on the relative independence of the bureaucracy and the army, with a third hierarchy, censors, used for safeguarding purposes (a prototype of the KGB). Later, this system of power was cemented by a unique form of religion/philosophy. In both cases, as in many other varieties of ancient totalitarianism, the hierarchy of money (wealth) was incapable of being formed independently, and so it almost totally merged with the hierarchy of power. The hierarchy of knowledge (science) was formed either within the hierarchy of priests or within the bureaucracy, and also was not independent. This is how the totalitarian system of society was created, in which

---

[1]Choice of profession, place of residency, as well as freedom to obtain and disseminate information - the ability and possibility to exercise free choice of alternatives is a key characteristic of human personality, which is rooted deep in its psyche.

the economy was based on public or state ownership of land, and on artisan work-shops, a partial or total enslavement of the population (a so-called "Asian" method of production).

The foundation for the political power of contemporary totalitarianism is created by different combinations of the three hierarchies: political party, army and security. When two of them dominate and are relatively independent (a two-hierarchical system), then balancing above is a "cult of personality", whose authoritarian, dictatorial rule does not differ much from that of a Pharaoh or Khan (such were Stalin, Hitler, Mao and other smaller cults). Also, there is very little variety in the way the property hierarchy (hierarchy of wealth) is subjugated: it is total nationalization ("collectivization") of all national riches and means of production, with their subsequent transformation into the collective (or "joint private", as in Ancient Sparta) property of the ruling class of the bureaucracy ("*nomenclatura*"). Such "collectivization", together with the prohibition of private property for citizens, transforms distribution into a controlling factor to enslave the entire population.

It is more difficult to deal with the hierarchy of knowledge. If before the Renaissance, science developed mainly "in the solitude of monasteries", now the hierarchy of knowledge embraces dozens of sciences, does not recognize state borders, and is often integrated into production. Hence, no government (a concrete hierarchy of power) is able to subordinate it and can only try to control it indirectly within its borders by controlling information, finances and education. But even such control is not always effective. That is why a contemporary totalitarianism, in its desire to be in total control of information, isolates the whole state from the outer world, and also totally enslaves scientists by depriving them of all independent (from the government) means of existence. The physical and economic coercion of scientists is complemented by an ideological one; i.e., by compulsory assertion of ideology above all sciences.

Contemporary totalitarianism, unlike totalitarianism of the past, is ideological rather than religious - which makes it more sinister and anti-human. Any religion makes all people equal before God thus excluding individuals from any earthly hierarchies. All great religions gave a person freedom of choice between good and evil (Augustinius: "Freedom of a man is freedom to do evil"), and freedom to choose a concrete faith (Kierkegaard: "Faith is not knowledge, it is an act of freedom, expression of free will"). The ideology of totalitarianism does not offer anything comparable to this freedom of choice, although it usually proclaims "freedom, equality and brotherhood". Implanted coercively, contrary to religion, it does not leave any freedom of choice to an individual in any sphere of human creative activity. Aggressively restricting and oppressing individuals, ideology retards human development, making men passive and infantile.

Ideology is a very important element of contemporary totalitarianism. It isolates (ideologically) society from the outer world, shapes party morals, creates a foundation for party ritual, forms a specific language (slang for communication between functionaries), and serves to distinguish between "us" and "them". Its key function is to ensure the directed hierarchical selection to the ruling top. Still, the main element of contemporary totalitarianism, the one which determines its special character, is not ideology, but "organization".

The contemporary epoch of scientific and technological progress with its electronics, cybernetics and computerization not only perfected means of communication and information, but also unimaginably perfected means of disinformation, espionage and conspiracy. This in its turn created unprecedented favorable conditions for successful activity of a small, tightly united and purposeful organization of a mafia-type and its capability to capture power in a contemporary state in periods of social cataclysms, as was the case, for example, in Russia, China and other countries. For the first time in the history of civilization, there appeared a possibility to scientifically manipulate human masses. For the first time, the proclivity of the party-state bureaucracy toward uncontrollable growth and conservatism was complemented by, and organically combined with, the dynamism and purposefulness of mafia (*partomafia*).

One of the most frequent misconceptions made is to assume that ideology is to blame for the accumulation of social, political and economic crimes, for horrible miscalculations and absurdities, for genocide, for rivers of blood and piles of corpses. In fact, ideology is secondary, and primary is organization. Any ideology was always formed - and is formed - on the basis of some teaching (Marxism, racism, panarabism, panslavism, for example), but it is a concrete political organization that transforms the teaching into ideology. The teaching is being stretched onto a rigid organizational structure as a caftan, which is then mended in the places of rupture and adjusted to the figure. In particular, it is erroneous to call Marxism an ideology (it is only a teaching), as there is no (and there never has been) a corresponding organization. But Marxism gave rise to Social Democracy (LaSalle, Bernstein, and others), various forms of contemporary socialism, as well as Marxism-Leninism, Trotskyism, Maoism and other "isms" adjusted to serve concrete organizations. It is they, and especially their leadership, that are responsible for crimes against peoples in our totalitarian century.

The organizational and functional structures of ruling political parties, cemented by ideology, make contemporary totalitarianism a unique phenomenon in human history. The ancient totalitarian regimes of Egypt and Sumeria were unable either to collectivize all lands and all production, nor totally control all spheres of human activity. They preserved spheres of private ownership and private interests. Totalitarian China always preserved local self-government and civil society by allowing various religions and philosophical schools to exist. Contemporary ideological and technological totalitarianism reached an unprecedented level of totalitariazation, leaving far behind not only all regimes of the past, but, to a certain degree, previously unimaginable anti-utopias of Zamiatin, Huxley, Orwell, and others. After the Bolshevik Revolution, it took totalitarianism only two to three decades to spread to all continents, but with the same rapidity it entered a phase of degradation - as soon as it exhausted its potential for inward expansion within the society and its outward expansion slowed down. This evolution is contained in its organizational structure, which combines elements of mafia (hence the dynamism of its expansion) and of bureaucratic absolutism with its permanent and inevitable "sluggishly progressing schizophrenia". A high degree of totalitariazation leads to the final destruction of all spheres of human activity, which in its turn accelerates the disintegration of society.

The combination of certain aspects of mafia dynamism with that of party-state bureaucratic conservatism is the most distinguishing feature of twentieth-century totalitarianism.

CHAPTER TWO
"DEMOCRATIC" BUREAUCRATISM

1. Introduction: On Terminology

Whatever is said about the present-day integration among sciences, exact sciences still differ, essentially by their study methods, from the "not exact" social sciences. That is why disputes about the origin and nature of bureaucracy, exacerbated over recent years, look rather strange to an exact scientist. The impression is that those involved in them are too much bound by their own social, political or group position and that their goal is a verbal victory over their opponents rather than the truth. Similar situations can take place in the exact sciences, too, but as a rare exception, and they would be considered a scientific pathology. Terminology is a good example: the meanings of terms can be "stretched out", or made ambiguous or otherwise manipulated. Let us consider, for example, the terms "democratic centralism" and "bureaucratism". They have been "paired" for more than seven decades and are frequently found in the pages of socio-political literature.

The first of them is defined as follows: "Democratic centralism, the organizational principle of construction of the communist and labor parties. It implies the electivity of the ruling bodies from bottom to top, their periodical accounting before their party organizations and higher organs, subordination of minority to majority, obligatory character of decisions by higher organs for their subordinates. <u>Democratic centralism also serves as the foundation for the construction and activity of the state, management, all social organizations both in the USSR and all other socialist countries.</u>" (*Big Soviet Encyclopedia*, 3rd edition, underlined by author).

This is one of the latest, most universally accepted definitions (although it has never been essentially altered). The underlined words that demonstrate the term's universality may put forward a question: is it possible that the total bureaucratization of all socialist countries can be linked to this principle of organization? A positive answer to this question would mean the recognition of the *definitio realis* (the reality of the term). Then, are not the principles of democratic centralism and bureaucratic centralism in fact identical?

By the rules of logic, the above definition can be considered a definition of a notion if it describes all its essential features, and they do not contradict each other. Only in this case, will the notion reflect reality or, in other words, will it satisfy the requirements of objectivity.

This is the formal side of the problem. But what do we have in reality? What we have is that over seven decades, whenever and wherever the term was applied to the organizations attempting to equilibrate centralization and democracy, centralization inevitably forced out democracy with the growth of the organization. Wherever democratic centralism was introduced (e.g., in a political party, state organization or trade union) the ultimate result was pure centralism. In other words, the electivity in such organizations was little by little substituted by appointments from above, which made any accounting of the minority to the majority void of sense, and the subordination of minority to majority evolved into its opposite. Somehow centralization "devoured" democracy, and therefore democratic centralism transformed into bureaucratic centralism. And there has not been a single exception over all these years. The question is - why? This question leads us directly to the formulation of the problem of bureaucracy (see Chapter 4, sections 1 and 3).

In what ways did the supporters of democratic centralism disguise this playing with the terms and the reality itself? They used (and still use) a variety of methods, including the vagueness of the term "democracy" itself. The principle of democratic centralism is always utilized by hierarchical organizations, for which the notion of democracy has to be essentially narrowed (see Chapter 4, section 2). The definition of "democratic centralism", however, does not even mention hierarchy as an essential feature,[2] although it hints slightly of it: "higher organs and their subordinate organs". This creates a possibility to manipulate the definition of democracy. Further, a centralized hierarchy is used for the construction of the army, bureaucracies, and other similar organizations for the very reason that this is a universal principle of making the majority obey the minority. This is why "hierarchy" is omitted on purpose from the list of the main features - to avoid an evident contradiction and undesirable analogies. Now the term "democracy" in its wide (hierarchical) meaning can be split into bourgeois, petty bourgeois, proletarian, peasant and other democracies, thus completely disguising the essence of the problem, its acuteness. Such splitting would be void of sense when applied to the closed hierarchical organizations.

As a second example, let us compare the terms "bureaucracy" and "bureaucratism". Bureaucracy is known since the origination of states, and by the beginning of this century its definition in Russian was: "It is the character of

---

[2]And not only hierarchy, but other important signs of a real democratic centralism as well, such as professionalism and conspiracy.

the state rule in countries where power is concentrated in the hands of the central governmental bodies, the latter acting by commands (from above) and through commands (sent down); also bureaucracy is a class of people totally separated from the rest of society and made up of these agents of the central power."[3]

From a contemporary viewpoint, it would be more correct to say "the system of the state rule", rather than "the character". Then the system and the people compose what is now called an "organization". One more detail should also be taken into account: the definition is too narrow as it refers only to state bureaucracy. There also exists another bureaucracy - not a state one. Nevertheless, the definition quite precisely reflects the essence of the phenomenon, but it took almost seven decades to admit it.[4] Soon after the revolution, such an approach to the term became politically disadvantageous because of the rapid bureaucratization of the state ruling apparatus. For this reason, Lenin began to instill another term: "bureaucratism".[5] Later, this derivative term began to force out the original one, and after being redefined, it became applicable only to the "pre-socialist" formations.[6] Much later, and only because of the intolerable and overwhelming dominance of bureaucracy, a slow

---

[3] And further: "Foreign term 'bureaucratic' fully corresponds to the Russian word 'scrivener'. In Western Europe, the development of bureaucracy was parallel to organization and the strengthening of state power. Administrative centralization accompanied the political one as its support. In a police state, bureaucracy achieves maximum prosperity. Decentralization and self-governing are the only ways to weaken it." (Brockgauz, Evfron, 1891, Vol. 9).

[4] See contemporary definition of bureaucracy in *Big Soviet Encyclopedia*, 3rd edition. "It is a specific form of social organizations (political, economical, ideological) in a society, where centers of executive power are practically independent from the majority of the society."

[5] It is an abstract noun derived from "bureaucratic" (*Dictionary of Russian Language* by Ushakov).

[6] In the second edition of the *Big Soviet Encyclopedia* (1951, edited by S. Vavilov) bureaucratism is considered the main term ("it is the system of ruling, adherent to exploitative states..."), and bureaucracy is mentioned only in the text of this definition as a "closed privileged layer of officials". Later, in the third edition of *Small Soviet Encyclopedia* (1958, ed. by A. Vvedensky), the term "bureaucracy" is not mentioned at all, and "bureaucratism" is defined as a "bureaucratic system of ruling, typical of slave-owning, feudal and capitalist formations...". Such an approach to bureaucratism as a system of ruling only in class society has been routinely preserved in many stereotyped editions up to the present day. See, for example, the *Ozhegov Dictionary*, 20th edition, 1988. The term "bureaucracy" has never been defined separately since then.

tendency back to the initial meaning of the term can be observed. In exact sciences, such manipulations with terminology would be considered pathologic.

Let us look again at the term "democratic centralism". It is known that the term was first introduced at the Sixth Congress (also called the "uniting" Congress) of the RSRDP (Russian Social-Democratic Labor Party) in 1906,[7] as a result of the compromise between the Bolsheviks and Mensheviks (the Bolsheviks wanted centralism, and the Mensheviks wanted democracy). The further evolution of democratic centralism went along the following lines: first, Mensheviks were forced out from the organization; and then all platforms, blocks, and groups as well; followed by the total ousting and extermination of all disagreeing or merely inconvenient members of the "democratically" centralized organization. All this resulted in extreme centralization, and totally bureaucratic monolithism. Such a development has been traditionally explained by the specific conditions in Russia: tsarism and the Civil War. But the fact that such an evolution was repeated later, dozens of times, in very different - economically, culturally and historically - states, points to the existence of a law which is defined by inner - more precisely, intra-organizational - patterns. In other words, within a hierarchically centralized organization, certain processes begin to unfold which distort the equilibrium initially created between centralization and democracy, with the result of strengthening the former at the expense of the latter (see Chapter 4, section 4 and Chapter 5, section 2).

Thus, the above definition of the term "democratic centralism" neither formally nor factually corresponds to the notion defined. Moreover, it deliberately (as it will be shown below) disguises a certain reality. What kind of reality and why? To answer these questions, one has to turn to the etymology of the word and the history of the term "bureaucratic centralism".

2. Birth of Chimera ("Democratic" Centralism)

Analysis of Lenin's approach to democracy, centralization and the principle of democratic centralism can start with his work *What is to Be Done?* (1902), which is almost as important in his heritage as *The Communist Manifesto* is to the Marx and Engel's one. This is how in this work Lenin explains his understanding of the intra-party democracy:

---

[7]See, for example, *CPSU in Resolutions*, 9th edition, 1983, Vol. 1, pp. 190, 206.

Everybody will probably agree that 'broad principle of democracy' presupposes the two following necessary conditions: first, full publicity (*glasnost*), and second, election of all functions. It would be absurd to speak about democratism without publicity, a publicity that is not limited by members of the organization. We will call the German Socialist Party a democratic organization because everything it does is done publicly, even party congresses are held in public; but no one will call democratic an organization that is hidden behind a veil of secrecy from everyone but its members. The question is, what is the sense of promoting a 'broad democratic principle', when the main condition of this principle cannot be fulfilled in a secret organization? (5th edition, Vol. 6, p. 138).

And further, Lenin describes in detail the conditions in the German Social-Democratic Party, and shows that they are impossible to be brought about in Russia, so therefore all discussions about intra-party democratism are a "useless and harmful toy". In Russia, "secrecy is such an important condition for an organization that all other conditions (e.g., number and selection of members, its functions) must all be subordinated to it."

Two years after *What Is To Be Done?*, in his article "A Letter to a Friend", Lenin explains in detail how centralization and publicity should be understood:

This brings us to a highly important principle of all party organization and all party activity: while the greatest possible centralization is necessary with regard to the ideological and practical leadership of the movement and the revolutionary struggle of the proletariat, the greatest possible decentralization is necessary with regard to keeping the party center (and therefore the party as a whole) informed about the movement, and with regard to the responsibility of the party... We must also (and for this very reason, since without information centralization is impossible) as far as possible decentralize responsibility to the party on the part of its individual members, of every participant in its work, and of every circle belonging to or associated with the party... (5th edition, Vol. 7, p. 22).

After that, the thesis of the centralization of leadership and the decentralization of responsibility is repeated many times, and the article ends with significant words about how publicity should be understood: "Under the autocracy we can have no other means or weapons of inner-party publicity than keeping the party center regularly informed of party events." (Ibid., p. 24). And this is how Lenin answered the accusations of anti-democratism:

> The only serious organizational principle the active workers of our movement can accept is strict conspiracy, strict selection of members, training of professional revolutionists. If we possessed these three qualities, something even more than 'democratism' would be guaranteed for us, namely complete mutual comradely confidence among the revolutionists. And this something is absolutely essential for us, as in Russia it is useless to think that democratic control can serve as a substitute for it. It would be a great mistake to believe, that because it is impossible to establish real 'democratic' control, the members of a revolutionary organization will remain altogether uncontrolled. They do not have time to think about the toy forms of democratism (democratism within a closed and compact body of comrades in which complete mutual confidence prevails), but they have a lively sense of responsibility, because they know from experience that the organization of real revolutionists will stop at nothing to rid itself of any unfit member. (*What Is To Be Done?*, p. 141).

Let us have a closer look at the formula of the extreme centralization of leadership combined with the extreme decentralization of responsibility. Where is this principle accomplished? In the army, the extreme centralization of leadership is accompanied by the extreme centralization of responsibility. Decentralization of responsibility is to a certain degree akin to any administration, and, in particular, bureaucracy. But even in this latter case, centralization is never extreme; it always co-exists with elements of hierarchical democracy and publicity. The answer is evident: the extreme centralization of leadership is combined with the extreme decentralization of responsibility in mafias, and any conspirative plot-making organizations, that struggle against state power or the whole society by terrorist methods. Lenin does not conceal it, though: "It would be extremely naive to fear the accusations that we, social-democrats, desire to create a conspirative organization." (Ibid., p. 136).

All reasoning about intra-party democracy refers to specific Russian conditions under autocracy. In reality, however, extreme centralization and conspiracy were the pivotal ideas of party structure, because the mechanism of the reverse evolution was excluded. Neither centralism, nor conspiracy, were revoked or softened after the revolution, when autocracy was dead, and specific conditions of tsarism did not exist any more. Soon the references to the special conditions of the Civil War were dropped too, which not in the least softened centralization or conspiracy. On the contrary, the Tenth Party Congress (1921) adopted two resolutions aimed at strengthening centralization and getting rid of intra-party democracy. Moreover, when Comintern was created, the extreme centralism, together with the conspirative party apparatus, were instilled in all communist parties, even in democratic countries. Written by Lenin and adopted at the Second Comintern Congress (1920), membership regulations said: "Parties - members of the Communist International must be built up on the principle of democratic centralism. In the present epoch of the acute Civil War, the communist party will be able to perform its duties only if it is organized in the most centralized manner, only if an iron discipline bordering on a military one prevails in it, and if its party center is a powerful body of authority enjoying wide powers and the general confidence of the members of the party." (5th edition, Vol. 41, p. 209). "They [communists] must create a parallel illegal apparatus everywhere, so that it could help the party in the decisive moment to carry out its duty before the revolution." (Ibid., p. 206).

References to the specific conditions in Russia in fact disguised and concealed a special goal: world revolution. Bolshevism is indissolubly connected with this goal and the idea that its exclusiveness and grandeur justify any extreme measures, including terror. Only beginning in the mid-1930s was this goal relegated to second place. It was accompanied by the destruction of the old bolshevist guard, and its verbal attributes (e.g., Comintern, Internationale, World Organization of Proletarian Revolution) gradually disappeared from the slogans. But it did not mean at all that the attitude towards the extreme measures changed. It did not, because the intrinsic structure of the ruling party did not change either. Hence a new "grand" goal was proclaimed: construction of socialism in "one, separately taken country".

In his work *What is to be Done?*, Lenin develops another idea, closely linked to the first one - the idea of two organizations: an organization of revolutionists and an organization of laborers, closely ("organically") connected between themselves. Lenin writes: "Organization of workers should, first, be professional; second, it should be as wide as possible; third, as little conspirative as possible (it stands to reason that what I say here and below refers only to autocratic Russia). On the contrary, organization of revolutionists must consist first and foremost of people whose profession is that of a revolutionist (that is why I speak of organization of revolutionists meaning revolutionists/social democrats)... Such an organization must of necessity be not too extensive but as secret as possible." (Vol. 6, p. 112). What should be the relationships between the two organizations? They should be like this:

> A small, compact core consisting of the most reliable, most experienced and hardened workers, with responsible agents in all principal districts and connected by all rules of the most strict conspiracy, with the organization of revolutionists, is able to carry out, with wide support of the masses, and without an elaborate organization perform all functions of a professional organization, and besides, perform them in exactly such way which is desirable for social-democracy. This is the only way to attain continuity and development, in spite of all *gendarmes*, of the social-democratic professional movement. (Ibid., p. 119).

The idea of two organizations is thus reduced to the absolute subordination of all professional labor organizations to the party by means of the disguised penetration of its representatives into these organizations.

Such are the origins of "democratic" centralism, as they are expressed in *What is to be Done?*. After the revolution, Lenin renounced neither the idea of leadership centralization together with responsibility decentralization, nor the idea of two organizations, of which the larger one is virtually playing the role of the periphery of the first one. Organization of revolutionists (party) is very centralized, hierarchical, professional and conspirative. While all labor organizations are subordinate to and controlled by it, they are also democratically centralized, but with a cut, controlled democracy.

All this was revealed to its fullest in the well-known discussion about trade unions, just before the Tenth Congress. A half-year after the Congress, in the draft theses on the role and tasks of trade unions under the NEP (New Economic Policy) Lenin wrote: "The Politburo directs the Orgbureau to set up under the Orgbureau of the Central Committee a special commission to check and replace some of the leading officials (and if possible, all communist functionaries) in the trade union movement for the purpose of intensifying the struggle against petty-bourgeois, S.R. (social-revolutionary), Menshevik, and anarchist influences and deviations." (Vol. 44, p. 355). These theses were written on January 4, 1922, and they were marked with a note "Not to be published". Throughout Lenin's work, there can be found quite a few similar directives to trade unions, soviets and other mass organizations with the same "Not to be published" note. Later, Stalin put all such statements together to give his own definition of dictatorship of proletariat, using references to Lenin. This is it: "Dictatorship of proletariat consists of guiding orders from the party plus their conveying by mass organizations of proletariat plus their implementation by the public." (*Problems of Leninism*, 11th edition, p. 123). Party is considered by him "the only organization able to centralize leadership of the proletarian struggle and thus transform all and every non-party organizations of the labor class into serving organs and driving belts, connecting it with the class." (Ibid., pp. 70-71).[8]

Under such a total subordination of all mass organizations to the party leadership, it was necessary to redefine the notion of democratism in these organizations. In his work, "Immediate Tasks of the Soviet Government" (March-April 1918), Lenin gives the following explanation by introducing a new term - "meeting democracy": "...the airing of questions in public meetings is the genuine democracy of the working people..." (Vol. 36, p. 202). And this is how he envisages the task of the party: "...To learn to combine the 'public meeting' democracy of the working people - turbulent, surging, overflowing its banks like a spring flood - with iron discipline while at work, with unquestioning obedience to the will of a single person, the soviet leader, while at work." (Ibid., p. 203).[9] Introduction of this term also made it necessary to introduce another one - that

---

[8]Lenin wrote: "Only such vanguard can exercise dictatorship of proletariat which concentrates in itself all revolutionary energy of the class. Thus we get something like a row of cogged wheels." (Vol. 42, p. 204).
[9]The term "meeting democracy" is also used later, see for example, Vol. 44, p. 165.

of a "socialist democracy". "The socialist character of soviet, i.e., proletarian, democracy, as concretely applied today, lies first in that the electors are toiling and exploited masses, the bourgeoisie is excluded; secondly, it lies in the fact that all bureaucratic formalities and restrictions of elections are abolished, the people themselves determine the order and time of elections of the best mass organization of the vanguard of the working people, i.e., the proletariat, engaged in large-scale industry." (Ibid., p. 203).

Lenin continues to develop the idea of special democracy of the masses. He writes: "The mass must have the right to elect itself responsible leaders. The mass must have the right to change them, the mass must have the right to know and check every, even the smallest steps in their activity. The mass must have the right to promote all - without exception - working members of the mass to leading posts." (Ibid., p. 157). These words give an impression that they describe common democracy, but this is not so, as earlier it was said that "mania for discussions and meetings - of which bourgeois media writes so much and with such anger - are the necessary stages of the transition of the totally unprepared masses to social construction, the transition from historical sleep to new historic creativity." (Ibid., p. 154). It meant that conventional democracy would be exercised only sometime in the future, while now "...<u>every representative of the mass, every citizen must be put in such conditions that he would be able to participate both in discussing state laws, in electing his representative, and bringing about state regulations</u>." (Ibid., p. 157, underlined by author). Put by whom? By the party of Bolsheviks. And how? By way of the extreme centralization of leadership: "Obedience, and unquestioning obedience at that, during work, to the one-man decisions of the soviet dictators, of the dictators elected or appointed by soviet institutions, vested with dictatorial powers (as is demanded, for example, by the railway decree) is far, very far from being guaranteed as yet...Iron discipline and the thorough exercise of proletarian dictatorship against petty-bourgeois vacillation - this is the general and summarizing slogan of the moment."[10] And to disguise altogether the contradiction between extreme centralization of the leadership and regular democracy, Lenin gives the following explanation: "The concept of 'masses' is changeable, according to the changing character of the struggle. At the beginning of the struggle it took only a few thousand genuinely revolutionary

---

[10]This is from Lenin's thesis to his work "Immediate Tasks..." sent to local offices for practical guidance (Vol. 36, p. 280).

workers to warrant talk of the 'masses'... Quite a small party is sufficient to lead the masses. At certain times, there is no necessity for big organizations."[11]

In his complete work, Lenin explains more than once how state democracy for the general public should be understood. Most characteristic in this respect are his letters to the Minister of Justice, D.I. Kursky. In one of them he writes (February 28, 1922): "Do not limit yourself to that (this is most important), do not follow the People's Commissariat of Foreign Affairs blindly. We must not play up to 'Europe' but move farther in intensifying state interference in 'private legal relations' in civil affairs... On the eve of Genoa we must not make a false move, show a lack of spirit, let slip out of our hands the slightest possibility of extending state interference in 'civil' relations." (Vol. 44, p. 411). In another letter in which he discusses the draft criminal code (May 15, 1922), Lenin writes: "In my opinion, we must extend the use of punishment by death (with its commutation into deportation abroad)... It must be formulated in the broadest possible manner, for only revolutionary law and revolutionary conscience can more or less widely determine the limits within which it should be applied." (Vol. 45, p. 189). And then Lenin formulates two versions of the later infamous 58th article of the criminal code, which was used by Stalin to its fullest form for crushing down his party and non-party adversaries. In Lenin's work, one can find many notes like the above in which he makes suggestions to introduce more severe forms of punishment - and all this at the time when the war was already over! (See, for example, Vol. 44, pp. 396, 398-401.) In his letter to Kamenev, at the very climax of NEP, Lenin writes on March 3, 1922: "It is a great mistake to think that NEP has put an end to terrorism. We will yet return to terrorism, and it will be economic terrorism." (Vol. 44, p. 428).

Such are, according to Lenin, the essence and contents of democratic centralism applied to the mass organizations of working men who composed the periphery of the party, as well as to the citizens of the country in general. The interpretation of the intra-party democracy was discussed earlier. In the Resolution of the Tenth Party Congress, the following is said about the situation that took shape inside the party by the end of the Civil War: "In this period the organizational principle of the party must be that of militarization of the party organization. Similar to the proletarian dictatorship, the party organization has taken (and should have taken according to revolutionary expediency) the

---

[11]Speech at the 3rd Congress of Comintern at the end of June 1921 (Vol. 44, pp. 31-32).

corresponding character. It is expressed all in all in the extreme organizational centralism and in the winding up of collective organs of the party organization." (CPSU in Resolutions, ed. 1983, p. 324).[12] This approach to democratic centralism is explained by the conditions of the Civil War. Nevertheless, the resolutions adopted by the Tenth Congress (already after the War) still enforce centralization and limit intra-party democracy. And although one of the resolutions mentions the necessity to overcome the heritage of war-time and to develop intra-party democracy in the future, the following reservation is given straight after it: "It stands to reason that the party must be flexible enough so that if need be it could quickly switch to the system of war commands." (Ibid., p. 327). In fact, such a need never disappeared. It was at this particular congress when Lenin pressed Bukharin back with the following words: "Absolute lashing the waves and bungling. Absolute misunderstanding of the fact that formal democracy must be subordinate to revolutionary expediency." (4th edition, Vol. 32, p. 65).

Such is the truth. But this is not all the truth. The militarization of the political party, hidden behind the harmless term of "democratic centralism", is not the main secret of the success of the Bolshevik party, though. For example, in the army, any commander and any officer, up to the Commander-in-Chief, bears complete responsibility for defeat in battle. As for the General-Secretary, he does not bear such a responsibility at all, as the degree of responsibility decreases with the ascension along the party hierarchy (decentralization of responsibility). This mafia-like element of Bolshevism, which itself is a consequence of the organizational principle (see Chapter 5) was unfolding very gradually, and was disguised more deliberately by way of complicating the intra-party structure.

By the end of the Civil War, the Bolshevik party was no longer a small compact group of partisans united by the common goal of seizing political power as it was envisaged by Lenin in *What is to be Done?*, and what it used to be before the October revolution. First, its membership levels grew

---

[12]In his book, *Origins of Partocracy*, A. Avtorkhanov gives the following quotation by Bukharin at the previous 9th congress: "We constructed our own party in such a manner that we have become the most militarized organization that has ever existed, as our party is a military organization almost in a literal sense, because spurs are not a necessary attribute of a war type." (p. 225 of a stenogram).

substantially.[13] Second, its infrastructure changed too: it was not homogeneous anymore. The old party guard was "driven out" to the upper levels of hierarchy and even partially disjoined from the rest of it. The principles of conspiracy and professionalism were observed only there, and only there the extreme centralization of the leadership of the whole party was concentrated. There are evidences to it by Lenin himself. In his letter to Molotov for the TsK (Central Committee) members, Lenin writes March 20, 1922: "If we do not close our eyes to reality, we must admit that at the present time, the proletarian policy of the party is not determined by the character of its membership, but by the enormous, undivided prestige enjoyed by the small group which might be called the Old Guard of the party." (Vol. 45, p. 20). Half a year later, in his Testament, Lenin writes: "Comrade Stalin, having become General Secretary, has unlimited authority concentrated in his hands" (Ibid., p. 345). Lenin, who himself sanctioned this appointment, undoubtedly had even greater authority. In connection with the disjoining of party leadership, democratic centralism acquires more complicated forms. Now the centralization of leadership and decentralization of responsibility becomes a more sophisticated, two-step phenomenon: first, between the leadership and the party apparatus, and then between the party apparatus and the state apparatus (the soviets). Complex processes of coalescence between the soviet and party apparatuses started. Chimera was gaining flesh and started to materialize. All this, together with the growth of centralization and the limitation of democracy, led to fast bureaucratization. The tempo of its growth could be easily traced by putting together all Lenin's pronouncements about it chronologically.

3. Materialization (Lenin on Bureaucracy)

In his work *State and Revolution*, which was written just before the October coup, Lenin, in his polemics with Kautsky, wrote: "The workers, after winning political power will smash the old bureaucratic apparatus, shake it to its very foundation, and raze it to the ground; they will replace it with a new one, consisting of the very same workers and other employees against whose transformation into bureaucrats the measures will at once be taken which were

---

[13]Between the February and October coups, the membership of the Bolshevik party increased almost fifteen-fold: from twenty thousand up to about three hundred thousand members, and still more by the time of the Tenth Congress - by the factor 2.5.

specified in detail by Marx and Engels: 1) not only election but also recall at any time; 2) pay not to exceed that of a workman; 3) immediate introduction of control and supervision by all, so that all may become 'bureaucrats' for a time and that, therefore, nobody may be able to become 'a bureaucrat'. (Vol. 33, p. 109).[14] But how to define wages for functionaries of different ranks? "All that is required is that they should work equally, do their proper share of work, and get equal pay." (Ibid., p. 101). It could be understood in a way that new proletarian administration would not be hierarchical.

In this last pronouncement, what is most striking is the absolute confidence that bureaucratism will be overcome easily after the dictatorship of proletariat is established. It can be explained by Lenin's desire to put off until later (and even to wave off) all other problems except that of seizing power. Lenin succeeded in sustaining this confidence through almost one whole year after the revolution. It can be traced in the above cited work "Immediate Tasks...".[15] But already by the end of 1918, the tone of his pronouncements changes, and the fight against bureaucracy together with the fight against speculation is given first priority. (See Vol. 37, p. 428.) In his report on the party program to the Eighth Congress he says:

> We have been hearing complaints about bureaucracy for a long time; the complaints are undoubtedly well-founded. We have done what no other state in the world has done in the fight against bureaucracy. The apparatus which was a thoroughly bureaucratic and bourgeois apparatus of oppression, and which remains such even in the freest

---

[14]Further Lenin continues: "Under capitalism, democracy is restricted, cramped, curtailed, mutilated by all the conditions of wage slavery, poverty and misery of the working masses. This and this alone is the reason why the functionaries in our political organizations and trade unions are corrupted (or rather tend to be corrupted) by the conditions of capitalism and have the tendency to become bureaucrats, i.e., privileged persons divorced from the people and standing above the people. That is the essence of bureaucratism, and until the capitalists have been expropriated and the bourgeoisie overthrown, even proletarian functionaries will inevitably be 'bureaucratized' to a certain extent... Under socialism, all will govern in turn, and will soon become accustomed to no one governing."

[15]"Our aim is to ensure that every toiler participate in practical governing... Our aim is to ensure that every toiler, having finished his eight-hours 'task' in productive labor, shall perform state duties without pay... in order repeatedly and tirelessly to weed out bureaucracy." (Vol. 36, pp. 204,206).

of bourgeois republics, we have destroyed to its very' foundation...
We dispersed these old bureaucrats, shuffled them and then began to
place them in new posts. The tsarist bureaucrats began to join the
soviet institutions and practice their bureaucratic methods, they
began to assume the coloring of communists and, to succeed better
in their careers, to procure membership cards of the Russian
Communist Party. And so, they have been thrown out of the door
but they creep back in through the window. What makes itself felt
here most is the lack of cultured forces... The result of this low
cultural level is that the soviets, which by virtue of their program are
organs of government by the working people, are in fact organs of
government for the working people by the advanced section of the
proletariat, but not by the working people as a whole... Bureaucracy
has been defeated. The exploiters have been eliminated. But the
cultural level has not been raised, and therefore the bureaucrats are
occupying their old positions. (Vol. 38, pp. 169-170).

This pronouncement looks strange compared to the previous confidence.
What is really strange is that a low cultural level, rather than the class struggle, is
referred to as the cause of bureaucratism: neither Marx nor Engels had that, and
as for contemporary higher ranking bureaucrats, almost all of them have higher
education. The reasoning about "creeping back in through the window" looks
also very strange in the conditions of martial law, the activity of so-called ChKs
(Extraordinary Commissions for the Suppression of Counter-Revolution,
Sabotage and Speculation), and so-called *Prodrazverstka* (surplus grain
appropriation system), and so on. The usage of the expression "advanced
section of the proletariat" instead of simply "party" is also strange. The
impression is that Lenin meant something different rather than the ordinary
bureaucracy that was very well-known to everybody, but was uncertain to say
that.

Another year passed, the Civil War was over and the threat of intervention
was over too. In his speech to the delegates of the Eighth Congress of Soviets
on December 30, 1920, Lenin, in his polemics with Trotsky about trade unions,
says: "...It is evident from our party program - this document is very well
known to the author of the 'ABC of Communism' - it is evident from this
program that our state is a workers' state with bureaucratic distortions. And we

should have stuck this sad - what shall I call it, label? - on it. Here you have, then, the reality of transition... Our present state is such that the entirely organized proletariat must protect itself, and we must utilize these workers' organizations for the purpose of protecting the workers from their own state in order that the workers may protect our state." (Vol. 42, p. 206). Here we see almost the same verbal rebus as above. Really, the "entirely organized proletariat" is nothing but the party (its advanced detachment), together with soviets, trade unions, Comsomol (Communist Union of the Youth) and, at last, non-party workers. Who are "we" then? And from whom should the proletariat be protected? Where is this monstrous enemy of bureaucratism hidden?

Partial answers to these questions can be found in another pronouncement of Lenin's a month earlier at the Moscow *Gubernia* Conference of RCP(B) - Russian Communist Party (of Bolsheviks) on November 21:

> The cultural level of the peasants and the working masses has not been high enough for this task, and at the same time, we have become almost totally accustomed to tackling political and military tasks, this has led to a revival of bureaucratic methods. This is generally admitted. It is the task of the Soviet government to completely destroy the old machinery of state as it was destroyed in October, and to transfer power to the soviets. However, our program recognizes that there has been a revival of bureaucratic methods, and that at present no economic foundation yet exists for a genuinely socialist society. A cultural background, literacy and in general a higher standard of culture are lacking in the mass of workers and peasants... It is natural that the bureaucratic methods that have reappeared in Soviet institutions were bound to have a pernicious effect even on party organizations, since the upper ranks of the party are at the same time the upper ranks of the soviet apparatus; they are one and the same thing. (Vol. 42, pp. 32, 42, underlined by author).

In this pronouncement, Lenin uses a new word - the "apparatus" (which is to be completely destroyed). One can assume that it is this apparatus that becomes the center and the hotbed of bureaucratism. It is also mentioned that the tops of the soviet and party hierarchies have amalgamated, and a conclusion can be made that the "apparatus" is the amalgamation of these two huge hierarchies. However, it still remains unclear what takes place at the middle and lower levels, as well as what is the link between this "amalgamation" and bureaucracy. The indication that it is the soviet institutions that play the role of the hotbeds for bureaucratism seems unconvincing.

Soviets, trade unions, industrial administration and all other mass organizations were established after the Revolution and were being formed under the strict and total control of the party apparatus. In the conditions of martial law and dictatorship, it meant that the party delegated its own representatives - with dictatorial powers - to all key posts in these organizations and conducted its policy through them. Lenin writes about it unequivocally in his work "Immediate Tasks...", and in many others. Quickly having gotten used to the intra-party extreme "centralization of leadership" they conducted this policy by command bureaucratic methods, getting a taste for uncontrolled power. Implanting bureaucratism in the soviets and other mass organizations, they then brought it back to the party thus accelerating the overwhelming process of bureaucratization of the whole amalgamated apparatus of power. This is the only way to interpret the above two pronouncements.[16] The amalgamation of all hierarchies at the middle and higher levels into a single apparatus of power and its accelerated bureaucratization, was, of course, something more important and much more dangerous than common, routine bureaucratism. It seems quite natural to assume that Lenin was aware of the approaching danger, but could not speak openly about it.

This first attempt of *perestroika* (destruction of "old apparatus" and the transfer of power to the soviets) failed. By the end of 1920, it became clear that the hopes for the world revolution did not come true, and now this mainly agrarian country, devastated by a three-year civil war, had to get prepared for a prolonged "peaceful co-existence" with its capitalist surroundings. It was necessary to eliminate the threat of total starvation and to revive the economy. Under these severe conditions, all echelons of the party and soviet apparatuses were seized by heated discussions which gave rise to multitudinous platforms,

---

[16]On the condition that we assume that the text of the Collected Work is authoritative and full, and also if we do not take into account Lenin's multiple warnings not to cite his speeches, but only letters and articles. (See, for example, Vol. 44, p. 246; Vol. 45, p. 170; Vol. 54, pp. 203 and 245). Many new materials have been published recently in connection with preparing a new, more complete edition, and they confirm the above conclusion.

blocks and groups. The very existence of the dictatorship of proletariat was threatened. The task of strengthening its pivot - the party - became a top priority, forcing out to the background all other tasks including the scheduled *perestroika*. The Tenth Congress fulfilled this main task by prohibiting any platforms and blocks, thus further strengthening the leadership centralization within and by the party apparatus. It also removed the last remaining element of control over the functions of this apparatus thus accelerating its bureaucratization. Besides, the amalgamation of the two hierarchies now acquired the character of absorbing one of them: the transfer of power to the soviets became still less probable.

What was Lenin's reaction to these deep-rooted processes? On his initiative, the Tenth Congress adopted the decision to purge the party and Lenin began to implement it straight away (see below). At the same time, he aggressed the bureaucracy and its concrete bearers in the upper echelons of the party apparatus, many of whom were directly subordinated to him through the Sovnarkom (Soviet of People's Commissars). For example, in connection with the case of the Fowler ploughs in his letter to the chief of the VSNKh (All-Union Council of National Economy), P.A. Bogdanov (December 23, 1921), Lenin uses - perhaps for the first time - the following sharp expression: "In future we will for such behavior send all such trade union and communist scoundrels (the court, perhaps, will express itself more mildly) mercilessly to jail." (Vol. 54, pp. 88-89). Beginning from 1922, his language becomes even more harsh. The most characteristic in this respect are his letters to the VSNKh deputy chief, A.D. Tsurupa. For example, at the end of January Lenin writes to him: "The most radical defect of the CPC (Council of People's Commissars) and the CLD (Council of Labor and Defense) is the absence of any checking-up on fulfillment. We are being sucked down by the rotten bureaucratic swamp into writing papers, jawing about decrees and drawing up decrees - and in this sea of paper, live work is being drowned." (Vol. 44, p. 364). And one month later again: "The main thing, in my opinion, is to shift the center of gravity from writing decrees and orders (our stupidities in this respect verge on idiocy) to selection of people and checking fulfillment. This is the essential point... All of us are sunk in the rotten bureaucratic swamp of 'departments'. Great authority, common sense and strong will are necessary for the everyday struggle against this. The departments are shit, decrees are shit. To find men and check up on their work - that's the whole point." (Ibid., p. 369). And to the same person again about his subordinates: "I am sending you a specimen of our vile red tape and obtuseness! Just think - these are our best men, Pyatakov, Morozov and others! If it weren't for the knout they would have ruined the whole cause!" (Vol. 54, p. 187).

Very characteristic in this respect is Lenin's reaction to the questionnaire sent to him for the scheduled re-registration of the party membership which contained as many as fifty-nine questions (see Vol. 44, p. 509). He reprimands Molotov with the following words: "Either you have a fool in charge of statistics, or there are fools and pedants sitting in important posts somewhere in these 'departments' (if the said institutions under the Central Committee are so called), and you have apparently no time to look into what they are doing. 1) The head of the Statistical department should be fired. 2) This and the Registration and Distribution departments must be given a thorough shake-up. Otherwise, we ourselves ('combatting red tape') breed the most disgraceful and stupid red tape under our very noses." (Vol. 44, p. 392). Evidently, it did not have any effect, as half a year later (September 25, 1922), in his letter to Rykov, Lenin writes: "Our apparatus is such an abomination that it has to be radically repaired. This cannot be done without a census. And the Central Statistical Board deserves being taken to task for its academism: there they are sitting and writing their 'tomes', giving not a thought to vital problems." (Vol. 54, p. 290). And that is what he writes to the Chief of Finances, G. Sokolnikov, about the work of the State Bank: "They slept in, they missed the bus, they waited, like real jack-in-office scoundrels for an order 'from above'." (Vol. 54, p. 167). To the same person on February 22, 1922: "All the work of all our economic bodies suffers most of all from bureaucracy. Communists have become bureaucrats. If anything will destroy us, it is this." (Vol. 54, p. 180). A week and a half later - to Kamenev: "But we find the idiots walking around and talking for two weeks! They deserve to be left to rot in jail instead of being given exemptions. The Muscovites deserve six hours in the bughouse for their stupidity. The *Vneshtorg* (People's Commissariat of Foreign Affairs) people, thirty-six hours in the bughouse for stupidity plus for 'central-responsibility'! That is the only way to teach them." (Vol. 44, p. 429). There are many pronouncements like these in Lenin's works.

As for the main causes of bureaucratism, now it is not the class struggle, not the lack of culture that are to blame, but the dispersal of the peasantry. And the time of overcoming bureaucratism is moved to the indefinite future: "Our program formulates the task of combatting the evils of bureaucracy as one of extremely long duration. The wider the dispersal of the peasantry, the more inevitable are bureaucratic practices at the center." (Vol. 43, p. 49).[17] Leaving alone the doubtfulness of such direct link between bureaucratism and the dispersal (Stalin's total collectivation and industrialization disproved it), such words of a political leader burdened by a variety of emergent problems, usually mean that the problem has lost its acuteness and that it is not emergent anymore. Is this the case with Lenin? This question gives rise to another one: is it true that the problem of the routine bureaucratism was so acute by 1922? The answer is no if we compare the bureaucratism of 1921-22 with what followed in the Stalin and Brezhnev periods. The administrative apparatus of that time, both the party and the state, was working very efficiently, which is justified by the astounding success of the NEP (New Economic Policy). Then, how can the sharpness of Lenin's above pronouncements be explained? Who or what did he fight against? Against what bureaucratism? Is it true that this efficient party-governmental administration began to tow already in a year? Why did Lenin never again return to the transition of power to the soviets? Here we are entering the area of surmises and suppositions.

4. Ousting the Creator

Decentralization of power and formation of local self-governing have always been considered the only effective means to limit and weaken the state bureaucracy (see definition on pp. 12-13). But it is impossible to find any suggestions of this kind in Lenin's words or deeds. He rather suggests the opposite. The matter is that these means are applicable only to ordinary bureaucracy, the one that can be controlled by outside power and is ruled from outside. Such was the state bureaucracy after the Revolution in its first period of activity, as it was controlled by the party. Such was partially the party

---

[17]This is from the Report to the Tenth Congress. More clearly it is put in Lenin's article, "The Tax in Kind", written soon after the Congress (April 21, 1921): "In our country, bureaucratic practices have different economic roots, namely, the atomized and scattered state of the small producer with his poverty, illiteracy, lack of culture, the absence of roads and exchange between agriculture and industry, the absence of connection and interaction between them... Bureaucratic practices, as a legacy of the 'siege' and the superstructure built over the isolated and downtrodden state of the small producer, fully revealed themselves." (Vol. 43, p. 230; see also a letter to M. Sokolov, Vol. 52, p. 190).

bureaucracy as long as it had the inner mechanism of control. Radical changes took place soon after the Tenth Congress, when this control was abolished and the process of the amalgamation of the party and soviet hierarchies into a single party-governmental apparatus took place. It is this term - apparatus - that can be seen more and more often in Lenin's pronouncements of this period (see, also, above - pp. 15-16). It is becoming more and more difficult to consider both these pronouncements and the above examples of very sharp language as merely a struggle against ordinary, routine bureaucratism.

In his report to the Eleventh Party Congress, Lenin says: "If we take Moscow with its 4,700 communists in responsible positions, and if we take that huge bureaucratic machine, that gigantic heap, we must ask: who is directing whom? I doubt very much whether it can truthfully be said that the communists are directing the heap. To tell the truth, they are not directing, they are being directed." (Vol. 45, p. 95). One half year later: "We have huge masses of employees, but not enough number of educated forces to be in real command of them. In practice it happens very often that here, on top, where we have state power, the apparatus functions anyhow, whereas on the grass-root level they run everything off-handedly, and in such a way that very often works against our actions." (Ibid., p. 290). Still more definitely and sharply he criticized the apparatus in a heated discussion about the republics' federation:

> The apparatus that we call ours is, in fact, still quite alien to us; it is a bourgeois and tsarist hodge-podge, and there has been no possibility of getting rid of it in the course of the past five years without the help of other countries and because we have been 'busy' most of the time with military engagements and the fight against famine... It is quite natural that in such circumstances, the 'freedom to withdraw from the Union' by which we justify ourselves will be a mere scrap of paper, unable to defend the non-Russians from the onslaught of that really Russian man, the Great-Russian chauvinist, in substance a rascal and a lover of violence, such as a typical Russian bureaucrat is. There is no doubt that the infinitesimal percentage of Soviet and sovietized workers will drown in that sea of chauvinistic Great-Russian riff-raff like a fly in milk. (Vol. 45, p. 357).

It was written five days after the "Letter to the Congress" with its famous phrase: "Stalin, having become a General Secretary..." and is evidently directed against him and the bureaucrats of "new formation" that were grouping around him. Although it talks about "bureaucrats" and bureaucratism here, what is really meant is "apparatus".

From the second half of 1922, in all Lenin's letters which are included in his so-called "Testament", the transition from fighting routine bureaucracy to fighting the apparatus can be traced even more distinctly. The term "apparatus" almost totally forces out the terms "bureaucracy" and "bureaucratism". For example, in his last article, "Better Fewer but Better" (March 2, 1923), Lenin writes: "We have been bustling for five years trying to improve our state apparatus, but it has been mere bustle, which has proved useless in these five years, even futile, or even harmful. This bustle created the impression that we were doing something, but in effect it was only clogging up our institutions and our brains." (Vol. 45, p. 392). And only occasionally about bureaucratism: "It should be mentioned in brackets that we have bureaucracy not only in the soviet, but in the party institutions as well." (Ibid., p. 398). This note, repeated in the above article on the next page, looks very strange after what has been said about the amalgamation of the party and state leadership. The same is in almost every article of his last period.

What deep processes were hidden behind this turn from the struggle against bureaucracy as "enemy number one" to the struggle against the apparatus? (and it *was* a "struggle", as it will be shown below). The system of state power which was formed by the end of the Civil War in the First Republic of the Soviets was unprecedented and was never repeated later. The ruling party which exercised the dictatorship of the proletariat expanded enormously and acquired the character of a territorially ramificated and vertically multi-level hierarchy of the party organs, beginning from a secretary of a party cell and ending with a supreme collegial organ: a periodically-sitting Central Committee and a constantly sitting Politburo. Another, equally overwhelming hierarchy - that of the *Ispolkoms* of the soviets (executive committees of the soviets)[18] -

---

[18]They got power directly from the Revkoms which are described in the *Big Soviet Encyclopedia* as follows: "Interim extraordinary organs of the Soviet power in the Civil War of 1918-20 - the central ones (republican and regional) and local (*gubernia, uezd, volost* and village; i.e., smaller administrative divisions). They concentrated in their hands all civil and

existed parallel to it, which was controlled by the party hierarchy at all important junctions. Formally, Lenin headed only the *Ispolkom* hierarchy through the CPC (Council of People's Commissars) and CLD (Council of Labor and Defense), but at the same time, he played a key role in the functioning of the whole system of power as he performed the link between the party and the state apparatuses at the very top level.[19] His special position as sole, charismatic leader, and his popularity, made possible a relative independence of the party and state apparatuses on the middle and lower levels and, consequently, their mutual control over each other.

Lenin's key role in the functioning of a two-hierarchical system of power and his, in fact, unlimited personal authority[20] were not only determined by his singular popularity among the party masses and general public, as the founder of the party and the leader of the October coup ("charismatic component of power", according to Weber), but by the relative unity of the ruling top ("Party Guard"), rallied by the common danger during the Civil War and the common goal of the world revolution. And, in the last analysis, it was also determined by the historically shaped unique two-hierarchical system of power, where the hierarchy of the ruling party, unlike the hierarchy of the state power, was governed by a collegial organ rather than by a "Gensek" (General Secretary) through a Secretariat that was subordinated to it, as was the case afterwards. The majority of the most influential members of this collegial organ (Central Committee and Politburo) were formally and factually subordinated to Lenin as a chief of the CPC (Stalin was the Narkom - People's Commissar - of Nationalities, Trotsky - Narkom of the Armed Forces, Kemenev and Rykov - deputy chiefs of the CPC). This distinguishing characteristic, which laid the grounds for a personal dictatorship and, at the same time, carried the elements of collegiality, was never repeated again, as it contained the possibility of a split in

---

military power. When the Soviet power was being established, they prepared the elections to the soviets and their power was taken over to the elected *Ispolkoms.*

[19]"The link between the CPC and the Politburo was mainly held by me personally." (Political Report to the Eleventh Congress, Vol. 45, p. 13).

[20]Whenever the famous pronouncement "Stalin, having become the General Secretary, has unlimited authority concentrated in his hands..." is cited, few understand its exaggeration. "Unlimited" authority, Stalin would acquire only one and a half decades later. Lenin's words only indicate the possibility of such concentration of power in one hand in a two-hierarchical system, in which not a single member of the collegial power enjoys autonomous power. Only Lenin's power was "unlimited".

the ruling party. It is this "double spiral" with a single pointed top that is hidden behind the word "apparatus".

Why did this "apparatus" start to tow in the climax of the NEP and only eighteen months after the end of the Civil War? There are many reasons. Some of them are outer - some, inner. The latter are the most important. The foremost of them is the impetuous and uncontrolled growth of the ruling party and, connected with this growth, changes in its composition.[21] The second one is the uncontrolled centralization of the leadership, which led to the autonomy of the ruling top, and its independence from the grass-roots members. The interconnection of these two processes is considered in detail in the next chapters. The operation of the apparatus also deteriorated because of the discords within the ruling top caused by the delay of the world revolution and the necessity of transition to the "peaceful rails". Adoption of the NEP aggravated these discords.

All of these processes upset the equilibrium of the two-hierarchical system of power. Such a system is unstable, if for no other reason than that two constantly and independently changing forces can never create a steady equilibrium. In a two-party system of a democratic society - to draw a distant analogy - the equilibrium between the two parties is supported by the stabilizing role of public opinion as expressed through the parliament and other democratic institutions. In the case of the USSR, this "third" force was lacking, and there was no way to create it quickly. The equilibrium in the system of political power began to become distorted as early as the end of the Civil War; a result of the above mentioned amalgamation of the party and state bodies. This distortion was further accelerated soon after the Tenth Congress. It was after this time that Lenin's key role began to change too, since the apparatus began to draw him away from power.

---

[21]Even periodical purges did not help. The decision about the first purge was adopted as early as in 1919, at the Eighth Congress. But instead of decreasing, the membership almost doubled over one year preceding the Ninth Congress. The Tenth Congress adopted the decision about the second purge, and over the next year almost half the members were "purged out". But already by the time of the Twelfth Congress, the membership had restored itself and continued to grow even faster ever after. The same took place in the state apparatus. To stop this overwhelming "flood", suggestions were made to suspend the admittance of new members (see Vol. 44, p. 285).

There are two popular versions of Lenin's removal from power: his illness, and the aggravation of the struggle for power at the top of the party hierarchy because of Stalin's intrigues. The first of them, and the oldest, relates to Stalin's orthodoxy,[22] and the second one originated after the Twentieth Congress. But neither of them, nor both of them combined (for example, aggravation of the struggle for power because of Lenin's disease), are able to explain all the known facts, and the number of these facts is growing as more and more blank spots in the history of Bolshevism are eradicated. We will restrict ourselves to considering only some of them.

Lenin's influence on the top echelons of power started to decline long before his first stroke (end of May, 1922), and there is much indirect evidence to support this. Further, his isolation after the second stroke looked more like an isolation from political activity rather than from worries and troubles, though it was disguised as such. And the second stroke itself, which determined the further development of the disease, took place after one such trouble (a meeting with Dzerzhinsky in connection with the so-called "Georgian case", December 12, 1922). And the most conspicuous fact is the fate of the "Testament". Some of its sections Lenin considered as absolutely secret, and he repeatedly warned his secretaries about it - but they became known straight away. This shows that by the end of 1922, the apparatus, together with his immediate surroundings, including secretaries, no longer considered Lenin a center of power. And lastly, the Testament of the leader ("A Letter to the Congress") was hushed up not only at the next Congress, but at all following ones as well. At the Thirteenth Congress it was announced "in delegations", and it was discussed somewhere in corridors. Nevertheless, over the whole next decade, there was not a single delegate to the Twelfth to the Seventeenth Congresses who denounced this hushing up openly! And all this was long before the repressions of 1937 which made them all "voiceless"!

It is also not very convincing to explain the "hushing up" of the Testament and Lenin's isolation by Stalin's intrigues: such actions against members of the Central Committee and Politburo became possible only a decade later. At the beginning of the 1920s, no one close to him could personally fight against Lenin. But the result of their combined effort and acts inevitably moved Lenin away from power, just like the result of the combined effort by Chernenko's

---

[22]It was rejected by all further developments: all rulers always remained in their posts even though they were much older and more decrepit than Lenin in 1922.

surroundings inevitably moved him towards the apex of the party pyramid, and neither his old age nor feeble health could stop it. Without doing anything distinguishing in all his life, he drifted slowly to the top of the power to die there ingloriously.

This is the property of all similar organizations, organizations hierarchically centralized, strongly soldered by mutual irresponsibility, and isolated from society. Their evolution cannot be reduced to the behavior of individual, even distinguished, members. Lenin's removal was the result of a joint effort of the party apparatus leadership, as he had become "inconvenient" long before his illness played any role in this process. His "Testament" was also buried by the joint effort of the apparatus.

The version "Lenin's illness plus Stalin's intrigues" is evidently weak too. It ignores the deep processes in the ruling party and concentrates attention only on the final stage of the process. In reality, already the Tenth Congress can be considered as Lenin's concession to the apparatus. General post-war devastation together with the threat of famine demanded extraordinary measures. The NEP took place, and it was impossible to carry it out without political concessions to the public. This was how Lenin's pronouncement about smashing the apparatus and giving power back to the soviets (cited above) can be explained, since the uncontrolled apparatus strangled every initiative. A strengthened and independent hierarchy of the soviets could restrict, in Lenin's opinion, the omnipotent party officials, and create the conditions of mutual control of the two hierarchies. But the process of amalgamation continued, and Lenin faced a demand by the middle and lower echelons of the apparatus to further concentrate the power.[23] After the Tenth Congress, the pressure on Lenin was becoming still greater, so one year later, at the Eleventh Congress, he had to state: "We have been retreating for a year. Now we must say on behalf of the party: enough! The goal pursued by the retreat is achieved." (Vol. 45, p. 87). Transfer of power to the Soviet was no longer mentioned.

---

[23]This is Lenin's own indirect evidence of the pressure from below: "In this discussion, the Party proved itself to have matured to such an extent that, aware of a certain wavering of the 'top' section and hearing the leadership say 'We cannot agree - sort us out,' it mobilized rapidly for this task and the vast majority of the more important party organizations quickly responded: 'We do have an opinion, and we shall let you know it'." (Report to the Tenth Congress, Vol. 43, p. 16).

Pressure from below was compounded by the pressure from the upper echelons of the apparatus, and a further concession followed. At a current plenum, Stalin took the post of "Gensek" (General Secretary), which had remained vacant for five years - an unprecedented case in the practice of all communist parties! Later, in his "Testament", Lenin would say: "Stalin, having become a Gensek...", stressing that the appointment was forced.[24] It had the effect of weakening Lenin's position in his struggle with the apparatus even more, as members of the Central Committee and Politburo who occupied state posts were now formally submitted not only to Lenin, but to Stalin as well. The process of amalgamation of the two hierarchies into a single apparatus of power was completed at the top. The growth of centralization and the appearance of a "Gensek" increased the authoritarianism of the top, making any pressure on it by means of appealing to the lay members of the party, to the party masses, less probable. All of it immediately affected Lenin's position: after the Eleventh Congress, his clashes with opponents in the CPC and the Politburo became more frequent, and he did not always win them.

Consolidation of the upper echelons of the apparatus probably took place at the Twelfth Party Conference (August 4-7, 1922) in Lenin's absence (he was on vacation in Gorky). At this conference, two very important resolutions were adopted, the impact of which can still be seen today. One of them inconspicuously revoked the decision of the Tenth Congress on "leveling".[25] In the resolution "On the Material Conditions of Active Party Workers", seventeen (!) categories of party functionaries (about twenty-five thousand) were established which not only fixed a salary for each of them, but also specified housing, medical care, and education for children. (CPSU in Resolutions, 1983, Vol. 2, p. 594). The top (seventeenth) category included members of the

---

[24]Stalin's appointment can be considered to a certain extent a formal act. The growth of the party apparatus centralization and subordination of *Ispolkoms* to it, inevitably led to the strengthening of the Politburo and the growth of the volume of its work. In the Report to the Eleventh congress, Lenin said: "On the one example, I have shown how every concrete small case is being carried to the Politburo..." (Vol. 45, p. 113). But who in the Politburo led all this growing organizational work? Undoubtedly, Stalin. It was he, the only member of the Central Committee, who constantly participated in both the Politburo and Orgbureau; who headed two Narkomats; who was a member of the *revvoensoviet* (Revolutionary Military Council); a member of the board of VChK-OGPU; and a member of the CLD.

[25]"The Congress altogether confirms its course of leveling in the material conditions of the party members." (CPSU in Resolutions, Vol. 1, p. 328).

Central Committee departments, members of regional bureaus, secretaries of *Obkoms* (regional party committees) and *Gubkoms* (*Gubernia* Party committees). For the Comsomol (Communist Union of the Youth) hierarchy, the provisions were two levels lower, correspondingly.

That is what resulted from Lenin's prophecy about new bureaucracy: "All that is required is that they should work equally, do their proper share of work and get equal pay." (Vol. 33, p. 101). Together with the principle of obligatory rotation of top party functionaries, which was established at the Tenth Congress,[26] it laid the ground for the formation of "*nomenclatura*" - a new privileged layer in the party and the state. Its gradual expansion and isolation from society finally resulted in the establishment in Russia of a state system, unprecedented in history, which was later called "partocracy".

The second important decision of the Twelfth Party Conference was the adoption of a new party charter, which rejected all Lenin's proposals for more severe conditions for admitting new members; an attempt at blocking party growth.[27] It in fact began to grow uncontrollably, hitting the millionth mark as early as the beginning of the 1930s, and altering its composition (see Chapter 4, section 4). It was just after the Twelfth Party Conference when the last and the most heated confrontations between Lenin and the party apparatus took place over the questions of the monopoly of foreign trade, and the so-called "Georgian case".

---

[26]"Having in mind the goal of fighting departmentalism, it is necessary to move comrades systematically from one branch of work to another under the condition, though, that every comrade can work a definite period of time at each place." (Ibid. , p. 329). They have been "moving" since then, creating the condition of total irresponsibility.

[27]Lenin's struggle lasted almost a year (see Vol. 44, p. 285; Vol. 45, pp. 17-18, 501; see also CPSU in Resolutions, Vol. 2, p. 547). It was Zinoviev's proposal that was adopted.

CHAPTER 3
PARTOCRACY

1. Pyramid of Power

The term "partocracy" was probably first used by A.A. Avtorkhanov in his book *Formation of Partocracy*. This is how he defined it: "...A system of absolute political, economic and ideological power and rule of a 'party within the party' - the CPSU apparatus, under which legislative, judicial controlling and distributive proprietary functions are merged together and are concentrated in the central apparatus of the Party; as for the ruling and distributive organs, they are dualistic: the ruling organs are located in the hierarchy of the party apparatus, executive ones - in the hierarchy of the state apparatus."[28] Elsewhere it is put more precisely: "An absolute dictatorship with a narrow oligarchic leadership on top, with a closed, vertically hierarchical party apparatus and a multi-million base of party spongers in the foundation of the pyramid - is a phenomenon unique not only in its class organization, but also in the depth and width of its influence and control over the whole population and each individual. These specific features make the Bolshevik state of a 'new type', an example of a totalitarian state unprecedented in world history."

This definition was formulated for the totalitarian Stalinist regime. At present, partocracy has become the system of state power in dozens of states and has spread over almost all the world. Its intrinsic structure has become more sophisticated as well. The party hierarchy is not always and not everywhere a dominant one. The army can dominate as, for example, in China, or the state security, or a combination of all three hierarchies that make up the framework of the pyramid of power. The vertical structure of the party apparatus has become more complicated, too; it is no longer two-hierarchical with a simple division into ruling and subordinate bodies. Nevertheless, in all varieties of contemporary partocracy, its three main characteristic features remain untouched. First, there is an extreme centralization of the whole system of power, under which all orders, instructions and regulations go from the top down, and those who rule are totally independent from the executives and are not accountable to them. Further, totalitarianism means not only the existence of the domineering hierarchy in the system of political power and the exclusion

---

[28]Cited by a 1974 "samizdat" version.

of everything that can restrict this power (religion, universal human morality, and traditions), but also the spreading of the hierarchical principle of rule over all spheres of public life. And, last, there is also a characteristic vertical in-homogeneity of the hierarchic party apparatus.

In contemporary partocracies, the party-state apparatus is not only a conspiratory inner party, but it also demonstrates a specific inner structure in which, besides an isolated ruling sub-system, one can distinguish a managing and a managed sub-system. Accordingly, the structure of the socium encompassed by the party apparatus becomes more complicated. This peculiarity of the vertical structure is the most specific feature of all contemporary partocratic regimes. Moreover, the separation of the initially centralized and conspiratory hierarchy into the three parts occurs mainly as a result of intrinsic rules of its evolution, and it depends very little on such factors as social cultural patterns of the state, or its history and traditions, as will be shown in the next chapter. It is for this reason that partocracy spread over all continents in such a short period of time.

Any modern scientific method exploits to a greater or smaller degree the idea of modeling. First, a rough, draft model of reality is created, which is gradually perfected and made more and more precise. Let us apply the idea to investigating the partocratic system of power using the Brezhnev-Chernenko regime as an example. The reasons for such a choice will be seen further. This period (1964-84) is characterized by the block of the three hierarchies: the Party, the KGB, and the military; the Party being the dominant one. Together they formed the main "backbone" of political power and exercised its total centralization.

In the stationary regime, the domineering party hierarchy was not only in control of the other two, but it totally subjugated them by, first, delegating its own representatives - who first of all carried out its policies - to their key positions and, second, by dubbing all major military and KGB departments in its own structure. The total subjugation was also ensured by a means of control over finances, economics and ideology. All these factors made the army and the state security the two "crushing teams" of the party apparatus, the first one being directed towards foreign enemies, and the latter towards the domestic ones. This was the system in calm (stationary) periods. In emergencies, each of the subordinate hierarchies could replace the party, examples of which are well-known.

Besides the three major hierarchies in the partocratic regimes of the type examined, three secondary hierarchies, also overwhelming, were formed (administration, trade union, and Comsomol), as well as a variety of specific ones (e.g., science, culture, sports), which, all together, encompass the whole society.[29] Every citizen, often before he comes of age, becomes a member of either a production hierarchy (department) or an agrarian one. ("All who do not work are parasites!") Male citizens are also liable for military service and at any time can be called to serve. Even in the reserves they, until nearly retirement age, are subordinated indirectly to the military department, and the system of military muster promotes them along the hierarchy of military ranks. The urban population is also included in trade unions, and the youth are included in pioneer and comsomol organizations. At a certain level, the hierarchy of local government bodies is merged with the administrative hierarchy, as well as the soviets with the state administration. All this web of departmental power safely entangles individuals, and residency permits deprive them of the right to freely change their place of living. Any uncontrolled and undesirable initiatives are, therefore, restricted and autonomy of local self-governing is done away with. As the existence of civil society is terminated, it leaves the individual in opposition to the whole state.

It is important to note one more peculiarity of the structural model of partocracy which will be discussed in more detail in the next chapter. No matter which specialized hierarchy is considered (science, culture, health care, education), in the ascension along its steps, the specialized tasks are gradually forced out by general state ones, and, consequently, by political ones. The process is facilitated by the development of individual links between functionaries, by working out common interests and agreements. The result is a greater closeness and, even, an amalgamation of the upper hierarchical levels in a single pyramid of power. This phenomenon is characteristic of any contemporary state. But in partocracy, it reaches its logical completion due to the fact that functionaries are not replaced personally: a socially and psychologically homogeneous medium originates at the higher echelons of power, cemented by common privileges, the spirit of incorporation, collective

---

[29]In fascist Germany, for example, besides the party, military and SS hierarchies, there were also those of student's and women's unions, the Union of Higher School Teachers, the German Labor Front, the Imperial Union of Functionaries, Doctors and Lawyers, the Union of German Girls, and many, many others. (A.A. Galkin, *German Fascism*, Moscow, 1967, p. 373).

responsibility, and other similar social and psychological links.   A natural
question arises: where in such a system is the ruling power localized?

In any hierarchical system created to furnish certain goals, the ruling
power is located in the place where the main goals are formulated and the most
important decisions are made. In the army, it is in the hands of the Commander-
in-Chief and his general staff. In a regular bureaucracy, it is in the hands of the
highest ranking functionary and his deputies. But these are simple ("linear")
systems. Partocracy is not one of them.

At first glance, it may seem (and this agrees with political orthodoxy) that
the Congress of the ruling party is the supreme body in the partocracy: it
outlines the strategy, puts forward the key goals, and makes key decisions. But
suffice it to familiarize oneself with the materials of any such congress and watch
the raised hands (always unanimously!), and, more importantly, the
expressionless faces of the delegates[30] when they make "responsible" decisions,
for it to become clear that important decisions are not made here. They are
made elsewhere; well in advance and long before the Congress. As for the
unanimity, it is attained by the special selection of the delegates.

The next candidate for highest body is the Central Committee. Unlike the
congresses, it gathers much more often and behind closed doors. But it is not at
all necessary to know its behind-the-scenes activities to understand that in
regular (not under restructuring) conditions, this body is not supreme and
decisive, which it must be according to its charter. The simple reason for such a
conclusion is that its staff, which is allegedly elected by the Congress, in reality is
not elected at all, but selected long before the Congress by another party organ -
the Politburo. And though, unlike delegates of the Congresses, members of the
Central Committee are not photographed with raised hands and phlegmatic faces
during their meetings, it is evident that before *perestroika* they, in the majority of
cases, voted unanimously and were always prepared to sanction any decisions of
their "electorate".[31]   So, the field of pretenders is narrowed down to the
Politburo.

---

[30]Over the last fifty years of the CPSU rule, there was not a single case of abstention or a
single debate at the Congresses - in spite of the glaring arbitrariness and permanent failure of
all adopted decisions, which is no longer concealed.
[31]At the beginning of 1989, almost half of the Central Committee's 303 members had more
than ten years' length of service, and 53 of them more than twenty-three years. About two-

The Politburo, unlike the Congress and the Central Committee, is a constantly operating body. It could, therefore, in principle, concentrate in its hands all political (and, consequently, any other) power in the state, formulate key goals, and make key decisions. However, many factors testify against this assumption about power concentration in the partocracy. To be such, it should not only possess all information (which it in fact does), but also be able to process and assess it professionally. In addition, it should control the implementation of the adopted decisions, analyze their results, and introduce corrections,[32] and many other things. And all this in a contemporary totalitarian state, where everything that can be centralized is centralized, beginning with defense and ending with sports and philately.

So, no matter how reasonably the functions of the Politburo members are distributed - no matter how many aides they have or how big an apparatus is assigned to each of them, or in how many convenient "signatures" colossal amounts of incoming and outgoing information is packed - still, any qualified leadership is above their physical and intellectual abilities. It is also impossible because they do not enjoy the freedom of choice necessary for effective leadership, because they are entangled and connected with the ruling layer by thousands of threads. Besides that, ascension to the apex of power is usually a very lengthy process, and it inevitably leads to the loss of originality and intellectual endeavor, without which no freedom of choice can be exercised. Finally, the Politburo is usually composed of people of a very advanced (or even ancient) age, burdened with various ailments.

Therefore, in the partocracy, in the conditions of its stationary functioning, there does not exist any definite localized ruling body. Something similar is observed in the contemporary gigantic international corporations which were studied, for example, by Galbraith (*New Industrial Age* and others). The ruling body in such corporations is the whole technical structure, rather than a person or a group, as it was in the past (Rockefellers, Fords, Duponts). It participates

---

thirds were people of retirement age. And all this in the fourth year of *perestroika*! (See "News of CPSU", N 1,2,5,and 6, and also "Arguments and Facts", March 9, 1990.)

[32]In the well-known manual of R. Johnson, F. Cast, and D. Rosenzweig (*Systems and Leadership*, Moscow, 1971, p. 35), the following functions of a leading organ are listed: 1. planning (selections of goals, politics and programs); 2. the organization itself (inter-connection and inter-relation of sub-systems); 3. management; 4. connection of sub-systems among themselves and with the outer world.

as a whole in formulating goals, making important decisions, and introducing corrections. The involvement of each member is proportional to the quantity and quality of information he possesses, such as information about the production process, external and internal conjuncture, state of sales, distribution of finances, and products. The technical structure does not demonstrate its power, rather, it disguises it in a variety of ways. According to Galbraith, a disguising role is also played by the owners of capital (shareholders), who enjoy the right of veto in emergencies only, when their dividends begin to shrink and their investments are endangered.

In partocracy, the role of technical structure of power is played by the "*nomenclatura*", an isolated privileged layer of functionaries.[33] It is its representatives who are on top of all key party and state institutions and bodies; it is they who participate in establishing major goals of the organization as a whole, in working out the structure of power, in forming the connections between sub-systems; it is they who process all incoming information and pack it into special signatures before sending it up to the supreme bodies, and who prepare decisions and exercise control over their implementation. *Nomenclatura* is the technical structure of the political, economic and social power of the partocracy.

What role do the Congresses, Central Committee and Politburo play in such a structure? To a certain degree, their role - if we continue the analogy with the technical structure - is a disguising one. The role of the members of the Central Committee and the Politburo is in a way analogous to that of the shareholders with the difference, though, that their "investment" is a devoted and irreproachable service to their clan all along their long and hard ascension on the hierarchical steps to the apex of political power. Another similarity is that all three official supreme bodies also possess the right of veto in emergency cases. With the exception of these features that follow from the analogy, the supreme bodies in the partocracy bear many other very specific features, and it is very hard to find their parallels at all in any other social systems.

Before *perestroika* (1985), such emergency cases in the Soviet Communist Party took place several times. If all the early congresses, up to and including the Seventeenth (1934), can be related to the period of the formation of the partocracy, then the congress of the ruling party adopted a non-trivial decision

---

[33]It is shown in detail in the book by M. Voslensky, *Nomenclatura* (1984). *Nomenclatura* will be discussed in more detail in the next chapter.

only once; it happened in 1956 (Twentieth Congress). The Central Committee plenum - three times: in 1957 (a case of the anti-party group), October 1964 (the dismissal of Khruschev), and, probably, 1982 (General Secretary Andropov). In all of these cases, the plenum was preceded by a non-trivial decision by the Politburo which sharply changed the party course. What all four cases had in common was the threat of a split in the ruling party after signs of a split appeared in the Politburo. The plenum removed this threat.

These examples show that the main function of the Central Committee is to prevent the threat of a split in the ruling party, in light of the existing or near-existing split in the constant body - the Politburo. What is the non-trivial function of the latter? Strange as it may seem at first glance, its major function is, firstly, to prevent the split of the Central Committee, and secondly, of the congresses. This is achieved by a thorough, multi-staged selection of candidates to the Central Committee and of delegates to the congresses. Also, the Politburo acts in the selection of candidates to the *nomenclatura*, in the definition of its size, composition, structure, and character of functioning and, consequently, in the selection of candidates to all key positions in the party and state. In other words, the major and non-trivial function of the Politburo members is the management of the cadre.

Even elderly honorary party functionaries, who make the majority in the Politburo of all partocratic states, are able to perform that. And not just able, but able to do it in the best possible manner, as over the years they worked out a special feeling, a "nose", for it. Add to that their considerable personal experience, as each of them ascended to their position over a long period of time. The task of selection is also facilitated by the fact that each candidate is being screened "in parts" from all possible angles. For over a half-century, this supreme party-state body has been fulfilling its priority task - not to let outsiders into positions of real power - with immense success. Not a single congress, not a single plenum, has suffered a split or even the slightest possibility of one. As for the hundreds of thousands of "*nomenclaturists*", very few of them turned out to be unreliable, and none at the higher levels.

Therefore, the priority function of all three supreme bodies in the partocracy is a mutual control over each other, aimed at the prevention of a split in the ruling party. And true, split is a real threat it faces after capturing state power. The second priority function is the formation of a homogeneous and consolidated ruling layer, as all unexpected inhomogeneities can create the potential for a split. Both functions are extremely important. Nevertheless, none of these bodies enjoys power over the other; none of them is in a position where the supreme power is localized. The latter is spread over the whole structure of the partocracy, and it is spread non-uniformly. How is this? According to what principles?

The model does not answer these questions. In fact, it cannot even be called a model, rather it is a draft, a first approximation of reality. The model does not even answer such a simple (but very important) question: in what place is the lower boundary of real power located? Evidently, it does not coincide with the lower level of the ruling party, as its grass-roots members, just like any grass-roots citizenry, are equally far from real power. Further, in the CPSU, its chief ideologist has always been considered as the number two - after the General Secretary - person, rather than as a Politburo member in charge of personnel, as it would seem to follow from the model. Why? What role is played by ideology and how is it linked to the power structure?

Ideology, as a factor of power, is not included in the model. Some other, equally essential factors are not included either. But even this approximated model of the partocracy illustrates its major property: all three organs are aimed, first of all, at preventing splits - at maintaining the unity of the ruling party and the privileged ruling layer. Hence, the totalitarian essence of partocracy is contained already, in the structure and functions of the supreme bodies. It is even apparent in the analysis of the vertical distribution of power as well as in the study of ideology; its specific role and specific functions.

2. Form of Rule

It is very hard to squeeze this weird form of rule into any classification. If we apply Aristotle's classification - autocracy, aristocracy (oligarchy) and democracy (republic) - and assume that partocracy is a special, fourth form of ruling (A.A. Avtorkhanov), then the cult of personality and collective leadership belong to different types. At any rate, the CPSU, the Communist Party of China, and other similar structures are elements of a state structure, rather than political parties in the general meaning of this word. Also, if we apply Montesquieu's classification (republic, monarchy and despotism), then it becomes difficult to find a place for "collective iniquity". (Evidently, a despot is lacking.)

It follows from the above model that in partocracy the political power is distributed throughout its whole structure, the whole organization. This does not mean, however, that we deal with democracy here, since the organization itself encompasses only a small portion of the population. The vertical distribution of power is not uniform; the bulk of it is concentrated in the *nomenclatura*. Again, by no means can it be called an oligarchy, as the *nomenclatura* itself is a mere list of names, positions of functionaries, totally or partially put above all public laws. Somebody must make these lists, change them and update them (the lists being different in different hierarchies). And they are constantly changing. The character of the partocracy changes too: under Stalin, it can be classified as an autocracy. But what about the Brezhnev rule? And, finally, any contemporary parliamentary regime is also a "partocracy", although it is subjected to constant control by the society.

All of this means that partocracy is not a Western form of rule, and, for this reason it does not fit any corresponding classification, which took its beginning with Aristotle and Plato. And it is not alone there. It is also very hard to squeeze into it the Chinese form of rule before the 1911 Revolution.[34] And this form existed for more than two thousand years! In fact, it still exists. It is not difficult to understand the reason for it: in China, a centralized bureaucracy (which comprises the foundation of the partocracy) has always been, not just a method of rule, as is the case in the Western societies, but rather a state super-bureaucracy, and the main political and social force of the society. The same is characteristic of partocracy. This is why comparing it with the Chinese state form is of more interest than the utilization of the Western classifications.

Partocracy was formed in Russia after the Revolution, the four-year civil war, the famine which followed the war in 1921, and the mass repressions. All these things together wiped out almost a quarter of the population, tore up the ties between generations, and created the atmosphere of the social and spiritual "vacuum". As for the first united Chinese state, the Ch'in empire (from 221-206 B.C.), it emerged after an almost two hundred year-long civil war (a so-called

---

[34]Unsuccessfully, even Montesquieu was trying to do it. In his work, *On the Spirit of Laws*, he more than once returns to this subject, and ultimately concludes that it is despotism. Though he makes an addition: "Maybe at the first dynasties, when the state was not that large yet, it slightly deviated from the pattern, but not any more." (1955 edition, p. 268). This is referring to the mid-eighteenth century (the period of greatest territorial expansion). Shortly after that, the character of rule changed again.

"Epoch of Fighting Kingdoms", 403-221 B.C.), and in similar conditions. At the origins of the Russian partocracy, we find Stalin's tyranny. Similarly, at the origins of Chinese statehood, we find the absolute tyranny of Ch'in Shih Huang-ti. In both cases, the empire was united coercively.

Under Shih Huang-ti, all China was divided into thirty-six districts, each of them ruled by three functionaries: a civil one, a military chief, and an inspector. All three hierarchies that made up the carcass of state power were joined in the person of the emperor. Further, all clans and tribes were abolished, and all residents of the empire were called "blackheaded" (an analogy of the abolition of classes and the transformation of all the population into a "working class"). All private property was nationalized ("expropriation of expropriators"), and all inherited ranks of nobility abolished: the emperor created his own new elite. All weapons were taken away from private owners and cast into bells. Again, a very good parallel - with the exception of the bells, of course.

To serve the new bureaucracy, new ranks of nobility were introduced (twenty of them, in all), as well as new conditions for functionaries. A new type of bureaucrat was formed. "In the Chinese society, three to four centuries before Christ, a new criterion by which an individual was valued, one sanctioned by the state, was created. Previously, in the Choi period, individuals were valued by their place in the system of clan ties, in which wealth and personal qualities did not play an important role. Under the new order, the value of a person was defined by hisr place on the ladder of the ranks of the nobility" (L. Perelomov, "Legalist Concept of Equality Before Law and the Khan's Bureaucracy" in *China, Society and State*, Moscow, 1973, p. 59). This concept was reinforced by the principle of equal opportunities for all in attaining ranks and promotions - under the condition of unquestionable devotion to the emperor. And, since all old possessions had been expropriated, new functionaries of all twenty ranks were "enjoying" total dependence on the state. They got their salaries in kind, thus being totally dependent on the graces of the emperor. Their additional zeal was also encouraged by additional payments in kind, and various privileges - among these, the allowed size of coffins depended upon the rank.[35]

---

[35]The highest functionary, for example, the prosecutor, earned two thousand dungs of grain (1 dung equals about 30 kilograms), the head of district earned six hundred dungs, and so it went down to the lowest functionary. (L. Perelomov, *Zing Empire as the First Centralized State in China*, Moscow, 1962, p. 61).

All this vividly reminds us of Stalin's reforms of his state apparatus, with the privileged *nomenclatura* at its top. Another similarity lies in the fact that these reforms were carried out in the atmosphere of total fear and mass repressions. Under Shih Huang-ti, a very complex system of punishment was introduced, including (for example) as many as twelve different types of capital punishment. Not only actions were punishable, but intentions and thoughts as well. Whole families and all direct relatives of condemned people were responsible for crime committed.[36] With such an approach, there were great numbers of criminals, and they were used (as the prototypes of Stalin's "great constructions"), mainly in the erection of the Great Wall of China.

Therefore, Hitler's concentration camps and Stalin's GULAG are not in the least original inventions of our times. Neither are some other ways of securing "the moral and political unity" of the population, such as relocations of whole nations,[37] the practice of genocide against one's own people, the burning of books, the persecution of scientists and professionals in general,[38] and many, many other things.

---

[36] "China represented a chain of jails, and so-called tasks of rule, with the exception of entertainment tours, constructions, marches to the North and South, and shipping of cargoes to the East and West, were evidently reduced to pronouncing verdicts... The condemned ones were subjected to cutting off all their hair ...and were sent to the Great Chinese Wall, which was under construction at that time. In the mornings and afternoons, they were protecting the wall against possible invasions, and in the evenings and at nights, they were building it. The whole of the Great Wall was built by these convicts. On these grounds, one can only estimate how many people were condemned. There existed so-called 'lists'. Those not included in them (in our times they are called 'residency permits' - A.K.) were pronounced criminals." (Go Mojo, *Philosophers of Ancient China*, Moscow, 1961, pp. 636-7).

[37] In the 34th year of his rule (212 B.C.), Ch'in Shih Huang-ti had seven hundred thousand criminals castrated and sent to the construction of the palaces Afang-tun and Lih-nyang. In the 28th year, he moved fifty thousand families of common people to the foot of the mountain Lang-Yetay, probably, to develop virgin lands. In the 35th year, he relocated thirty thousand families to Lii, fifty thousand to Yah-Yang, and thirty thousand to Hubey (see Go Mojo, p. 660).

[38] In 213 B.C., the emperor came to the conclusion that sciences brought too much dissension into the brains of his people and he issued an order to burn all books. This order contained the following items: "1. to burn all books that are not related to the Ch'in history...;3. to execute in public all those who dare to discuss between themselves the Book of Odes and the Book of History [the ancient book of songs and the history book, canonical book]; 4. to execute, together with the families, all those who, looking back at old days, dare to criticize the present...; 6. to exile to the construction of the Great Wall all those who will not burn their

What do we know about the personality of the first Chinese emperor that could be helpful in explaining his unlimited power over the Chinese people? It is known that he - unlike, say, Alexander of Macedonia or Julius Caesar - did not demonstrate any special attractive features either in appearance or character. On the contrary, he had a deformed chest (*osteomalacia*), a "jackal's" voice (because of the constant inflammation of the larynx), he was lopsided and utterly homely and frail. Neither could he boast fearlessness or bravery. On the contrary, in his last years, he was in constant fear of attempts on his life, and he concealed his location from everybody. Under the threat of the death penalty, nobody in the palace should have known in what exact part of it he stayed. That is why, when he died (at about fifty), he was discovered only by the smell of his decomposing body. The description fits Stalin almost perfectly.

Neither was Shih Huang-ti a legitimate heir of the Ch'in state; he found himself on the throne accidentally.[39] He was not, and did not try to be, a religious leader. China, unlike Egypt or Sumer, did not develop any religion - neither before nor after the formation of the single statehood - that could have become a unifying factor. Then, how could such an unattractive person build up such absolute power?

The same question asked about Stalin makes the similarities of the two systems of power even more noticeable, and it thus justifies their comparison. In Stalin's case, the answer is almost self-evident. War, ruin, famine, disintegration of the civil society, total anger - under these forces a new system of state power was formed in Russia. By the will of fate, as a result of a combination or a series of circumstances and his specific characteristic features, Stalin found himself in the most vulnerable and crucial place of this newly forming system, and - knowingly or unknowingly - took over the role of spokesman of one of those

---

books thirty days after the order is issued" (Ibid., p. 560). Still, he did not succeed in eradicating science, because there still remained some scientists. Then , two years later (one year before his death), he issued an order to exterminate all scientists: 460 reputable scientists were gathered together, from all ends of the empire, and buried alive.

[39] As the result of the machinations of an influential merchant, Lu Pu-wei, who was selling horses. In his striving for power, he found, in the small kingdom of Chao, one of the numerous illegitimate sons of the then Ch'in ruler, and when the latter died, he managed to put him on the throne in 246 B.C. This protege died one year later and the throne was inherited by his thirteen year-old son, Ing Cheng. It was this Ing Cheng who, when he became older, got rid of his mother, as well as of Lu Pu-wei, and became emperor Ch'in Shih Huang-ti.

forces. Now we know quite a lot about the nature of these forces and how they were formed in Russia after the revolution. They were: a political party that captured power, a newly born state bureaucracy, an army, and a security apparatus. They were clearing up their relationships, defining the borders of possible compromises and possible blocks. As for China, in the period of the united state formation, such forces were: the remains of the old privileged layer, a new bureaucracy under formation, and the army.

Such was the first Chinese "cult of personality" at the origin of Chinese statehood. It took the state several hundred years to be formed, but it was Ch'in Shih Huang-ti who laid the grounds for this process by introducing so-called "feedings"[40] for the two uppermost ranks. This way he distinguished them from the rest of the military and bureaucratic hierarchies. This was the beginning of the Chinese "*nomenclatura*", which later became hereditary.[41] The on-going rivalry between the ruler and the bureaucracy became less sharp and less devastating as soon as this third buffer party was put between them. The elite became a hereditary bearer of culture, habits, traditions and also of an ideology. The upper levels of its hierarchy were mingling with the emperor's clan and with the tops of the bureaucratic and military hierarchies, the bottom ones - with the local self-government.

The process of the formation of the partocratic power was accompanied, as is known, by the reformulating of the Marxist teaching to adjust it to the task of fortifying the power of a party-state apparatus, and to make it an obligatory and coercively instilled ideology. A similar process can be traced in the period

---

[40]"Feedings" was the right (which could not be inherited) to collect part of the taxes from a given number of households without possessing these households.

[41]In the first years of the Han dynasty (206 B.C. - 220 A.D.), the rank of feeding was lowered down to the eighth one, whereas the numerical value of the "*nomenclatura*" increased sharply and its position was strengthened. In the year 200 A.D., the privileges of the military were expanded; to sue even the lowest ranking military, the emperor's permission was required. Five years later, an additional order removed a number of categories of functionaries from under the regular laws. The order said: "If persons having the fifth rank of nobility, functionaries who receive six hundred dungs of grain and more, and also those who serve the emperor and whose names he knows, will commit a crime and will have to be put in shackles like robbers, a condescending attitude should be worked out towards them." This order was followed by other similar ones, thus nullifying the equality of citizens before the law, which was proclaimed at the formation of the single state (see L. Perelomov, "Legalist Concept of Equality Before Law and the Khan's Bureaucracy" in *China, Society and State*, Moscow, 1973, p. 55).

of Chinese statehood formation. It started under the Han dynasty, together with the formation of the elite, but it was accomplished much later, under the Sung dynasty (960 -1279) - that is, it was a very lengthy process. A single ideology absorbed the concepts of all Chinese major philosophical schools: legalism, Confucianism, Taoism, Maoism - but in a severely revised form. This revision ended up such that their synthesis proved able to justify and substantiate both an extreme centralization of all state power in the emperor's hands, in emergencies (legalism), and the rule of a hereditary privileged top formally headed by a ruler - a servant of the ruling top (Confucianism) - in the quiet periods. A single obligatory ideology encompassed and absorbed the remains of the ancient beliefs and took over the major functions of religion in the consolidation of the society, by substituting God with His earthly "deputy". By isolating China from the rest of the world, ideology not only saved it from the destructive external influences, but also impeded all internal changes, thus preserving the society. But are not the same functions performed by Marxist-Leninist ideology in the partocracy?

The Chinese statehood existed more than two thousand years. Over this period about twenty dynasties succeeded each other. Each of them started with the dictatorship of a military ruler and ended up as a decaying bureaucracy, with a puppet emperor on top of a pyramid of power. The existence of a third force - an elite - lent stability to these swings, lessened their amplitude and frequency, ensured the continuity of power, and perpetuated the system. A multiplicity of nations and states perished over this period, but China - almost within the same borders - not only remained unshakable, but its population increased almost ten-fold, and now it makes up a quarter of the world's population. Indeed, it is a flourishing state!

Summing up this brief digression into Chinese history, let us point out the main characteristics of a Chinese (Eastern) statehood: a total independence of state power from the society, which converts the people into mere objects of rule; all regulations, orders and laws of this power are deprived of any religious or moral sanction; and arbitrary rule is not restricted by anything. This is characteristic of any alien invasion, when a conqueror coercively establishes his own rules and then coercively maintains them. For this reason, each of the numerous conquerors of China (Turks, Huns, Tunguts, Mongols and Manchurians) usually established a new dynasty: As for all other rules, they left them untouched. The consequence of such a specific approach was a constant opposition between the state power and the people,[42] which periodically flared into an open fight.

All other characteristic properties are linked to the ways in which the population was subjugated, and to the reproductive mechanism of power. First, it is an uttermost concentration of the legislative, executive and judicial power in the hands of a single centralized ruling hierarchy headed by an emperor. This hierarchy is formed by the amalgamation - at the upper levels - of bureaucracy, hierarchy of military ranks, and the elite of the society. Second, a single, coercively instilled state ideology is aimed at creating a uniformity of views. Total bureaucratization and hierarchical selection into the upper echelons of power make up a mechanism of reproduction of the system.

If the rulers are totally independent of the ruled, and the people are a mere object of rule, then in such a society, an individual cannot exercise any demands and interests other than those of the state. In such a society, there is no such thing as individuals with their individual problems. Moreover, there are no citizens there, but only subjects of the state (there is no civil state). There are no political parties, in the Western meaning of the word, therefore there is no political struggle - only rebellions and mutinies. Hence, there is no struggle of opinions and nothing that we call pluralism. Dynamism of the society is supported only by the struggle between the emperor's clan and bureaucracy and local governments (softened by the elite), change of dynasties, intra-bureaucratic squabblings, and its evolution is reduced to the swings between "cult of personality" of the emperor and the "collective lawlessness" of the ruling hierarchy.

Western statehood, the origins of which can be traced through Rome and Greece back to Sumer, has an absolutely different character. Although some of the above considered characteristics of Eastern statehood can also be identified in Western history, they have never been united in such an overwhelming combination, which would make it possible to put an obligatory ideology in the

---

[42]The founding fathers of the Chinese state did not conceal this characteristic feature, and that is what made them different from the fathers of partocracy. This is an example of a statement of one of them: "When the state is strong, the people are weak. Therefore, a strong state which follows the right road, strives to weaken its people... If the people are strong, the army is half that strong... If the people are stupid, it is easier to force them to do hard work, and if they are clever, it is not..." (Shanuang, *The Book of the Ruler of District Shahn*, Moscow, 1968, pp. 157, 172, 221). There are many statements like this.

place of religion, and turn citizens into the objects of a bureaucratic apparatus. The crowning achievement of Western evolution was a parliamentary democratic republic, characterized by the total or partial separation of the legislative, executive and judicial powers; their total or partial independence and, as a consequence, their mutual control. For that reason, in such states a centralized bureaucracy, no matter how strong it becomes, is unable to transform into super-bureaucracy and become the only power of the state. Its second characteristic is real, not imitative, elections to all organs of power. Therefore, no matter how strong the position of a head of the state becomes, he is always restricted by the term of office, and he cannot turn into a permanent dictator. For the same reason, people are subjects rather than objects of power. This is opposite to the conception of power in the Eastern states and partocracies, and it represents a real political force. And although power in such a state belongs to one political party, it is always the political parties - rather than bureaucratic squabbling in the partocracy - that create the dynamism of the whole society.

At first glance, partocracy may seem to stand as an interim stage between the Eastern and Western types of statehood. Indeed, together with well-known features of the Eastern type - a single state hierarchy, extreme centralization of power, a layer of privileged ruling bureaucracy, a single ideology instead of religion - it bears some features of a parliamentary republic. separate bodies of legislative (Supreme Soviet), executive (Council of Ministers) and judicial (Supreme Court) power. But it is only a semblance of separation of powers; these organs are neither supreme nor independent. Real supreme powers are someplace else, and these are nothing but imitations. Moreover, the elections are again nothing but imitations of elections: their result is always known well in advance. That is why there is no need for more than one candidate who is indicated from above. And it is natural, since it is imitations of power that are elected, and therefore, there is no struggle of political forces behind the elections, as is the case in the Western states. Further, all power in the state is concentrated in the hands of one political party that delegates its representatives to all branches of the state apparatus from top to bottom. It seems to be the main characteristic of Western partocracies. But in the investigated case a party exists, even though there is no struggle of parties which lends dynamism to the society. Also, there is no opposition. The ruling party is not really a party in the conventional meaning of the word, as it does not represent and defend interests of any social layer of society, but only its own.

Therefore, intermediacy is non-existent: in reality, all principles typical of Eastern (Chinese) statehood are present in the partocracy. This is why there is no place in it for individuals with their unalienable rights, nor for citizens. There are only subjects of the state, and coercive ideology instead of religion. This is why its evolution is also reduced to swinging between the "cult of personality" and a "collective leadership". And if not for the above imitations of power with the comedic elections; if not for the fact that the ruling bureaucracy is called, for some reason, a "party", and its head is called "Secretary General" (but what "secretary" is he?), rather than emperor, or say, khan; or that the ruling layer is peculiarly called "*nomenclatura*" (literally, "calling by name", or "list of names") and is hiding from its people and the outer world together with its privileges - "feedings"; and, last, if not for the name of the state ideology which is for some reason "Marxism-Leninsim" (what Marxism is it?), rather than, say, legalism, then there would be all grounds to call this form of rule "an Eastern partocracy" and reckon it as a variety of a Chinese one. And this investigation would be finished at that. But then the reason for the above named peculiarities would remain unclear, and numerous new questions would be added to the already formulated ones.

CHAPTER 4
ADMINISTRATION AND BUREAUCRACY

1. Formulation of the Problem

The phenomenon called bureaucracy can be traced back to the origination of states. But bureaucracy became a real social epidemic only in the twentieth century when, in a majority of states, its numerical strength began to grow faster than population, national income, and many other indexes as well.[43]

One can distinguish three major directions in the flux of investigations of this universal social evil: scientific studies using tools of sociology and social psychology; universal denunciation as of social disease; and satiric literature ("Parkinson's Law", "Peter's Law", and others). The latter places bureaucracy together with such universal phenomena as, for example, stupidity. The second one connects bureaucracy with the nature of state power. In this case, general denunciation can be illustrated by numerous pronouncements about bureaucracy made by Marx, Bismarck, Lenin, Kafka, Dostoevsky, Spencer and many others, in whose views, other than that, there is nothing else in common.

What catches the eye in the growing stream of scientific studies on bureaucracy is a multitude of mutually excluding viewpoints on its nature. It can be explained both by the complexity of the phenomenon, and by the ambiguity of the term "bureaucracy", which embraces three main meanings: a system of management (ruling); its representatives (functionaries); and a method of ruling ("red tape"). (As many as eleven meanings of the term are given in M. Albrow's *Bureaucracy*, London, 1970, p.85.) Another reason is that there exist two forms of it, one being able to transform into the other. Together with the conventional ("routine") one, controlled by society and a strong central authority, there is another variety uncontrolled by anything or anybody, which was called "monocratic" by Weber.

But the major limitations of most investigations is that they do not take into account the dynamics of the phenomenon. The bureaucratic apparatus will never stay the same; it is always subjected to evolution and it changes (and this is what is important) for the worse. Below, main attention is given to this feature, i.e., to the process of bureaucratization. Its symptoms can be traced in

---

[43]Approximately 4-5% annually, twice as fast as in the nineteenth century. Some statistical data are given in V.P. Makarenko, *Faith, Power, and Bureaucracy*, Moscow, 1988. Data on Russia are given in Zaionchikovski, *Government Apparatus of Autocratic Russia in the Nineteenth Century*, Moscow, 1972.

any administration as soon as its numerical size exceeds a certain threshold and problems of management become more complicated. In other words, the task of bureaucracy investigation is inseparable from problems of management.

Indeed, no state can exist without administration as an apparatus of management. But no matter in what sphere of public life hierarchical administration is created (politics, economy, education, health care, science), no matter how precisely its tasks are formulated at the outset, or how strictly it is controlled by the state or society, certain typical negative symptoms, which are considered as related to bureaucracy, inevitably appear. These symptoms begin to progress in it with time, the process of deterioration being very weakly dependent on national, economic, cultural or other factors. Bureaucratism turns out to be inseparable from administration, which gives rise to a notion that bureaucracy is a "shadow" of any administration, its specific "disease" or deformation. This fact is even reflected in everyday language. We say "administration", "administrator" or at least "functionary" when we are pleased with him, and "bureaucracy" and "bureaucrat" when we are not. This fact is consciously fixed in sociology, where these two notions (bureaucracy and administration) are usually not separated.

Let us for example address a well-known book on sociology by Jan Shepanski (*Major Concepts of Sociology*), where bureaucracy is defined as a:

> method of work by an administration (management and control), based on aligning functions to persons who specialize in them and on creating fixed rules of subordination when a functionary is subordinated to only one superior and gets directives directly from him. A functionary performs his duties within the frames of rationalized division of labor, and his labor is totally separated from his private interests. He works and solves problems strictly within his competence, qualification and his hierarchy, and is constantly controlled. The system does not depend on private links between functionaries, superiors and their subordinates. Promotion and career opportunities depend entirely on the quality of performance and level of qualification (Moscow, 1969, p. 158).

This definition enlists both principles of organizational structure (hierarchy, centralization and professionalism) and conditions of effective functioning (control of performance, independence from extra-office relationships). Furthermore, Shepanski says that "bureaucracy is the system of organization of labor aimed at effective functioning of institutions and goal-oriented groups as a whole. When the above conditions are present, the work exclusively furnishes the goals of the institution or association, and is guided by its interests and permanently controlled. All in all, the administration or institution serves as an impersonal machine kept in good working order." (Ibid.)

Such an approach to the study of bureaucracy was formulated as long ago as Weber. There are many works critiquing it. In particular, they point out that in real life it is impossible to observe all nine named conditions simultaneously. Even in such a highly professional and relatively small administration as a scientific department, it is extremely difficult to keep professional labor apart from private matters and personal relationships. It transforms any administration into a community of competing individuals. It becomes increasingly more difficult to observe the named conditions with the numerical growth of an organization, with the interference of political influences, and with the growing complexity of tasks. As for such highly politicized bureaucratic departments as the Communist Party of the Soviet Union, the majority of the named conditions were never observed there at all. That is why Weber's bureaucracy will be considered below only as an initial, or ideal, model. Also, a systems approach and modeling method will be used, in the way they are used in the natural sciences.

2. The Principle of Hierarchy and Hierarchical Democracy

The term "hierarchy" is usually associated with a multi-layer pyramid with a wide foundation and a steep apex. Its mathematical presentation is a geometric progression defined by two parameters: the quantity at the initial level (basement), and the progression denominator. But this image is a static presentation of a hierarchical society. Such societies of live organisms do not exist in nature. Real hierarchical societies are very dynamic due to the universal upward tendency ("lifting force") of its members, and the magnitude of parameters usually change with time. In human societies, the personal assessment of the probability of the next promotion, together with the emotions caused by such a probability (mobilization of the will, competition, and others), creates the dynamics of the hierarchy, and the psychological atmosphere in which it functions. This demonstrates the mutual influence of the human and organizational factors.

The principles of the hierarchical societies were thoroughly studied using the example of the highly-developed animals and, in particular, primates (sociobiology). The main principle is that of the distribution of all benefits of joint life strictly in accordance with the occupied level. When this principle is violated, the "lifting force" (striving for upward movement) disappears because competition declines, dynamism drops, too, and the society degrades rapidly. Another, less evident, principle is that all benefits of joint life are unalienable in the quiet periods (between restructurings) since they are awarded, or "paid", for the previous effort in ascension, for previous labor. When this principle is violated, instead of the orderly, peaceful existence of the group, there will be constant rivalry, competition, scuffling, exhaustive fights and, ultimately, the same result: degradation. These two principles were worked out in the evolution of species.

Hierarchical societies of animals possess their own hierarchical "democracy" and hierarchical psyche. Hierarchy is always established as the result of aggressive acts, and the hierarchical position gained, together with its benefits, has to be constantly defended. At this point, the second principle is enacted: it is always easier to defend than to attack. When the hierarchy is established, acts of aggression are substituted by rituals of aggression (poses of dominance and subordination), and an orderly life is set in the group. Rivalry and quarrels start anew only when the hierarchy is restructured, when the hierarchical psyche is revealed to its fullest: chase the weaker one and obey the stronger one. Hierarchical "democracy" is implemented in the freedom of vertical advancements in accordance with the physical and psychological qualities of an individual, and also in the freedom to join the hierarchy at its lowest level or to quit it. As a result, being in a group proves to be useful for both the strongest and the weakest.[44] Even though it implies that an individual has to be in a permanent tension; has to constantly train such qualities as strength, aggressiveness, endurance, and psychological stability. Everyone acts

---

[44]Its advantages are studied in great detail and they are: better protection against predators, better access to food, more effective protection of the habitat, favorable conditions for offspring, and so on. The advantage enjoyed by the group as a whole is that the strongest, the better fit ones lend viability to the whole group as they contribute comparatively more into the heredity fund of the generations to follow.

to his own benefit, but it turns out that everybody benefits. The apex of the pyramid in such a society is occupied by a leader. The degree of centralization in such a society is minimum, and the leader is not in the least a tyrant in the human meaning of this word.

Such hierarchical groups are native to almost all primates, almost all close relatives of man, and probably were typical for his direct ancestors. As it is now well-known, elements of psyche and behavior are also inherited through genes, so humans also carry part of this "forgotten" past. The question is where we can expect it to be revealed and what shape it can take. Among particular cases, an army and a mob are the most characteristic: in both of them common elements of psyche and behavior are tuned in unison (resonance), and therefore, they increase with the growth of the numerical value.[45] Such a hierarchical "legacy" is undoubtedly very individual, and it varies within very wide limits among humans. But any human organization, depending on its intrinsic structure, goals and methods, absorbs "human material" selectively, and this leads to the accumulation of certain human types and the demonstration of certain elements of psyche and behavior. Below, this regularity will be illustrated using the examples of the army and bureaucracy.

Now let us return to "democratic centralism". As any administration is built on the hierarchical principle, then, when we speak about democracy and centralization in it, they should be understood as a hierarchical democracy and a hierarchical centralization of hierarchical constructions. That means that if any reality at all exists behind the term "democratic centralism", elements of democracy should be hierarchical. According to what was said before, they are as follows: formation of the hierarchy from the bottom up (as, for example, is the case in local self-government), freedom of vertical movements according to individual qualities, freedom to join or quit, freedom of competition. This principle can be observed in an organizational structure only if any stable and

---

[45]The more numerous the group (and, in particular, a human organization), the less the influence of individual differences of its members, and oppositely, the greater role in its evolution is played by deep, ineradicable, common to the majority, features of individuals. With the growth of the numerical value, the latest cultural differences are repressed, "averaged" and erased first, then go the group and class differences, still later - the racial, ethnic, and biological ones. This law of large human groups is probably true of all numerous human organizations, including bureaucracies, in relatively quiet periods of their evolution. When equilibrium is distorted, it is not true any more, and individual features, especially those of a leader, come to the forefront.

relatively long-lasting equilibrium is possible between democracy and hierarchical centralization in it.

Such stable states, if they exist, must be somehow connected with the hierarchical psyche which is formed within a particular group. In the case of humans, they should also be connected with elements of the hierarchical "morale". In a hierarchical psychic society, justice means inequality and freedom means freedom from competition. In the societies of animals it is controlled only by the unconditioned reflexes which not only forbid killing of their own kind, but even injuring them to any serious extent. Such societies also enjoy the cult of an individual (subordination to the stronger ones, and especially, to the leader), as well as poses of dominance and subordination. Could it be that "cults of personality" are growing from a similar root? Principles of such a "democratic centralism" are really unique as they are worked out by the whole evolution of species.[46]

A hierarchical society such as the one considered above enjoys minimal centralization. An opposite extreme is of interest for the study of bureaucracy: that of maximum centralization. Let us consider the example of the army, where all orders and commands issued by a superior are a must for their subordinates at all levels. They can even be given over the heads of intermediate chiefs. Their unquestionable implementation is first of all ensured by the trinomial (more rarely a quadruple) structure itself: any disobedient or mutinied detachments can be brought to obedience by giving the corresponding orders to the two other detachments. Though such conflicts are rare, the possibility of such a solution acts as a permanent deterring factor. Implementation of orders and commands is further guaranteed by the parallel hierarchies of the controlling and punitive organs: special divisions, trial courts, places of detention and incarceration. The degree of centralization is also enhanced by the secretive character of its functioning, especially in war-time. And lastly, the army is always formed from above, and any restructurings in it are also performed from above. All this transforms the cadre staff of the army into a special sub-system, contrasted with

---

[46]To highlight their originality, let us compare them with the organization of societies in the world of insects. There the principle of societal construction is not based on individuality and hierarchy, but rather on morphological differences: between the queen, working bees and drones. Principles of hierarchical democracy or hierarchical psyche are lacking altogether, and the cult of community stands for cult of an individual. You will not find individual demands here. All demands are public.

the rank-and-file soldiers who are direct executors of the orders and who usually compose more than ninety percent of any army.

The army is not only the simplest example of extreme hierarchical centralization; its intrinsic structure and its mechanisms of functioning have been elaborated over millennia in a wide variety of local conditions, and therefore they can be considered universal. Further, the influence of a human factor is reduced to its minimum, therefore, the influence of the organizational factor becomes dominant and visual. In war-time, the army is probably the only example of a numerous, hierarchically centralized administration which is able to function very effectively and without the typical bureaucratic perversions or at least with very few of them, as long as in a regular civil administration these perversions are difficult to separate from the processes of normal functioning. On the contrary, in peaceful periods, the army acquires some negative features typical of regular bureaucracy. When the state power is weakened, the transformation of the army into a military bureaucracy can evolve to its logical completion: capture of the state power. It happens almost annually in some African and Latin American countries, which provides us with good examples of all stages of the degradation of centralized hierarchies, i.e., the degradation of an administration into a bureaucracy. Another example is military settlements within the borders of a country.[47] Below, the army will be used as an illustrative example in a number of cases.

3. Evolution of Administration (Bureaucratization)

Bureaucratization is spoilage of administration: a violation of optimum functioning, a shifting of goals and tasks of management, and so on. To study it is to study the causes and character of this spoilage, i.e., using more scientific language, the study of direct evolution. Lastly, it is an investigation of the

---

[47]In Russia, they were introduced by Alexander the First, and they existed from 1816 until 1857. Common barracks, uniforms for all members of the family beginning at six years old, all worked by command, and even marriages were arranged on command. Such settlements encompassed five regions and by the end of his reign, amounted to four hundred thousand (fifty regiments). They were abolished because of their total ineffectiveness: agricultural works never started in time, grain was crumbling, hay rotted from rains, corruption and bribery were flourishing. Above all, from the beginning of the 1830s, these settlements were repeatedly, and with increasing frequency, stricken by mutinies and uprisings (see F. Brockgaus and I. Evfron, *Military Settlements*).

inevitability of such evolution, which converts an optimally working administration into a parasitic bureaucratic department. These are the questions studied below.

First, a word about causes. The main cause is incompatibility of the principles of organizational structure. The principle of centralized hierarchy demands distribution of payments and all other benefits strictly in accordance with the occupied hierarchical level, as long as a principle of professionalism implies that payments are related to professional training and quality of performance at work. Violation of the first principle inevitably leads to a drop in dynamism, as stimuli to ascension also drop, competition declines, the number promoted goes down, which cannot but lower the optimum functioning. Violation of the principle of professionalism leads to the same result. As stimuli to enhance qualifications and to gain experience weaken, and incompetence grows, the process reduces responsibility for concrete results of work.

Therefore, it is possible to keep the initial optimum level of functioning only in a case when a stable compromise between these two opposite tendencies can be found. In other words, when dynamism goes down (a violation of the principle of hierarchy), there should exist some inner processes that are able to restore it. The same is true of a violation of the principle of professionalism.

Such stable compromise is impossible, because the principle of professionalism implies decentralization of responsibility, which is very difficult (if at all possible) to combine with centralization of leadership in any stable manner in the same hierarchy. To do so, at least two interrelated hierarchies are needed, as is the case for example, with local self-government in a democratic society. Therefore in any administration, it is impossible to keep its initial optimum state without duress from outside.

Weber himself pointed out that to make bureaucracy function effectively it must be supplemented by "special force established by society, i.e., such force that is legitimate and makes an individual sometimes do what he does not want to do" (see R. Johnson, F. Cast, and D. Rosenzweig, *Systems and Leadership*, Moscow, 1971, p. 94). That is not enough, though: duress from outside has to be increasing to compensate for the incompatibility of the principles described above. To explain that process, it is necessary to pass from general reasoning to consideration of elementary processes within an administration, the most important being the relationship between a superior and his subordinate.

Let us first consider how it works in the army, where all processes are simplified to their utmost. Orders and commands are always formulated as specifically and in as much detail as possible and at the same time briefly, and the subordinate must implement them quickly and accurately. Such orders usually contain not only what is to be done but also how it is to be done. If the latter component is lacking for some reason, a serviceman must use statutes, which are worked out in great detail and utilize the experience of all times and all nations. Statutes restrict the field of individual initiative, risk and enterprise, and at the same time release the executor from the responsibility for unforeseen negative results of his actions. Commanders take the responsibility for them. Only in rare cases which are not foreseen or cannot be foreseen in the statutes, is a soldier allowed to act on his own initiative and to bear personal responsibility for it. Only in this very narrow field does decentralization of responsibility exist, along with the total centralization of leadership.

This is how matters stand with the army with its relatively simple and negative tasks, where individual qualities of a serviceman are a mere addition to the general ones - namely discipline, efficiency, punctuality, and obedience. In civil life, where regular administrations have to work, tasks are much more complex and diverse, concrete situations are much more tangled. Here it is usually impossible to foresee all diversity of situations, all possible turns of events, all varieties of human types. Hence, numerous regulations and rules, recommendations, explanations, and specifications are used here rather than commands and orders. They are as a rule formulated rather loosely, dimly, flexibly and loquaciously, leaving an executor some space for initiative, for maneuvering among unforeseen circumstances and unexpected difficulties. A subordinate is expected not only to be professionally fit, but to possess certain initiative and prudence - to a much greater extent than in the army. Who then is responsible for unforeseen and unfavorable consequences of the orders? And associated with this, how is additional risk compensated for?

First, about responsibility: in the ideal administration all responsibility rests with the executor (utmost decentralization of responsibility). In all imperfect administrations, this responsibility is divided between the superior and the subordinate. Evidently, the greater the centralization the greater the responsibility invested in the chief, until almost all of it goes to him with the growth of the degree of centralization - as in the army. Concrete patterns of the distribution of responsibility are not only non-existent, they cannot be established for all cases of life with its infinite variety of human characters, conditions, and tasks, which all demand different degrees of leadership centralization and responsibility decentralization. So, in any administration, at any level, issuing orders is in fact a joint act carried out by a chief and his subordinate. They both bear responsibility for their execution and possible unfavorable results.

From here follows the inevitability of the growth of centralization over time, the main initiator of it being the subordinate rather than his superior as, for him, greater centralization means lesser responsibility for the unfavorable result of their joint action. It is more natural for him to acquire the "pose of subordination", to ask for more detailed instructions and to wash his hands if the result is not quite what it was planned to be. Large contemporary administrations are administered by rather ordinary or average people, the majority of whom would not take risks. That would then result in upward pressure from below on the scale of the whole hierarchy. This inevitably leads to the growth of leadership centralization and, consequently, results in a reduction of a subordinate's responsibility. A tendency to escape individual responsibility and merge into the collective one gradually becomes universal. This process goes even faster if the outer power uses the administration to strengthen its own prestige, its influence or stability, rather than for the administration's direct goals. This is usually the case in authoritarian and totalitarian regimes. In this case, pressures from below and above are summed up.

Another consequence of shared responsibility is that the selection of immediate subordinates becomes a crucial task. Decisive criteria in this selection involves such qualities as loyalty, respect, and personal devotion, rather than professional ones, since in the long run they will have to share responsibility "amicably". But this violates two conditions of effective administrative management: professionalism and de-personalization. The apparatus of power gradually converts into a group of interconnected and inter-dependent functionaries with all the shortcomings, vices and contradictions typical of the majority of human societies. The human factor comes onto the stage.

What about rewards for additional initiative and risk? They are "additional" because, according to the principle of free hierarchy, any payment and all benefits and privileges must be distributed strictly by hierarchical levels and should be unalienable. Without it, hierarchy loses its dynamism and stability. How is it rewarded in the army? Every member (except rank-and-file) is simultaneously a commander and a subordinate, and is included in two hierarchies: military ranks and military positions.   Ranks are awarded for irreproachable service (by virtue of long service).   To move successfully up the hierarchy of ranks, it is necessary to demonstrate unquestioning obedience and discipline.   Demonstration of initiative or other similar qualities is not needed. The principle of hierarchy is totally observed here.   To perform the duties of a commander, however, is not enough.   It is necessary to demonstrate an ability to rule and to exert initiative, and to possess endeavor and prudence.   It is in this hierarchy that problems with reward for additional effort arise, as it is extremely difficult to account for all such qualities.   Awarding orders, medals and diplomas would not solve the problem, as they also have to be distributed by hierarchical levels, and it could be effective only when they enhance chances for the next promotion.   The latter is possible only when enough vacancies are available. Vacancies are available in sufficient quantities only in war-time (physical losses) or during fast growth of the army in a pre-war situation.   When these two factors are lacking, additional effort and risk remain, in fact, unpaid, and slowly but steadily the army transforms into a military bureaucracy with all the vices of conventional bureaucracy.

Consequently, in the army the two hierarchies are, so to speak, organically amalgamated, one of them playing the main role in the centralization of leadership (hierarchy of power), and the other in the decentralization of responsibility (professional hierarchy).   It solves the problem of rewarding additional work, but solves it satisfactorily only in times of rapid growth or severe losses.   The situation is more complex in civil bureaucracy.   It is even more complex if three parallel hierarchies (as is the case in science - those of positions, ranks and degrees) are created, because it is much more difficult to assess the individual contribution of any functionary, as was discussed earlier. That is why the promise to promote a functionary becomes a conventional way to pay his additional zeal.   This is again a joint act of a superior and a subordinate, as their joint promotion is the most natural way to settle the matter. If a vacancy opens up elsewhere, a superior is interested in filling it with his man and preserving relations with him, because he himself has chosen him from among the most eligible.   That is how the inner collectivism begins to sprawl this time horizontally, rather than vertically, giving rise to clanism and corporativism.

No administrative apparatus based on the principle of centralized hierarchy and professionalism can operate effectively, as it is with the army, unless it constantly expands.   Then a promise to promote gives rise to real expectations and corresponding emotions. This is the case when promotion is realistic or very probable. If not, and there are not enough vacancies, then a functionary who estimates the prospect of his own promotion negatively, begins to reward himself on his own for his additional initiative, risk or effort by using his position (his "property") for private purposes. That is how grounds for malfeasance in office, corruption, and similar phenomena are furnished.

Therefore, expansionism, together with the growth of centralization, is a second process accompanying bureaucratization. The promise of promotion plays the role of a promissory note with an unguaranteed payoff. The probability for it to be paid off is enhanced with the growth of the number of vacancies, i.e., when a department is expanding. Both superior and subordinate are equally interested in it, which leads to an extended reproduction of bureaucracy. As soon as it slows down, promotion of functionaries also slows down, and many of them begin to assess the chances for promotion pessimistically, thinking that their additional zeal remains unrewarded. It cannot but affect their attitude to their duties. Such functionaries will increasingly think that they work "for free". Thus, they will face an alternative: whether to reward themselves on their own or to stop exerting any additional effort at all, abiding themselves, just as it is in the army, by direct implementation of all instructions, insisting upon their more detailed and exact formulation.

As soon as the initiative and energy of such functionaries is concentrated on the latter course, forcing official promotion out to second roles, they turn into the category of "stopped" bureaucrats, forming a "reserve army" of administration. Gradually, their activity is reduced to passing orders and commands from top to bottom, and to demanding new recommendations, explanations, and clarifications. Having surrounded themselves with all this, such "stopped" functionaries accompany their every official step, every order, with justifying papers, justifying references and requests. Paperwork and paper waste are snowballing, which is an indirect indication of growing centralization. Gradually, efforts to enhance professional qualities decline resulting in de-personalization and the decline of dynamism.

The population of the "stopped ones" (in sociological literature they are often called "settled", as opposed to "nomads") plays a very important role in the transformation of administration into bureaucracy. Stopped ones are, in a sense, real bureaucrats, which are opposed by another population, that of "pacing" ones ("nomads"). The pacing ones can take risks (they are paid by promotion for that), suffer defeat, ascend, and descend. This population is dynamic and its dynamism is conveyed to the whole administration. Pacing ones compete with each other for the best prospective positions. Stopped ones, on the contrary, avoid initiative and risks, as they consider them unjustified ("initiative is punishable"). Therefore, they easily form various informal groups and groupings, clans and corporations. Their upward promotion is usually a group one rather than individual. Unlike pacing ones, they are not individualists, they are collectivists. To them, "self-preservation" means not only preservation of the achieved, "conquered" hierarchical level, as is the case with the pacing ones, but also preservation of a group, clan, and established informal structure; the whole order.

At first, the equilibrium between these two populations is static, and a relative number is subjected to frequent fluctuations (one who is stopped today can start moving tomorrow and vice versa). This state exists for some time. Later, though, they transform into two permanent psychic commonalities, two sub-systems of bureaucratic department: a dynamic one and a conservative one. This disintegration of a single hierarchy into two different populations and their gradual transformation into two hierarchical sub-systems can be considered as a completion of the first stage of bureaucratization. The conservatism of the stopped ones cements the whole structure of administration. It lends it rigidity, stability, and resistance to all restructuring from the outside. This property is expressed in a well-known phrase: "bureaucracy won't sink". As for the dynamic sub-system, it makes administration more mobile, elastic, better able to adjust to changes in the environment. And as long as the numerical value of this sub-system remains high enough, the administration manages to carry out its main tasks more or less satisfactorily.

4. Departmentality

A department is an administration under the command of some organ or an individual. As for its derivative - departmentality, it bears a negative connotation, and implies an element of spoilage. This is understandable, as departmentality is an inseparable companion of bureaucratization.

In the scheme given on page 93, it is seen that administration can evolve towards the growth of centralization (to the right on the graph), or vertically - towards the growth of autonomy. The processes of the growth of centralization and autonomy are interrelated and further each other. In the previous section, we highlighted the first of them, now let us concentrate on the second one.

The initial degree of an administration's autonomy is set forth by the principle of confidentiality. In totalitarian conditions, confidentiality inevitably transforms itself first into secrecy and then into permanent conspiracy. Growth of centralization strengthens vertical links between functionaries at the expense of weakening horizontal ones, thus increasing autonomy. Its further evolution is determined by hierarchical selection, the collective character of functionaries' activities and their consolidation, and other factors. These processes, linked to the growth of the conservative sub-system and alteration of the administration's composition, lead to the alteration of the uniting goal (below: goal reduction). Growth of autonomy, alteration of the composition, and goal reduction compose departmentality.

The key process in departmentality is hierarchical selection. If we throw a glance at huge contemporary bureaucratic apparatuses that rule industries, trade unions, education, health care, culture, and sciences in a totalitarian state and ask what human types dominate at the upper levels of hierarchical pyramids, this is what one will see: not in the least, do bright and strong personalities, with either wide cultural or mere human horizons, nor enthusiastic idealists or moralists dominate there - neither do talented professionals, carried away by their professions. Typically, upper levels of hierarchical pyramids are occupied by regular administrators, not so much specialists as politicians in the broad meaning of this word. Some of them could have been talented scientists or engineers or teachers. But the road to the apex of knowledge is very long, sometimes it takes decades to cover it. And, since the development of contemporary sciences and different special fields is so rapid, sooner or later it leaves any professional behind, depreciating his knowledge and experience. Also, long ascension cannot but deform his demands, interests, and, even, his world outlooks. Exceptions, though not rare, sink in the mass of mediocrity and they rarely influence the functioning of the bureaucracy.

Hence, at the upper levels of contemporary bureaucratic apparatuses, the dominant human type, as a rule, will be a commonplace, mediocre, average person, who, for some reasons, has chosen the profession of ruling others. If we look at them closely, though, they all have some common features. What are they and how are they formed? And why and how do administrators become bureaucrats?

Any hierarchical administration provides power for a few over the many, thanks to its hierarchical structure. Growth in the degree of centralization strengthens this power, since it lowers the demands for professional adequacy. That is why those move most successfully up the hierarchical ladder who seek power and have corresponding inborn inclinations, rather than those who aim at professional refinement. Such individuals compose a certain small percentage in any human population. But with time they accumulate and begin to dominate at the top of any hierarchy. And the closer an administration is to the core of totalitarian power, the higher their percentage and the more effective their dominance is.

Additionally, those who hunt for power as a means to get material benefits, as well as mere careerists, moved by ambitions, vanity and other stimuli accumulate at the upper levels. These three related categories, accumulating as the result of hierarchical selection, will gradually become a dominant contingent in any hierarchically centralized administration. They will make up a single psychic entity, which, in the process of its growth starts to affect natural hierarchical selection, imparting to it some features of the artificial one. Gradually, the composition of the whole administration changes. It is accompanied by a change (simplification) of initial goals and tasks.

For any of numerous administrations, the simpler, more understandable, more "tangible" the goal is, the higher the aims at integration, dynamism, and effectiveness are. The army again provides the clearest example. Its controlled and easily manageable dynamism is bought at the expense of the simplification of tasks, by reducing them to the negative ones (to intimidate, browbeat, surround, destroy). Military administration is effective only for such tasks for the very reason that the specific nature of the goal in the process of hierarchical selection is forming the corresponding composition of the whole administration. The characteristic type of a military man, filtered out and polished by hierarchy and "educated" in the process of long ascension is a good illustration of the connection between goal and composition. It can be traced in any administration of sufficient size, and, consequently, the effectiveness of hierarchical selection is high too. Reduction of goals inevitably changes the composition and vice versa.

Its most important consequence is the further intensive growth of the autonomy of the department, which is achieved by forcing out the controlling influence of the outer power. In totalitarian states such control is performed through a specially selected and periodically replaced ruling top, together with the administration's leader, and a parallel controlling hierarchy in the ruling party ("shadow" departments in the hierarchical party apparatus). Alteration of the composition of the top, and, as a result, replacement of the leader (appointed from outside) by an administration's own protege, weakens or even altogether eliminates the first type of control. Then starts deliverance from outer control at all levels by a means of coalescence with the controlling hierarchy (formation of a single party apparatus). Further evolution of the antagonism between a department and outer power depends on the strength of the latter, on the general situation and on other factors. And if the controversy is won by the department, then special processes typical of the so-called self-organized systems begin to unfold: forcing out of the outer control, formation of self-government, and alteration of relationships with the environment.

Let us illustrate it with examples. The reduction of goals can be traced in the evolution of the department of Goskomsport (State Committee on Sports and Recreation), using evidence of the world ex-champion in weightlifting, Yuri Vlasov, as an authoritative source. When this department was first created, its goal was to organize health improvement programs and facilities for the entire population by involving it in different types of sports activities in schools, colleges, and sports clubs; at work and at home. In the name of this goal, working places were created and funds were obtained. Years and decades passed. An extensive hierarchy of sports management was formed, followed by changes in its composition, especially in the ruling top. Simultaneously, a reduction of goal took place and gradually the initial goal of the department was reduced to the training of a relatively small number of "prospective" sportsmen in a relatively small number of first-rate sports facilities. Such a task was definitely easier than the one initially chosen. It was also easier to assess the ultimate result by the number of champions, medals, and victories. However, the initial goal is not revoked, but just moved aside, converted into a parade; money and vacancies are still obtained for implementing this task. As the expansion of the department is still cloaked in the name of the improvement of the health of the entire population, professional sportsmen are disguised as amateurs, and this is done with great success.

Another example, which has now become a classic, is Minvodkhoz (Ministry of Water Economy). The original goal of this administration was to organize a single country-wide system of irrigation, watering, and draining of soils with the ultimate result of enhancing crops, making water usage more effective as well as creating other economic and ecological benefits. The department grew, a goal reduction took place and all of these economic benefits were gradually forced into secondary roles: it is not easy to carry them out and to assess their results and the effectiveness of the department. The mere digging of the soil, and redistributing waters from one region to another soon became the main occupation of the Ministry. The effectiveness of the department was evaluated by the number of erected dams, the volume of elevated soil, and the cubic kilometers of redistributed water. Behind it the real goal of a swollen bureaucratic apparatus was hiding: joint self-preservation.

This example vividly demonstrates the almost fantastic vitality of the department. Even "the dictatorship of the proletariat" was unable to stop its expansion or, at least, to slow it down. In the period of *perestroika,* when the majority of society stepped forward in defense of the environment, it became possible (only) to slightly "curb" the monster! Even then it was reborn under a new "signboard".

In the evolution of the Bolshevik party, one can trace a short period when it was developing as a subordinate to Lenin's department of general and ideological management in the system of state power. With this example, we can see both ways of ousting outer control: hierarchical control of the soviets was forced out by way of an amalgamation of the party apparatus with the soviet executive bodies into a single state-party apparatus, thus making them subordinate to the party. Additionally, the influence of the leader was removed by forcing him out from the party apparatus and by replacing him with a party protege (Stalin).

CHAPTER 5
COMMANDOCRACY

1. Commandocracy[48] - Model of Administration

Any administration is a goal-oriented organization with a homogeneous inner structure, controlled from the outside. The goal of inner structure (together with rules defining relationships and decision-making procedures), along with a means of control and corrections from outside, this is what defines the main facets of its activity at the early stage.

But no social organization remains homogeneous if it increases in size over time. Its initial structure inevitably undergoes change. In the previous chapter, it was shown that it is these changes that determine the process of bureaucratization, and they include the following: the initial goal is simplified ("reduction of goal"), the original composition is changed (the result of "hierarchical selection"), the inner structure is rebuilt (a ruling top separated and isolated), autonomy is increased (independence from the outer power and society). Evidence of corruption becomes the first sign of the dominant socio-psychological links and the transformation of the administration into a specific community of functionaries - bureaucracy.

Mainly, it is inner reasons that cause and determine the above processes. That is why bureaucracy is so universal and the image of a bureaucrat is so typical - they have been the same over centuries (and even millennia), even in completely different types of social order, systems of government, economic, social or cultural levels of the society and other outer conditions. The expansion of bureaucracy in our times is a mere consequence of the complication of the tasks of management, which, besides other reasons, is also connected with the general growth of the world population and, what is more important, its density.

The main inner reasons for bureaucratization are considered below at a little different perspective and in more detail than in Chapter 4. Additionally, the initial model of administration is constructed on the assumption that two hierarchies - the professional one and that of power - are organically combined. The hierarchy of power is responsible for the centralization of leadership, and the professional hierarchy for the decentralization of responsibility. The latter is a hierarchy of knowledge and skills, whereas the former is one of will and

---

[48]Commandocracy differs from partocracy in the transformation of the ruling party into an element of the state structure. In Russia, this process was completed by the beginning of the 1940s.

coercion. Each of them has its own characteristic inner structure, its own rules for procedures and relationships, its own degree of democracy and centralization, and its own ways of rewarding. Their interconnections, interrelationships, and interactions, which define the process of bureaucratization, are described with the help of five parameters of the state: degree of centralization, professionalism, de-personalization, dynamism, and autonomy. The choice of such parameters (see below, section 2c) contains the same degree of arbitrariness as the choice of the model itself, since in the modeling method they are mere "tools" of investigation.

a. Hierarchy of Power

The inner structure and characteristic features of the functioning of this hierarchy can be most easily examined by looking at the army, where it dominates. Here the main decisive parameters are the degree of centralization and autonomy. Centralization is created in the army by its very hierarchical structure, its specific rules and procedures, and by the existence of the parallel hierarchies of the punitive organs; control and correction. Autonomy is created by confidentiality, secrecy, mechanisms of self-government, and isolation from society. It grows as the degree of centralization grows, which indicates a direct correspondence between the two parameters. Another factor that unites these two parameters is that each of them characterizes the organization as a whole, and this is not so with all other parameters of state (see below). Such a property is traced in any centralized hierarchy, and it is characteristic of any bureaucracy in general.

In the army, centralization characterizes the degree of subjugation, and ultimately, the degree of de-personalization of a serviceman. The degree of de-personalization depends on the hierarchical level. Isolation of the army from the society, a system of secrecy, an utmost centralization of coercion, an obligation to implement quickly and unquestioningly all orders and commands, and a specific system to ensure such an unquestioning obedience, result in the creation of the image - especially among the lower levels - of the leadership as an almighty and tightly-united hierarchy of direct and indirect bosses, which is enforced by the hierarchy of intimidation (guardhouses, jails, penalty isolation wards and court-martials). The power of such an enforced hierarchy cannot but cause a permanent fear, which, in war-time, can even exceed fear of the enemy.

A rank-and-file soldier is in fact opposed to the whole army, and his individuality is dissolved in the collective almost in the same manner as it would in the crowd. In view of all this, we can say that the army represents the utmost embodiment of centralization and de-personalization, where an individual is totally subjugated and transformed into a machine. It is the only variety of human organizations in which the terms hierarchy, power, and authority[49] are understood so closely to their literal meaning.

Such is the mechanism of extreme centralization, autonomy, and de-personalization. Now let us consider the dynamism of the army. It is ensured, first of all (and again!) by the hierarchical structure itself. In the army, just like in any other hierarchy, each member is paid strictly in accordance with his hierarchical position. This makes servicemen move along the ladder of ranks in such a manner as if there exists some "pull" acting upon them. Also, the army enjoys a "buoyant" force as well. It is an oppositely directed (downward) growth of hardships of service and punishments. Both of these forces, when added together, increase the intrinsic energy, and the stability in the community of army servicemen. The pattern for the distribution of the hardships of service, punishments, encouragements and awards, and material benefits for each hierarchical level is found experimentally in such a manner that maximum effectiveness in the achievement of the organization's goal is attained at the minimum expense. Evidently, as long as the goals are different in war and peace times, the encouragement and punishment packages will also be different.

b. Professional Hierarchy

The hierarchy of knowledge and skills, unlike the hierarchy of power, is a free hierarchy which is formed naturally from the bottom. It is characterized by freedom to join and to leave, freedom to disseminate information and freedom to compete for positions in the hierarchy. Therefore its geometry (the number of levels, their interconnection, the numerical value of each level) reflects the dispersion of individualities according to their natural abilities (talents) and personal qualities, and it also takes into account the individual contribution of each one into the aggregate knowledge. Any restrictions of any of these three

---

[49]"Authority" - from the Latin *auctoritas*: power or influence. "Hierarchy" - from the Greek *hieros*: sacred, and *orche*: power.

freedoms will restrict the free influx of talents, their free realization, and depth of ideas; it will lower the general effectiveness of the hierarchy.

Free autonomous scientific communities of the past are the best example of the hierarchy of knowledge. But in the present-day epoch of the scientific and technological breakthrough, when science has become a productive force of society, scientific communities have lost their autonomy[50] and the principles of the free hierarchy have inevitably been distorted. On the other hand, a qualified and effective management of any sphere of contemporary life in our society requires direct inclusion of professionals into the apparatus of rule rather than mere consultations with them at all levels of the administrative hierarchy as it used to be in the near past. In other words, the principle of professionalism, to a certain limited degree, should necessarily be incorporated into any contemporary administration. What is this degree and what are the limitations?

Of the three above listed freedoms, the limitations are inevitable and necessary in the first one, the freedom to join or quit. It takes years, and sometimes even decades - as in science, for example, where it becomes an all-state task - to prepare a contemporary higher professional. The stage of direct training, which utilizes the systematized experience of the previous generations, is followed by the stage of preliminary accumulation of individual experience (on-the-job training), and only after that starts the ascension on the hierarchy of knowledge. At this stage "free" exit is undesirable and often even impossible. Inevitable, but not necessary, is also the limitation of the third freedom, that of competition: it lowers the dynamism of the hierarchy and hence should be minimalized. But really impermissible is the limitation on the free dissemination of information because it makes it impossible to assess the individual contribution and, consequently, the fair reward for it.

All of this imparts to the professional hierarchy a number of specific characteristics which are non-existent in the hierarchy of power. It has to have the minimum degree of centralization and de-personalization and at the same time, the maximum degree of autonomy and professionalism. Accordingly, the character of its intrinsic dynamism undergoes changes: it is no longer a

---

[50]As an example, one can consider the priority areas of contemporary research: thermonuclear fusion, space exploration, and AIDS. Each of them has, besides a scientific aspect, a social, a political, a philosophical, and many other aspects as well. Thousands of researchers, engineers, and public activists are involved in solving each of them. The same is in other areas of science as well.

compulsory dynamism of an organization, rather it is a dynamism of free competition of individuals which reveals and encourages all their talents and personal merits. In such a hierarchy, individual demands, interests, and goals are domineering rather than those of an organization, like in the hierarchy of power. It enjoys a distinctive hierarchical democracy and hierarchical psyche.

c. *Two-hierarchical Model*

In any contemporary administration one can detect, as it was underlined above, a very complicated combination of two hierarchies: that of power and the professional one. They are organically united by common goals, common tasks, and a common ruling center. Under these circumstances, the functions of each of them are partially redistributed between the two, and a complicated system of compromises between functionaries' duties - those of power and the professional ones - is established. The above introduced parameters characterize the most important of these compromises.

How can this system of compromises be achieved? What conditions can ensure its equilibrium and stability without the ever-growing correcting interference of the outer power? First of all, let us consider two boundary cases: the army, and the administration of the local self-government. For these two the answers will be relatively simple. A general case of administration will be considered in the next section and it will be shown that its bureaucratization is the result of violation of the equilibrium; violation of compromises.

Of all varieties of administrations, local self-government enjoys the most harmonious combination of the principles of hierarchical power and that of professionalism. Hierarchy of power is elective there, it is periodically replaced and is under the total control of the society at all levels. As for the hierarchy of professionals, it is completed from above by the specially trained functionaries. Periodical replacements, different ways of completion and the constant control from the society prevent their amalgamation and restrain the process of bureaucratization. Their relative independence creates an opportunity for mutual control and at the same time for a favorable combination of positive properties of each of them: simplicity and effectiveness of management with professionalism, dynamism of the organization with the dynamism of a free community. Stability of such a two-hierarchical administration and its effectiveness is further enhanced by the presence of some characteristic features of self-organized systems, namely continual adjustment to the changing outer conditions, to changes of goals, population, and so on. This mechanism of the "social homeostasis" is ensured by the stable compromise between the interests of an organization and the interests of an individual.

In the army, due to a very special character of its tasks, the power and professional functions are very difficult to separate. Nevertheless, it does have both hierarchies, but in an amalgamated form, as every military man belongs to both of them simultaneously. His promotion on the hierarchy of knowledge (the analogue of the professional hierarchy), though, and hierarchy of posts can occur with different speed. Such a degenerated two-hierarchical system has a deep meaning; it originated very long ago, it is used in all contemporary armies, and it deserves some additional explanations.

His ability and preparedness to quickly and unquestioningly implement all orders and commands from above is usually considered as a principle quality of a military serviceman. However, each serviceman (with the exception of rank-and-file) is at the same time a subordinate to some people and a superior to others. But the latter needs to have quite different qualities than when a mere implementation of orders is involved. These both sides of his activity are taken into account, assessed and rewarded in a different manner. This is what creates a necessity to merge both hierarchies.

It is assumed that to be a subordinate no talents are needed and this "formidable" science can be easily mastered by everybody. That is why in any army there exists a so-called "virtue of long service" which defines a time interval needed to get promoted to the next military rank. It is required that during this period the serviceman demonstrates no serious violations of the codes or any other major misdeeds. The hierarchy of posts (hierarchy of power) is established parallel to the hierarchy of military ranks, but promotion along this one is based on different criteria, which involve personal abilities, initiative, and zeal demonstrated in commanding others. Each military rank corresponds to a definite post only approximately ("on average"), for example: lieutenant corresponds to the commander of the platoon, captain - to the commander of the company, major - of the battalion, colonel - of the regiment, and so on. Also, for different types of troops, as well as for peace and war times, this chain of accordances is different. It defines an average type of a serviceman, who normally "paces along the ranks" and whose abilities to command and to obey are balanced. Such a double hierarchy doubles the number of encouragements and punishments, coordinates the "pull" and the "push", improves control over them, thus enhancing the regulated dynamism in the army.[51]   The importance of the double hierarchy is also illustrated by the fact that a separate reward for the rank is in fact the pay for the past effort to ascend, and it is reflected in the retirement laws for servicemen.   Therefore, deprivation of a rank or its delay is one of the most severe punishments, and the longer the service, the more he loses when a serviceman is dismissed or quits service on his own.   On the scale of the whole army, it is the way to retain experienced cadres, a means to accumulate the organizational experience.

In an army which is based on compulsory conscription (it is the case which is of a paramount interest in this study), the professional hierarchy consists of cadre officers only, who are trained in specialized schools.   And as this hierarchy is inseparable from the hierarchy of power, then their mutual control - which plays a very important role in all other varieties of administrations - is also lacking.   Also lacking - or very weak - is control from the society, due to the considerable isolation of the army.   Therefore, unlike, for example, local self-government, the army does not enjoy the properties of self-orgnaized systems and it cannot function properly without strict control from an outside power (national government).   The passive character of the professional hierarchy constitutes another difference.   The rule of "virtue of long service" is in fact excluding the competition among the professionals which is typically present in any other administration.   It means that in the army, free dynamism is minimal, and it is almost forced out by the organizational - the coercive one.   It simplifies the task of payments, but this simplification is achieved at the expense of

---

[51]Zealous servicemen surpass the norm, lazy ones lag behind.   The first ones are encouraged to greater zeal, the latter are urged on making up.   For example, a colonel who is appointed to be in command of a division, will read in the eyes of his colleagues: "What a fine colonel!"   But among his new colleagues - generals - he will feel a renegade, as he is allowed to wear only a general's tall fur hat, but not trousers with stripes or any other general's regalia.   When meeting them, he should be the first to salute.   All this stimulates his additional zeal to get an out-of-turn rank, since his only general's clothing - a tall fur hat - constantly reminds him of his "intermediate" status between the two layers of servicemen, one of which he already left, and the other he has not yet reached.   On the contrary, the same colonel who is punished by suspending his next promotion, and who, for example, is in command of a battalion, will always hear behind his back: "What a bad colonel!"   And he will zealously try to do his best until he removes this discrepancy and becomes again "like all others".   This mechanism acts automatically and it is not always realized.

lowering the personal responsibility of a serviceman, which was discussed in detail in the previous chapter.

The more complex the tasks and goals of a department, the higher the demands of professionalism and the more complex are the interrelationships between hierarchies in the system. For example, consider departments engaged in creating nuclear weapons in the US and the USSR. In both, a hierarchy of power had a regular organizational and functional structure characteristic of the army, headed by generals (Groves in the United States, and Beria in the Soviet Union). Professional hierarchies were headed by scientists (Oppenheimer and Kurchatov). Relative independence of these hierarchies and, as a result, possibility of mutual control, was ensured by submitting each of them to a single, very complex superior organ which comprised both military and scientific personnel.[52] The similarity between these two departments - in countries otherwise absolutely different in governmental structure, social order, traditions, and cultures - justifies the universality of a two-hierarchical system of management when applied to solving complex problems.

2. The Integration Processes

Let us formulate the problem of bureaucratization in a different manner than it was done in Chapter 4. We will consider administration as a goal-oriented system which consists from the very beginning (after formed by the outer power) of two sub-systems described above as hierarchy of power and professional hierarchy. Let us further assume that the relationships between the sub-systems are balanced in a manner which maximizes the effectiveness of administration in the implementation of the pre-set tasks. Then violations of such an optimum and equilibrium will define the further evolution of administration and, in particular, its spoilage, or bureaucratization.

First of all, some explanations are needed to clarify the term "a two-hierarchical system" as applied to our task. A metal worker can improve his

---

[52]In the United States, it is a "Provisional Military and Political Committee" subordinated to the President through the Secretary of State, which included three generals and two scientists (W. Bush and D. Conant). This example is interesting also for the reason that the complexity of tasks demanded an extremely broad "field of selection" of specialists. In the United States, the professional hierarchy was completed with scientists from the entire democratic world, while in the Soviet Union, from the whole country, including Gulag.

professional skills by moving from the first (the lowest) to the seventh (the highest) rank, and all this time he still remains a mere laborer. But in his ascension, he can step away from this route and become a senior master, a foreman, a head of a sector, or a shop. And if at the beginning he is capable of performing both his professional improvement and his administrative duties of ruling others, further on to do both would become increasingly difficult. Earlier or later, he will face an ultimate choice and at a certain level, he will have to abandon his professional advance. A doctor will be a more sophisticated example: he (or she) can cover all possible ranks of the profession up to the rank of "distinguished doctor of the republic", being at the same time a rank-and-file doctor, but he can also - at a certain level - switch to the hierarchy of power and end up as the secretary of the country's health care, gradually reducing his individual medical practice. Any contemporary administration has to take into account and utilize the professional skills of its functionaries and their administrative abilities as well.[53] Therefore, one can always detect two fluxes of functionaries (two hierarchies) in an administration, one of them being dominated by the professional interests and goals and the other one by the administrative, organizational ones. Combining both of them in one person will be typical only at the lower levels. It is this factor that is taken into account in a two-hierarchical model.

In such a system then, what defines the speed of functionaries' promotions and their transition from one hierarchy to the other? The defining factor is the inner structure and dynamics of the hierarchy itself, as well as the personal qualities of functionaries - their orientation. In other words, it is defined in each concrete case by the relationships between the organization and the individual, and on the scale of the whole administration - by the compromise between their corresponding interests and goals. The change of the parameters of state characterizes the inner restructuring of the administration. It means, that when the two-hierarchical model is used, the study of the bureaucratization process can be generally reduced to the study of the accompanying structural changes described by the parameters of state.

---

[53] All examples of this paragraph refer mostly to the totalitarian society, though many conclusions bear a general meaning. It is important to remember, though , that the ruling party and, linked to it, hierarchies (KGB and army) have their specific features, and below they will be pointed out.

a. The First Stage (Bureaucratization)

The distortion of the optimum equilibrium established at the beginning starts, as it was shown in the previous chapter, with the increase of the degree of centralization, and the greater the isolation of the administration from the society, the faster it increases. For that reason, in a totalitarian state, the principle of "democratic centralism" which is embodied in this or that form in any administration, transforms into bureaucratic centralism: the growing centralization inevitably forces out the hierarchical democracy. Factors that make such a process irreversible were considered in the previous chapter. Let us briefly list these factors.

In the hierarchically centralized administration, the defining process will be that of the relationships between the superior and his/her subordinate; the first one issues orders and the second one implements them by way of issuing new orders to his own subordinates. And in such a manner it goes through the whole hierarchical pyramid from top to bottom. It creates two insoluble problems. One of them is connected with the responsibility for the decisions made, as it has to be divided in some way between the superior and the subordinate. The mechanism of such a division is lacking in the part of the administration where the professional hierarchy is amalgamated with the hierarchy of power. The result is an increasing degree of centralization, and decreasing professionalism and de-personalization.

The second problem is the reward for additional risk and initiative. The reason is that the subordinate faces two options: he either merely passes the same order down or he can reformulate it in more detail or alter it to fit the concrete conditions, and he usually knows them better than his superior. The degree to which he changes the initial order can also vary. How can it be taken into account, and in what manner can the additional effort and risk be awarded in a hierarchical organization, where all rewards should be distributed exactly in accordance with the hierarchical level? If the latter principle is violated, such factors as the dynamism of the organization and the striving for promotion begin to decline. Impossibility to solve these problems leads to the accumulation of inner tensions and the subsequent decay of a single hierarchy into two sub-systems: a dynamic and a conservative one. Hence, the effectiveness of the administration drops. To sustain it at an acceptable level, it is needed to increase its numbers.

Let us explain this prevailing and irreversible tendency using Marxist-Leninist phraseology. Proceeding on the principle of the strict correspondence between all privileges and the occupied hierarchical level, the conflict between a superior and his subordinate is analogous to the conflict between a capitalist and his worker. The only "capital" of the first one is vacancies, and the only "property" of the latter one is the ability to show initiative and to take a risk (the analogue of manpower). The higher the degree of centralization, the greater is the "capital", and the higher the degree of dynamism, the greater is the "property". It is natural to assume that the functionary will try to get the reward for each and every fact of demonstrating his initiative and for the risk taken. Moreover, he considers this reward as an addition to his salary, and the salary should correspond to the hierarchical level and is, in fact, the pay for the previous effort on ascent. Therefore, the superior can reward the additional effort with a "promissory note" for the next promotion.

All administrators keep service records of every functionary where they list all facts of his additional zeal, his specific achievements, as well as all earned awards, ranks and bonuses. Accumulated, they increase his chance (his "stock") for promotion. But no "promissory note" guarantees the payment with one hundred percent reliability. In the considered case, an acceptable degree of guarantee is possible only in the periods of the administration's inward and outward expansion, when the number of vacancies is growing. It means that both a superior and a subordinate are interested in such an expansion, which can also be called an expanded reproduction of bureaucracy during which all "class conflicts" are smoothed over or even disappear. An alternative to the expansion is that the subordinate suffers an oppressive feeling of "working for free", and a superior suffers a no less oppressive feeling of uncertainty in the expectation of "bankruptcy".

These two "psychic tensions" in each elementary "cell" of the administrative system are the deepest source of the major bureaucratic distortions: corruption, bribery, malfeasance in office. Only under the condition of the "expanded reproduction" of bureaucracy does the "inflation" of promises disappear, and vacancies become a valid, convertible "hard currency". But if the expansion is impossible and the promotion of the functionaries is determined by the natural mortality rate, then the majority of the issued "promissory notes" remains unpaid. Then many functionaries begin to reward themselves for their "above the norm" work on their own, and their regular salary acquires the character of unemployment benefits. As soon as their initiative and energy is concentrated on the latter, forcing official promotion out to secondary roles, the functionaries turn into the category of the "stopped" ones, forming the "reserve labor army".

Thus, in an administration isolated from society, a series of processes originate and develop which determine its further evolution into bureaucracy. The key to these processes is an irreversible growth of the degree of centralization. Its main cause is the lack of mechanisms for separating responsibility between superiors and subordinates, and for additional reward for initiative and risk. Moreover, such mechanisms cannot be worked out at all, for the reason that it is impossible to simultaneously combine in one hierarchy both centralization of leadership and decentralization of responsibility. To achieve it, at least two hierarchies are needed, as is the case, for example, in the local self-government. It is impossible because the hierarchical centralization suppresses and forces out the hierarchical democracy, and, together with it, readiness to risk, to demonstrate initiative, independence and enterprise. As a consequence, the individual ("personal") responsibility for the decisions and their results is substituted by the collective one, and the latter inevitably evolves into universal irresponsibility. Which is the direct road to the well-known bureaucratic distortions. Behind this whole series of causes and effects stands the incompatibility of interests of an organization and an individual.

The increasing intra-organizational tensions inevitably lead to the inner restructuring of the administration. The growing population of the stopped ones converts into a special conservative sub-system. Its demands and interests are gradually reduced to the collective bureaucratic parasitisms, and joint self-preservation becomes its priority goal. From now on only the dynamic sub-system becomes the bearer of the initial goals and tasks of the administration. In the once single administration there originates, so to speak, two directions of activity, each with its own goals ("splitting" of goal), and, correspondingly, two directions of the hierarchical selection. This, in turn, defines the further evolution of administration and the second restructuring.

b. The Second Stage (Departmentality)

Until now, we have not distinguished between professional hierarchy and hierarchy of power because at the first stage of bureaucratization they are closely linked and the processes under way in each of them are similar. At the second stage, the stage of formation of inner self-governing, they become different, but this difference should be accounted for only in dynamic sub-systems. Conservative sub-systems of both hierarchies can be considered now as a single conservative sub-system of the administration (a department under formation).

Indeed, the advancement along the hierarchy of power implies the development of the ruling skills and accumulation of the corresponding experience. As for the hierarchy of knowledge, it implies the development of the professional skills in the selected narrow field, needed for the tasks and goals of the whole administration. In either case, a "stopped" one - the one who, for this or that reason, assesses the probability of his promotion pessimistically, - will spend minimum time and effort doing his official duties and he will gradually switch to doing his private matters, matters of his family, relatives, or just friends. Or doing his professional work in the area not related (or weakly related) to the tasks of the organization to which he formally belongs. Therefore, in both conservative sub-systems (the power and the professional one) the degree of professionalism and de-personalization decreases, the differences between them are gradually obliterated, and goal reduction furthers their integration into a single conservative sub-system.

Now let us consider in more detail the relationships between the two dynamic sub-systems. To do that we will return to the analysis of the differences between them. In any large enough hierarchically-centralized administration, in the course of a functionary's promotion, the number of his subordinates grows as well as the range of his administrative duties. It reduces the resources of his free time and energy, which he could use to advance his professional level. It cannot but slow down his ascension along the hierarchy of knowledge. So, sooner or later, he will face a dilemma: to reconcile himself to this slowing down and continue to improve his professional level, or to concentrate totally on the administrative duties and administrative career. The second option means, in fact, his transition into the hierarchy of power, where the demands for professionalism are usually lower and have a different character. The road to the apex of power is thus dichotomized, the relationship of power and professionalism undergoes changes, and the character of hierarchical selection changes, too. These changes prepare the inner restructuring of the department under formation.

In the totalitarian state, former professionals in the hierarchy of power possess a specific psychology. They gradually lose qualities considered typical of true professionals: devotion to truth, enthusiasm, unselfishness; hence, their desire to present "yesterday's knowledge" (half-knowledge) as today's, their pretentiousness, self confidence bordering on impertinence, and other well-known features. Nevertheless, they still contribute at least some elements of knowledge into the hierarchy of power, which enable control of all spheres of professional activity of the administration. With their help, the top of the hierarchy of power gradually places under its command the professional hierarchy, converting it into an executive sub-system of administration. Later, it helps the top become a dominant (command) element of the whole two-hierarchical system of the department.

The conclusive process in such a restructuring is the separation of the ruling top. How and why does the rupture of a single body of the hierarchy of power, which is formed by the amalgamation of administrators and former professionals, happen? The model cannot answer such questions, as it is very general and designed to describe slow, gradual processes rather than the revolutionary, restructuring ones. But using the two-hierarchical model of administration, it is possible to indicate processes that contributed to the separation of the top, as well as the place of this separation.

The most important of such processes is a rapid consolidation of the functionaries at the upper levels of the hierarchy of power where they form a single psychic entity, which opposes the rest of the hierarchy[54] by way of contrasting between "us" and "them", because former professionals (teachers, engineers, doctors, scientists) who switched to the hierarchy of power, have much more in common, much more mutual understanding and common interests, than working professionals. Power, as a uniting goal, furthers their consolidation with "pure" administrators. Power by itself or as a means to get something (privileges, material benefits, and self-assertion). In time,[55] hierarchical selection creates the homogeneity necessary for such a consolidation.

---

[54]Opposes, for the most part, the over-populated lower levels. This is why isolation of the department from the society, which furthers the over-populating, also furthers the decay.
[55]In the Bolshevik party, it was about fifteen years. The same in the Fascist and Maoist parties.

Another process is linked to the relationships between the professional hierarchy and the hierarchy of power: the first one is weakened by the on-going outflow of functionaries, whereas the second one starts to strengthen at its expense and ultimately subjugates it. As soon as the professional hierarchy loses its independence, the possibility for professional control in a two-hierarchical administrative system is also lost. On the other hand, the alliance between functionaries-administrators and former professionals turns out to be a very effective way for the department to neutralize outside influence and to increase its own autonomy.

Now let us locate the place in the hierarchy where the separation takes place, and the specific role of the intermediate layer. Described in the previous section, the splitting of the administration into conservative and dynamic sub-systems is related almost exclusively to the intermediate level of the hierarchy: in the separated top they are almost amalgamated, and on the lowest levels, they are not distinguished yet. Their relationships considerably affect the further restructuring of the whole system, the further evolution of the administration and, consequently, the key role of the intermediate layer. Later on, inside this layer, under the leadership of the separated top, a ruling (managing) and a ruled (managed) sub-system is formed, together they will make up the apparatus of the newly born department. It is the intermediate layer rather than the other two, which shapes the ideas of the general goals for the whole system, its current tasks, key strategies and tactics. And it is the layer in which later, and again under the control of the top, the foundations for the corporate spirit are laid down, and paradigms of ideology are formulated. In this layer a non-stop battle between professionals and illiterate "potentates" goes on. It is the "reactor" of the department, its supplier of energy. The main reason for its constructive dynamism lies in the special combination of sociality with hierarchism: the top layer due to its low numerical value does not enjoy much sociality, and the bottom layer does not have much hierarchism. Therefore, the process of the separation of the ruling top probably starts somewhere at the upper levels of the intermediate layer in its dynamic sub-system.

In conclusion, let us cast a brief look on the general structure of the totalitarian department and point out its most distinguishing features which will be instrumental in the analysis of commandocracy. In the hierarchical system of power of any department, one can detect three sub-systems: a leading one, a ruling one and a ruled one. It well agrees with the division of the community of functionaries into higher, intermediate and lower layers, the boundaries between them only approximately coinciding with the differentiations in the system of power. Therefore, those who make the key decisions (the leading sub-system) do not have direct contact with executors, since they are separated from them by the ruling sub-system. For that reason the executors are totally removed from the procedure of decision making. The second distinguishing feature is the character of the boundaries between the sub-systems; at each of them the selection of a functionary is taking place by written and unwritten laws. Thus the natural hierarchical selection acquires features of an artificial one, and it creates the opportunity for the leading top to form a desired staff.

Due to these features a mature department becomes not just a large administration or a conglomerate of many administrations, but it becomes an autonomous and closed administration, which is hostile to any "outsiders". The existence of inner self-governing, together with the feedback mechanism, lends it the property of adaptability, i.e., the ability to react to changes in the environment and to adapt to them by way of complicating its inner structure (the beginning of self-organization). This "inward expansion" is supplemented by the outward one. At the stage of departmentality, the regular striving of the bureaucratic administration for reproduction of bureaucrats acquires the character of a purposeful outward expansion: a department serving a certain part of the population is trying to subjugate this part to its own interests using any available methods. Outward and inward expansions enhance its autonomy and ability to survive.

c. Scheme of Evolution

Organizational and functional structures of any administration are constructed on four principles: hierarchy, centralization, professionalism, and confidentiality. The character of hierarchy, the degree of centralization, professionalism, and confidentiality are defined by the goals and tasks of management set from outside and aimed at optimum functioning in a given social environment. When all of them change, the structure changes too. In the simplest model of an administration, these changes can be taken into account with the help of parameters of state: degree of centralization and degree of professionalism. These two are not enough, though, as the character of a hierarchy can also change, and confidentiality can transform into secrecy or conspiracy. That is why below three more parameters are introduced: degree of dynamism, degree of autonomy, and degree of de-personalization.

Some explanations are needed for these additional parameters. The degree of dynamism of any hierarchical community has two different sources. Freedom to join and leave the group, as well as freedom of vertical movements (hierarchical democracy), creates the dynamism of an individual D_i. On the other hand, in a free hierarchical group, hierarchical geometry (the number of levels, their inter-connection, and the numerical value of each level) is formed from below and reflects the dispersion of individualities, of their pressure upon each other ("lifting force"). It creates the dynamism of the organization D_o - its ability to adjust to constantly changing inner and outer conditions. Both dynamic components are of course inter-connected: the individual one can be manifested only through hierarchy in the striving for upward movement, and the organizational one is inseparable from the hierarchical democracy. The self-organization of a free hierarchical group means that in it, the combination of these two components automatically achieves its optimum. This is how a compromise between the best satisfaction of individual demands and the vitality of the group as a whole is achieved.

The parameter "degree of autonomy" sums up the whole chain of changes: confidentiality, secrecy, conspiracy, isolation, and self-governing. It characterizes the degree of independence of an administration from outer power and society. It will be shown below that the natural evolution of an administration and its transformation into a bureaucratic department is accompanied by the growth of this parameter.

The last parameter - "degree of de-personalization" - is the most difficult to comprehend. Any human organization restricts individuals - limits their possibilities and abilities in choosing alternatives of behavior. But any goal-oriented and centralized hierarchical organization does it in a certain direction, purposefully, by both subordinating them to a common goal and by forming their special interests and demands. Degree of de-personalization (deprivation of personality) sums up all possible restrictions, thus reflecting the compromise between developing individuality and the proper functioning of an organization as a whole. It is often more convenient to split this parameter, as well as those of the degrees of dynamism and professionalism, into two components: an individual and an organizational one.

Obviously, all five parameters are inter-related, and alteration of any one of them entails changes to the others. But they are not equitable: the main one is degree of centralization, changes in which start first and then trigger the whole chain of processes that determine the administration's evolution. Linked to it is degree of autonomy. These two parameters characterize an organization as a whole, and determine the degree of its totalitarianization. The three others characterize both organizations and individuals.

Such a method of constructing approximate models can be applied to all hierarchical social systems with an aim to their classification. Let us illustrate this with several characteristic examples. Let us start with biology. Here, principles of hierarchical societies are well studied in the case of highly developed animals and, in particular, primates (see Appendix, section 2). The main principle is that of distribution of all of the benefits of joint life strictly in accordance with one's occupied level. It is this principle that creates the desire to strive for upward movement and the necessity to defend the achieved level (hence, dynamism of the group). In such a group, everybody is "a professional", since all the rest are filtered out by natural selection, and the degree of autonomy is extremely high. Such individual qualities as physical strength, adroitness, foresight, endurance, aggressiveness, and psychological stability are constantly tested and trained, and are consolidated in a series of inherited features and behavioral stereotypes by hierarchical and natural selection. It makes the whole group strong and competitive. In other words, in such groups, hierarchy acts as a filter for outstanding individuals (specimens). Therefore, in such groups, "de-individualization" is minimal. It is displayed distinctly only in cases when some outside conditions hinder the possibility for an individual to freely quit the group, and the size of the population exceeds some threshold level, beyond which degradation starts.

In human society, the closest analogy would be a free professional community (group), which is not directly connected with ruling bodies, or production, or distribution. In the past, such were scientific societies - until science became "a productive force". Here, as in the previous example, degrees of centralization and de-personalization are minimized, and degrees of professionalism and autonomy are maximized. All military and semi-military systems represent the opposite case.

The scheme below sums up different individual cases of hierarchical systems. On its left side, besides a free society, one can see Weber's ideal bureaucracy, and on the right-hand side - besides the army, different mafia systems, characterized by a high degree of centralization and autonomy. The dotted-line rectangle indicates the limits of all other real cases. One of them is the administration of local self-government. Arrows show the direction of the irreversible evolution towards the increase in totalitarianization. For example, the army differs from mafia systems by having a lower degree of autonomy; it is a variety of state administration, created and controlled from outside, and designed for very specific tasks. This difference exists only when the army is solving these specific tasks. In peace time, with no outside threat, this difference begins to vanish, and the army evolves into a typical military bureaucracy, acquiring many features of a mafia system.

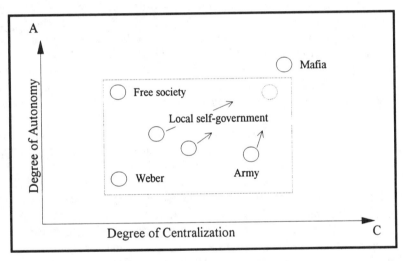

Strictly speaking, the parameters introduced are not quantitative characteristics, although some of them (for example, the degree of centralization) can be assessed quantitatively without difficulty. They can be useful only when the dynamic processes that define the direction of irreversible evolution are investigated (arrows on the diagram).

Each hierarchy of local self-government is characterized by its own set of parameters of state (on the scheme, the local self-government hierarchies are spread apart for a better view). In all other known cases, the differences are less significant, and for the most part they are demonstrated at the middle levels of the dynamic sub-systems, as it was already pointed out earlier. With the growth of parameters A and C, differences between the hierarchies are further decreased. Degeneration of the two-hierarchical administration takes place.[56] The department-mafia hybrid is the ultimate result of such evolution (see dashed circle on the graph). Mafia, placed outside the rectangle, is distinguished by the lack of a doubled hierarchy, as well as by the combination of high centralization with high dynamism.

3. Mafiazation

Mafia organizations belong to totally self-organized systems. They serve specific goals, possess dynamism, and are at the same time stable. Their organizational and functional structure sensitively reacts to environmental changes and adjusts to them - it enjoys the property of adaptivity. All this favors their high effectiveness: with membership of only several dozens, rarely hundreds, such organizations can challenge cities with multi-million populations, or even whole states (as in present day Colombia), and fight them successfully over decades.

A combination of purposefulness, dynamic stability and adaptivity is characteristic of all self-organized systems studied in biology and cybernetics. Without delving deep into the theory of self-organizing, let us only note that in living self-organized systems, such as cells, organisms, populations and biocenosis, dynamic stability is ensured by the mechanism of homeostasis, and it results in a combination of openness of these systems, as well as their autonomy. (The mechanism of homeostasis connects the structural organization with the functional, thus ensuring the system's dynamic stability, which is far from equilibrium.) The existence of special regulated barriers between the system and

---

[56]The utmost degeneration is observed, as it was underlined earlier, in the army, where a single set of parameters can be used. In the general case, the degree of integration of the two hierarchies can also be taken into account by introducing generalized parameters. In this case, the parameter "degree of centralization" will reflect the compromise between centralization in the hierarchy of power and decentralization in the professional hierarchy (i.e., between centralization of leadership and decentralization of responsibility). The degree of autonomy will reflect the compromise between confidentiality (conspiracy) in the hierarchy of power and freedom of informational exchange in the professional hierarchy. The same is true for other parameters.

the environment, through which exchanges of energy, matter and information goes on, preserves the structure "in essence". Self-preservation is a universal goal of such systems. It unifies all parts (sub-systems) into a single entity.

Mafia organizations are also united with a similar goal. They are characterized by dynamic stability, existence of barriers, and a self-restoring vertical structure (dome, apparatus, buttons). Is it possible then to find there some analogue to the homeostasis mechanism, which would connect its functional and organizational structures? When this analogy is applied to social systems, it is important to take into account the fact that they get information, material values (analogue of energy), and human material (analogue of matter) from their environment. Therefore, a mechanism of social homeostasis should support optimum inter-relations between these streams, and at the same time, restore their stable structure "in essence". Moreover, extremely complex relations between the system and its environment, and many other difficulties, make any direct way of studying its stability rather unprofitable, so it is necessary to find some roundabout ways. One of them is a speculative model suggested below.

First, let us note that the trinomial mafia structure reflects a universal structure of management: command element, apparatus, executors. Further, self-governing of the system means that the command element belongs to the system itself, and the apparatus provides two channels of information: direct and reverse. The first serves to pass orders and commands; the second collects, processes and prepares information about how an order has been implemented, and about the state of the environment. An isolation barrier between the command element and the apparatus should serve to differentiate composition according to different functions, as well as support the optimum ratio of their numerical sizes. Preliminary selection of an eligible contingent is ensured by the lower barrier, the one that separates all organization from its environment. The existence of these two regulatory barriers is one of the main conditions for preserving a universal trinomial structure necessary to support self-governing.

It is not enough, though. On the lower barrier, the reward should considerably outrate individual risk (as assessed subjectively), to attract as many candidates as possible. It would make selection into the apparatus and, what is even more vital, into the dome, more effective (future cocaine barons, "godfathers"). In the apparatus, individual responsibility and risk, as a rule, grow with the hierarchical level, but collective responsibility and collective risk grow even faster, and they begin to dominate at a certain level. This is the lower boundary of the upper barrier. The dome is formed above this barrier on the basis of collective responsibility and risk (smaller membership, better conditions for conspiracy).

Let us assume that the influx through the lower boundary begins to decrease. The field of selection is then narrowed down, the quality of the apparatus deteriorates, and the quality of information relayed upwards deteriorates too. It results in the deterioration of the decision-making process, and the quality of the decision's implementation. As a result, the influx of money that "fed" the mafia begins to deplete. The organization goes into a stage of aging and withering. Gradually, an idea of its "restructuring" begins to formulate and permeates all levels. And, as its first step, the idea of "liberalization" is born on the lowest levels, aimed at enhancing the influx. It gradually materializes into corresponding command decisions. If, on the contrary, the influx through the lower border is too high (reward is too high, and risk is minor), then the organization starts to swell, conditions of conspiracy deteriorate, competition in the apparatus and the dome sharpens, and fights between various groups, groupings and clans unfold. It lowers the effectiveness of directed hierarchical selection and the effectiveness of the functioning of the organization as a whole. Again, the idea that "it is impossible to go on like that" is formulating and spreading throughout all levels, generating this time ideas of more severe selection, eradication of "opportunism" both in the apparatus and the dome, of stronger unity, and so on. The existence of all stable and self-regulated mafia organizations oscillates between these two borders of withering and splitting.

Hierarchical selection starts within the apparatus of mafia and is completed in the dome. Severe competition during hierarchical ascension is, in fact, competition for survival (free exit is limited from below and is impossible on top due to conspiracy). All the weak and old, clumsy, not vigilant, including the unlucky and failures, are excluded, thus clearing the apparatus and regulating its size. Thus formed, the composition of all three parts of a mafia ultimately defines the structure of the organization and its most important functional links. Therefore, hierarchical selection which takes into account - through feedback - all changes in the environment, is the main element of social homeostasis.

Now let us go back to a bureaucratic department. Its mafiazation includes, first of all, the restructuring of the vertical structure described above, and the formation of an inner self-government. Further, since a department is a goal-oriented organization formed to rule somebody or something, then goal reduction for it will mean its splitting, not just its simplification. The initial goal gradually transforms into a formal, "legalized" deception - a "facade", which implies an element of falseness. Hence, natural evolution of an isolated department results in its degradation as a goal-oriented administration and its strengthening as an organization of a mafia type, a parasitic one. Departmental bureaucracy transforms into "bureaumafia".

In conclusion, let us point out the difference between a bureaucratic department as a mafia-type hybrid and a real mafia. As long as the department stays in the system of the totalitarian state power, it has to combine a mafia-type parasitism with performance of certain functions in the system. The necessity to implement orders, regulations, and commands that come from above restricts its autonomy. A totalitarian department transforms into a departmental-mafia hybrid only when it frees itself of all these fetters, or at least of their greater portion, as it happens, for example, in the case of a ruling political party in a totalitarian regime isolated from the outer world. In this case, its rank-and-file members become an inner environment of a sort for a mafia apparatus, and the entire society becomes the controlled outer environment of the ruling *nomenclatura*. This completes the processes of the department's self-organization, and this is where an analogue of the homeostasis mechanism described above comes into effect.

4. Pyramid of Departments

Any state administration is always created as a number of separate administrative apparatuses. In time, with the growth in numbers of each of them, such apparatuses transform into relatively independent departments with the structure and distinguishing features described above. Further evolution of departments depends both on their relationships with the outer, federal power (i.e., on the form of rule), and on their inter-relations among themselves. The result will be a hierarchy of departments of a higher order - a hierarchy of hierarchies. But in totalitarian states, such a hierarchy is formed as a single self-organized system which encompasses political, economic, and social spheres of the society, whereas in democratic states the process of its formation is stopped at an intermediate equilibrium stage due to periodic changes of the higher apparatus of the ruling power, and due to control from the democratic institutions of the society. The term "commandocracy" is applied to describe the first of these cases.

Two varieties of commandocracy are known: the two-hierarchical one, which was first created under Lenin and perfected by Stalin, and the collective one, the most typical example of which is the Brezhnev-Chernenko "stagnation epoch". In the first of these two varieties, two relatively independent hierarchies of power create conditions for the individual dictatorship of a charismatic leader, and in the second one, a so-called "collective leadership" disguises the tyranny of the "inner party", formed by the ruling tops of several consolidated departments. The first can be considered as a transitional stage to the latter (Stalinism, Hitlerism and Maoism are examples). Therefore, below only the second, main form is considered, which by now has spread over all continents.

Real political power in a commandocracy is spread, as it was shown in Chapter 3, over its whole structure, but its vertical distribution is not uniform; it reflects the structure of the individual departments. The second addition to the first approximation model is the existence of a horizontal hierarchy of departments. In the Brezhnev period, this model looked approximately like the following: CPSU, KGB, MVD, the army, the system of the most important departments, trade unions, agroprom, and so on down to the sciences, arts and sports. It created one more direction of centralization, and it provided a variety of ways to the apex of power, thus changing the pattern of hierarchical selection. Now, besides a routine ascension and transition from the professional hierarchy into that of power, a horizontal "drift" in the direction of greater centralization also becomes possible. The character of the inner insulating boundaries also becomes more complicated, since they are different in different departments, and as the departments integrate, they broaden and blur. Finally, the third direction of centralization and ascension to power is in the territories, dependent on their social and economic importance and distance from the center (territorial-production principle).

At first, let us consider the vertical structure of a commandocracy. The integrated ruling tops of the departments form a so-called "*nomenclatura*", or, more precisely, special bureaucracy. Special bureaucrats differ from regular bureaucrats in three ways. First, they are never fired, but always transferred. Second, they are appointed rather than elected. And last, they are isolated from the rest of the functionaries in all possible ways: informational (access to information), economic (special salaries, special distribution, special snack bars, special clinics, special rest homes), legal (exception from all acting laws by way of secret instructions, "telephone right"), and many others. This isolation is furnished by two boundaries - inner and outer, the latter one separating the whole apparatus of rule from the outer ruled sub-system (i.e., the general public). So, the vertical structure of power in a commandocracy reflects the vertical structure of a mature department, together with its key characteristics: those who rule and manage do not have direct contact with those who are ruled and managed, and therefore, they are independent of them.

The vector of hierarchical selection is directed towards special bureaucracy. But now, unlike a department, the needed contingent can be selected from the whole society due to a number of roads leading to the apex of power. Each functionary can start his ascension in any hierarchy (department) and from any region, and then, by drifting through the system of departments, end up in the main *nomenclatura*. This drifting furthers the development of the needed qualities which are important for the enforcement of the system of power and which are not linked to professionalism. The intensity of selection is enhanced by the following structural feature: rank-and-file functionaries of the main hierarchies (zero level), unlike those from the secondary ones, are not regular citizens, but they have certain privileges and are delegated (or disguised, as in KGB) to other hierarchies, thus keeping the horizontal drift under control.

These special functionaries have families, and are surrounded by relatives, friends, acquaintances, spongers, and servants. Due to the character of their activity (rule and management) they have to keep in close contact with the top of the intermediate layer. Therefore, their isolation, especially informational, is only effective if all these categories of the "working" people are included. It means that besides special bureaucracy, a corresponding socium is inevitably developing along with it, and a corresponding vector of social selection is working parallel to the hierarchical selection of the functionaries. It also means that the inner isolating boundary separates off not only functionaries, but a part of the intermediate layer of the bureaucracy as well. The social medium above this level, far outnumbering the *nomenclatura*, forms a distinct inner environment for the special bureaucracy, characterized by its own psychology, ideology, channels of socialization, and outlooks.

It is much more difficult to locate the lower (outer) boundary of commandocracy. This difficulty, however, is connected with the major problem of the systems approach in general: it is the separation of the studied system from the environment (see Appendix, section 1). For self-organized systems, this boundary is a place where very complicated interaction processes with their environment take place, and as a result of which, the state of self-organization is sustained by way of the on-going complication of the inner structure. This boundary is vague and changeable. Therefore, only limits within which the displacement of the boundary occurs are indicated below.

The upper outer boundary of commandocracy is easy to understand if to glance at it, figuratively speaking, from the bottom upwards. Then, the common outer boundary can be seen in the place where horizontal connections between functionaries of different departments are established and their inter-dependence is developed. At a certain level, common demands/interests and common socio-psychological connections will inevitably build up between a scientist and an artist, a KGB member and a medic, a military man and a sports leader, and so on. And not only connections will be established, but also a feeling of corporativism. And this is the place in a commandocracy near which a functionary usually switches from the professional hierarchy to that of power, as political interests of the functionaries from different departments will unite them better than professional ones.

It is more difficult to define the location of the lower outer boundary. The affiliation of a functionary with a commandocracy as a system of power is defined not only by the existence of his subordinates, but also by his independence from them (the condition of commanding). Therefore, a rank-and-file soldier, or a rank-and-file trade union or comsomol member, will definitely belong to the outer surrounding (zero levels of secondary hierarchies). This cannot be said about the more domineering departments, though, as their representatives can be delegated or inserted into other hierarchies, and their independence is based on the horizontal centralization of departments. These delegated/inserted rank-and-file members of the ruling party and sympathetic domineering hierarchies are parts of the "apparatus", the lower boundary of which defines the location of the lower outer boundary of the whole commandocracy.

5. *Gangocracy*

Natural growth of any bureaucratic apparatus of rule (any department) is determined by the growing complexity of the administrative tasks inevitable in any contemporary society, due to complications of the economy and growth of the population. Therefore, the minimum influx needed is defined by summing this natural growth and the natural mortality of functionaries. In reality, any bureaucratic department is increasing its size much faster and, what is more important, in excess of the minimum growth needed. The increase in numbers is a forced measure by the outer power in an attempt to compensate for a drop in efficiency. This is a surface reason, but there exists an intrinsic and more important reason for such an uncontrollable and irrepressible reproduction of functionaries, and of the whole non-productive portion of commandocracy in general. It is linked to the amalgamation of the apparatus of power with the socium and their joint isolation from the society (considered above). Hence, it is sooner revealed to its utmost in the special bureaucracy and the special socium.

Functionaries from the *nomenclatura* are not indifferent to the fate of their offspring, relatives, close associates, or their habitual circle. So, all these should be provided with vacancies and places within this isolated social layer too. Such a closed population increases in size, as it is known, exponentially. In the same manner, the number of vacancies should also grow, and, consequently, so grows the special socium and the expenses to support it. This results, in its turn, in the growth of an alienated public. A similar process of growth of the non-productive population takes place in the rest of commandocracy as well, although not as rapidly (lesser isolation). So, as the loss of functionaries is defined only by their mortality, then the optimum number is achieved very quickly. After that, the degeneration processes described above unfold: namely, an increase of the population of the "stopped" ones, malfeasance in office, corruption, aging of the ruling top, and so on.

Only outward or inward expansion is able to slow down the degeneration of the system. And not just any expansion, but only such a one which unimpedes the free upward movement of functionaries and the free expansion of the corresponding socium, and at the same time supports hierarchical selection, as well as renewal and rejuvenation of the special bureaucracy. For that reason, no matter where the commandocracy regime is established, from the very start it begins to expand outward and also inward, into the society, trying to win control over all its spheres. The best example is provided by the Brezhnev regime, which was attempting to expand over all continents. The outward expansion begins even before domestic relations are stabilized; even before inward expansion is completed. Cuba, Vietnam and Ethiopia illustrate this fatal regularity. Ideological explanations of the necessity and inevitability of such an expansion are nothing but a routine camouflage aimed at disguising the expansionist nature of commandocracy.

But both outward and inward expansion have their limits in our days, upon achieving which commandocracy enters its specific variety. To denote this variety, the term "gangocracy" is used below. Impossibility to expand into the special bureaucracy and into the intermediate level reduces the influx of a new contingent of functionaries below the minimum needed to support self-organization. At that point the metamorphic processes will unfold. Inward expansion gets the character of creating unneeded departments; their numbers outpace optimum levels; the corridors of power are stretched beyond the point needed for effective management; autonomy of departments also increases at the expense of weakening the central power. Outward expansion acquires a one-sided character, with accents on politics and ideology, without supporting them with military, economic or technological expansion. Gradually, all constructive functions of the central power are lost, and only conservative ones survive, together with functions of oppression and retention. Processes of self-organization are little by little reduced to processes of self-preservation, to the preservation of the special bureaucracy and the special socium. In the ruling layer, tendencies to parasitism are becoming dominant, and in the society, shadow economies and politics come into being and flourish. Corruption becomes an everyday phenomenon and it encompasses all levels and all spheres of power. Again, the Brezhnev-Churbanov regime is a good example, and, to a lesser degree, the rule of the "Gang of Four" in China can also illustrate it. A similar process of degeneration, as it is now known, was going on in Romania and other "hotbeds" of gangocracy.

But why was such an odious term picked up? In the general meaning of the word in the majority of European languages, "gang" means a group of people bound by a common goal of feeding off the society. The same goal binds the degenerating commandocracy. The narrow meaning of the word with its odious connotation, relates to the case when this parasitic goal is attained by means of robberies, burglaries, murders, blackmailing and racketeering.

However, gangocracy has never hesitated to use to the fullest extent all these ways to achieve its goals, although it usually prefers "peaceful" coexistence and "detente". The same preferences are characteristic of all large, extensive gangs such as the Italian Mafia or the Colombian Medellin cartel, who use murders and explosions for their self-defense only as measures of last resort.

Anyway, all this is still not enough to justify the usage of the term for the degenerating commandocracy. But similarities can be found in many other aspects as well. A gang (mafia) is, just like a gangocracy, a self-organized system with a strict, and even universal, inner structure, universal traditions, ideology and even its own dialect in any language. Also, similarities in the vertical structure of mafia and a mature department have already been pointed out. Also, the principle of "democratic centralism", with its "unanimous consent" of minority with majority is not alien to mafia-type bureaucratic organizations at all. Always and inevitably, this principle leads to corporativism and collective responsibility, and it is accompanied by hierarchical centralization and conspiracy. Gangocracy, like any gang, is not a party - it does not represent a part of anything, rather it exists by itself separately from the society. It represents nobody except itself, and does not protect anybody's interests except its own.

This parallel can be developed further when a gang and gangocracy are considered as systems having many features of self-organized structures, whose intrinsic patterns and principles of functioning are simple and universal in essence. In large and extensive mafia-type organizations, a ruling top is always separated and detached from the rest of it. It is a so-called "dome", whose analogue in gangocracy would be the special bureaucracy. Below it an intermediate stratum is located, in which managing and inner managed sub-systems can be distinguished (so-called "organizers"), and still below there are regular executors ("buttons"). A very similar vertical structure can be identified in gangocracy. In both cases, there exists a very sophisticated system of feedback from the environment, through which self-preservation by means of parasitism is ensured. In large and extensive mafias, one can find even the horizontal structure similar to that of the "hierarchy of departments".

A few words about parasitism. By definition, parasitism is association between organisms of two kinds of which one (a parasite) obtains benefits from the other (a host) using it as food and environment and usually injuring it. In the case of a regular mafia, it is not difficult to discriminate between a parasite and a host. Mafia is the parasite, and the part of the society in which it functions is its host. But even this simplest case of a self-organized parasitic social system needs some clarifications: a part of the host totally controlled by mafia should be considered separately. First of all, it is the part of the state apparatus which receives direct benefits from mafia activities (inner environment, for the Medellin cartel, for example, it is the essential portion of the state bureaucracy). Also, the part of society should be distinguished which is composed of those intimidated, terrorized and blackmailed individuals which have to serve it, provide information, or assist it in some way (the controlled outer environment). In gangocracy, the parasite is the special bureaucracy and the special socium. The rest of it, down to the lower outer boundary (see page 99), can be considered the inner environment. As for the rank-and-file citizens, they are the controlled outer environment. Together, they make up the whole environment of the parasitizing gangocracy.

The most characteristic property of parasitism is lack of concern about the state of the "host". In a degenerating commandocracy it is demonstrated, in particular, in unlimited production of armaments at the expense of all other branches of the economy and its gradual slowing down, in a progressing deficit of everything needed for life support, in plundering exploitation of natural resources, in destruction of nature, in universal apathy and passivity of the population, and ultimately, in such well-known satellites of a sick society as alcoholism, thievery and corruption. In its attempt to preserve itself, gangocracy asphyxiated society, while at the same time asphyxiating itself. This is the characteristic feature of the most sinister of all the varieties of parasitism, typical, for example, of viruses.

Any parallel certainly has its limits, and relationships between gangocracy and its inner and outer environment is much more complicated and cannot be reduced to sheer parasitism. There are other differences as well. One of them is corruption; there are no official posts in mafia and other like organizations, hence there cannot be malfeasance in office in its conventional meaning. However, in this particular case the parallel can be extended as in gangocracy, corruption acquires a specific form. It has become evident with the fall of many partocratic regimes when attempts have been made - for the most part, futile - to sue the higher party functionaries. In gangocracy, regular corruption is replaced by a system of written and unwritten rules that connect into one whole the regular and shadow economy, as well as the hierarchy of the political and economic departments.   Here it becomes impossible to determine in each concrete case who bribes whom; a superior his subordinate, or vice versa.   It is also impossible to figure out where the state economy ends and the shadow one starts.

What is the key difference between gangocracy and the classic mafia? Why would it be a mistake to use the term "mafiocracy" instead? To answer, let us look again at the scheme of evolution given on page 93. The proximity of the departmental-mafia hybrid as a main structural element of gangocracy and mafia is a result of simplification; only two parameters are utilized, the degree of centralization and the degree of autonomy, and differences between the remaining three are not taken into account. In all bureaucratic departments, the decrease of dynamism and professionalism accompanies the increase of centralization and autonomy, as it was pointed out above. Such a peculiarity which is characteristic of bureaucracy in general, is lacking in the classic mafia; its high dynamism and professionalism are combined with high centralization and autonomy. This is why a departmental-mafia hybrid should be considered as a final stage of evolution, which is reflected in the fact of placing mafia outside the rectangle encompassing all real cases. This is why gangocracy cannot transform into mafia, it cannot become a "mafiocracy".

The main reason for such a radical difference is the narrowness of the goal and tasks of a classic mafia, which defines the very focused direction of the hierarchical selection and its high effectiveness. The existence of the two isolating barriers controlled by the dome gives the hierarchical selection some features of an artificial selection of those best fit for the active parasitism, and that ensures a highly homogeneous composition. This homogeneity is furthered by the well worked out system of expulsion and eradication of all undesired deviations, dissidents and informal groupings. The ideal solution has also been found for the problem of the top's aging; the top is simply exterminated in the on-going squabbles. Another difference is connected with the structure of the inner environment, which is formed by way of incorporating into the state organs of power and economic structures. Mafia-type organization not as much prepares its members for handling concrete, specific tasks, as it selects them in this environment with the subsequent rejection of the unfit ones. The wider the sampling (i.e., the deeper the mafia's penetration into the economic and political structures of the society), the higher is the mafia's effectiveness and vitality. It would be a mere gang rather than a mafia without such a penetration and incorporation. A focused direction of the artificial hierarchical selection, high homogeneity of composition, and the deepness of penetration that secures the broadness of sampling - this is what explains the enigma of mafia's striking effectiveness. This is what makes it "immortal".

These two reasons account for the lack of incompatibility of the demands, interests, and goals of the entire organization as a whole and of its individual members, which is so characteristic of all varieties of a ripe and over-ripe bureaucracy. Unlike a bureaucratic department, the degree of de-personalization in mafia is small, and therefore the discrepancy between possibilities and abilities is lacking for the majority of its members (see Appendix, section 4).

Now let us digress from details and consider commandocracy-gangocracy from a more general point of view, as a complex system characterized by a number of specific features common for all self-organized systems. We will use the analogy with live self-organized systems such as an organism, population, or ecological system. For each of them, the state of self-organization is supported by the existence of a specific inner environment which plays the role of a buffer, and also by specific relationships with the environment which can be conventionally divided into the processes of extraction from it of all components, energy, and information needed for self-organization, and of excretion into it of all unneeded ones.

From general considerations it follows that any organized system is able to extract all needed components and elements thus enhancing its stability, its "order", only out of a less organized system. For live systems, for example, for an organism, it is performed by means of destruction of food with the help of ferments followed by assimilation. For commandocracy, the needed "elements" and "components" are people. Therefore, reasoning analogously, the process of extraction should be preceded by the process of decomposition of the surrounding socium to such an extent that extraction becomes possible. In the boundary case, it is decomposition of the outer social medium into separate individuals - the restriction, suppression or eradication of everything that binds individuals into society: religion, morals, legal norms, and traditions. And it is really being accomplished, and accomplished with an astonishing consistency and mercilessness in all known cases of the commandocracy formation. Ideological irreconcilability in all these cases is the effect rather than the cause of such an organizational irreconcilability, and it also serves as a means to break down the socium.

Methods of such disintegration are also universal: selective repressions, total terror, disinformation in the conditions of isolation from the outer world, and so on. Slaughterous revolutions, military defeats, civil strifes - all these contribute to the socium disintegration too. All these factors are effectively utilized in each concrete case.

An analogue of assimilation is more complicated. In the case of Bolshevism, the formation of an inner medium started straight after the Bolsheviks arranged themselves into an independent party. A large and extended legal organization of professional workers, which enveloped and concealed a small and conspiratorial organization of professional revolutionaries, played the role of such a medium (see Chapter 2, section 2). At this first stage of its formation, up to the 1917 Revolution, ideology played a very important role. The charter of the Bolshevik Party, with its "infamous" first paragraph and principle of democratic centralism, laid the foundation for the hierarchical selection into the inner party. After political power in the country was captured - and it is then that the commandocracy, and its punitive organs, started to form - the act of entering the party became irreversible. At that point, inward expansion became the main task of the organization, and, in particular, restrictions on or complete removal of all alternatives of human activity which it was unable to bring under its control; and not only in the political or social sphere, but in any other one. Together with isolation and ideological indoctrination of the population, it created the initial impulse for ascension along the newly forming state hierarchical system of departments, thus shaping the directed and regulated flux of the "human material". In this process, the free dynamism of each hierarchy has turned into the coercive dynamism, and the energy of the socium's destruction has turned into the controlled energy of ascension along the official or social hierarchy. Artificial hierarchical selection became, therefore, an analogue of assimilation. Judging by the results, it worked very effectively.

Now let us discuss the process of excretion. The excessively swollen population of the "stopped ones" lowers the dynamism of commandocracy and the professionalism of its apparatus, as it clogs the channels of ascension and limits the influx of fresh "human material". Getting rid of this population, or at least reducing its size, as well as getting rid of all harmful and dangerous elements, becomes a permanent task of commandocracy. In live self-organized systems this task is solved, in principle, very simply: everything harmful and unneeded is thrown out into the environment. Commandocracy cannot do the same with the harmful and socially dangerous elements, as they remain to be socially dangerous to it also beyond its borders. The world has become too small, all its parts are interconnected; as for the colonization of the moon and the planets, this possibility is discussed only as a very remote and uncertain future.[57] For that reason, to get rid of their "social" waste matter, all varieties of contemporary commandocracy prefer to use a traditional GULAG, located on their own territory.

This is how matters stand with all harmful and dangerous elements. It is more difficult, though, to do away with the "stopped ones". Because of the lowering of competition among them, they cluster together into a conservative sub-system, which is enforced by strong inner corporative connections, and at the same time, it remains an organic part of the commandocratic structure. In the commandocracy, there are no forces that would be able to remove, restrict or at least neutralize the damaging role of such a sub-system, which becomes a hotbed of corruption and other similar phenomena, as well as the accelerator of the aging of the apparatus.[58] Moreover, origination of such a population takes place everywhere and in a continuous manner. Therefore, the process of extraction in relation to it has forced individual character campaigns which resemble the convulsions of a sick organism. They are usually aimed at lowering the size of the conservative sub-system to an acceptable level. For that reason, commandocracy has to drag along the major part of its social wastes with it to the future. Their decay and rot poisons the whole society, and to a certain point determines the degeneration of commandocracy and its conversion into gangocracy.

Commandocracy as a socio-political system has been existing in Russia for more than seven decades. Over this period, it "ground" three generations of its citizens, and even now, in the period of *perestroika*, it desperately resists any changes. Live self-organized systems exercise their self-preservation using special mechanisms which provide stability and reproduction. What is preserved

---

[57]Huxly chose the Falkland Islands for that purpose. In the 1930s, they seemed to be very far, somewhere at the edge of civilization - not any more.
[58]A more radical way to rejuvenate bureaucracy was used by Stalin and his "predecessor" Chi'h Huang-ti (see Chapter 3): eradication of functionaries before they achieve the stage of the "stopped ones" combined with total fear, which delayed this stage.

in commandocracy, and what are these mechanisms that lend it stability and reproduction?

To answer these questions, it is necessary to consider the role of ideology, which not only determines the direction of the hierarchical and social selection, but also ensures the constancy of the inner environment, the "species composition" of functionaries, and the isolation of the whole commandocracy and its ruling top. It also serves a number of other functions which all contribute to the reproduction of commandocracy.

CHAPTER SIX
SCIENTIFIC THEORY AND IDEOLOGY

The next two chapters occupy a special place in the work for several reasons. They were written earlier than the rest of the manuscript - and at a time when any criticism of Marxism-Leninism was forbidden and prosecuted. Therefore, the place and time of their possible publication seemed very vague, and mere preservation of the manuscript was the number one task. At present, a considerable portion of the old text has become outdated and has lost its acuteness. Therefore, I have reduced its volume by half. This might have affected the coherence of the presentation.

Another exceptional feature of the chapters is their explanatory (of Chapter 5) and introductory (to Chapter 8) character. For that reason, the investigation of Marxism-Leninism as a scientific theory (Chapter 6) is limited to accessible and well-known sources, and to those of its aspects which are of importance in understanding contemporary totalitarian organizations and ideologies, and their interconnection as well. From here one more distinguishing feature follows, namely simplification. In a similar manner, Chapter 7 considers the genesis of only that part of the communist ideology which is linked directly to the evolution of the organization, beginning from the Communist League, through the First International, and up to Bolshevism.

1. Marxism

a. Notes on the Main Part of Marxism

Marxism as a scientific theory is multi-lateral, immeasurable, and wordy. But many of its parts are already history. Below only the main part of Marxism is considered, the one which was later developed by Lenin into the core of contemporary communist ideology. It is considered in its interpretation which was used in the period of monolithism, i.e., the thriving of the socialist camp and its ideology. Deviations from this interpretation, such as Trotskyism, Maoism, and Eurocommunism will be mentioned only in passing. This considerably simplifies the task of the author which otherwise would have been enormous.

The brief formulation of this part is contained in the *Manifesto* and in Engels' prefaces to its 1883 German and 1888 English editions. To further narrow this main part, let us refer to the words of Marx himself, in his letter to Weydemeyer:

> As for me, I should not be given credit neither for discovering the existence of classes in contemporary society, nor for discovering the struggle between them. Bourgeois historians described the historical development of such a struggle long before me. What I did do was that I proved the following: 1. the existence of classes is connected only with certain phases of the production development, 2. class struggle inevitably leads to the dictatorship of the proletariat, 3. this dictatorship composes a mere transition to the abolition of any classes and to the society without classes. (*Complete Works*, 2nd edition, Vol. 22, p. 424, cited from a Russian edition).

Lenin was even more specific: "Only those are Marxists who disseminate the recognition of class struggle leading to the dictatorship of the proletariat... On these grounds only the true understanding of Marxism should be recognized..." (*State and Revolution*).

Therefore, the teaching about class struggle under capitalism, about proletarian revolution as its inevitable consequence and dictatorship of the proletariat as its final result, forms the main part of Marxism. Leninism is the development of only this part. It is this part that later on was simplified and dogmatized into the core of contemporary communist ideology. Marx's development of the political economy in his primary works (*Das Kapital*, *Critique of Political Economy*, and others) was aimed at placing a scientific foundation under this part of his teaching. The fact that the teaching was proclaimed before its scientific explanation was usually considered by the communist literature as evidence of Marx's ingenious intuition. However, this scientific theory, which placed an economic foundation under the political teaching on revolution, was formulated in such a manner as to justify the necessity and inevitability of revolution and the dictatorship of the proletariat as its natural consequences (this will be shown below). This is why it is possible to limit ourselves to considering only the most important part of Marxism, and to refer to his economic teaching and other parts only in connection with its substantiation.

b. Teaching on the Proletarian Revolution and the Dictatorship of the Proletariat

Even this part of Marxism, together with comments to it, is, as it is well known, enormous. For that reason I will introduce its formulation in a simplified form - the form which is utilized in the ideology (see Chapter 7). There, this "symbol of faith" is formulated in the form of the following four statements:

1. The class struggle is the driving force of human history, and revolutions are its pinnacles.
2. The main cause of revolutions is the conflict between productive forces and productive relationships. Their main goal is to remove this conflict by a revolutionary method.
3. The present epoch - that of capitalism, is the eve of the proletarian revolution which will inevitably lead to the dictatorship of the proletariat.
4. Two main characteristics of it (the present epoch) are:
    a. the proletariat performs on behalf of the whole society and it frees the society forever from exploitation (i.e., this revolution is the last for every and each country),
    b. this revolution must be worldwide (i.e., this is the last revolution in history).[59]

Any scientific theory, no matter in what particular sphere of knowledge it is worked out, always contains certain basic statements and consequences, logically deduced from them. Without it, it is a teaching rather than a science (for example, *Mein Kampf*). Since Marxism is claimed to be a science by its followers, then its first trial will be the logical analyses. Of the above four statements, the first two are evidently related to the foundations of the theory, and the last two are the consequences, which are to be tested by "experience".

Let us first concentrate on the consequences and see how they were derived from the main statements in *Manifesto*.[60] Why, for example, should the

---

[59]"The bourgeois relations of production are the last antagonistic form of public production... Therefore, the pre-history of humanity is completed with this form." (Marx, *On the Critique of Political Economy*).

proletarian revolution bear a world-wide character? In *Manifesto* we read: "Combined effort of at least a number of civilized countries is one of the main conditions of the proletariat liberation." (The answer is: because such a character is typical of the capitalist production - unlike, for example, the feudal one). Because there exists an international market and international solidarity of the bourgeoisie; for that reason the proletarian movement rapidly outgrows the national boundaries and becomes an international one. It follows from here that "the proletariat does not have a fatherland" and "proletarians of all lands unite!"

Why does the proletariat perform on behalf of the whole society? Simply because, as capitalism advances and its contradictions sharpen, all other classes except the proletariat and the bourgeoisie disintegrate and disappear. The *Manifesto* says: "...The society progressively splits into two hostile camps, into two major classes that oppose each other - the bourgeoisie and the proletariat... Among all classes that confront the bourgeoisie today, the proletariat alone is really revolutionary. Other classes decay and perish at the rise of large-scale industry...". It follows then that "the proletarian movement is the movement of the immense majority, in the interests of the immense majority."

Then how was it concluded and justified that the middle of the nineteenth century became the eve of the proletarian revolution (the third of the earlier given statements)? The *Manifesto* justifies it by explaining that in the developed European countries, by the mid-nineteenth century, the conflict between the productive forces and the relationships of production sharpened right to the extent which precedes a revolution. It says:

> The modern worker, instead of rising as industry develops, sinks even lower in the scale, and even falls into conditions of existence below those proper to his own class... This plainly shows that the bourgeoisie is no longer fitted to be the ruling class in society or to impose its own social system as supreme law for society at large. It is unfit to rule because it is incompetent to provide security for its slaves even within the confines of their slavish existence; because it has no option but to let them lapse into a condition in which it has to

---

[60]According to Lenin, "This small book is worth volumes: until now, all of the organized and fighting proletariat in the civilized world is inspired and led by its spirit..." (*Complete Works*, Vol. 2, p. 10, cited by Russian edition). This source has never been an object of criticism or doubt in communist literature.

feed them instead of being fed by them. Society cannot continue to
live under bourgeoisie rule.   This means that the life of the
bourgeoisie has become incompatible with the life of society.

It also adds that bourgeoisie itself has decayed and is continuing to decay,
whereas the proletariat becomes more united, more educated and more cultured.

All this reasoning, together with the conclusions about world revolution in
the developed industrialized countries, turned out to be erroneous. The slogan
"Proletarians of the world, unite!" still exists today, because since the days of the
Manifesto, nationalism did not disappear at all, but on the contrary, it is
continuously growing. Every proletarian still has a "fatherland" which he still
defends. International "unity" and "solidarity" of the proletariat, having reached
its maximum in the epoch of the cult, is starting to weaken. Over one hundred
thirty years after the *Manifesto*, nowhere in the world did the splitting of
industrially advanced capitalistic society into only two classes, irreconcilable and
hostile towards each other, take place, because all other classes whose death was
predicted in the *Manifesto* still exist.

Disintegration of the class of capitalists did not happen and is not
happening either, at the background of the growing unity of the working class.
Neither does the latter become impoverished. The opposite trend is taking
place. All of these and many other processes turned out to be opposite to the
predicted ones. Hence, naturally, not in a single well-developed capitalist
country did the predicted proletarian revolution take place, and communism has
moved (Russia and China) and is still moving to backward, feudal and semi-
feudal states.

All this became common knowledge and it belongs to history.[61] But on
these grounds only, it is incorrect to conclude that Marxism is not a science and
that life disproved it. It is incorrect, first of all, for the reason that the above

---

[61] All of these arguments were revealed in the heated discussion at the end of the last century
and at the beginning of the present one, in connection with the works by Bernstein. Defenders
of the orthodox Marxism, including Lenin and Plekhanov, were mainly accenting the fact that
the above tendencies are of a temporary character, and Bernstein attaches too much
significance to them. Later, when it became difficult to deny their real existence, the
conclusions had to be fixed up and a theory of a revolution in one, separately taken country,
had to be elaborated.

tendencies have appeared in world history only a century ago - a period negligible on the history scale. Further, the conflict between the conclusions and real life does not yet mean that the scientific theory is not good. It is possible that the conclusions derived are wrong, or they may be equivocal. Then the equivocality needs to be removed, the conclusions need to be corrected, and the arguments should be altered, as it was first done by Bernstein then by Lenin and others, on the grounds that "Marxism is not a dogma, it is a guidance to actions." Finally, the *Manifesto* is not a scientific investigation, rather it is a program of a political party. Therefore, strict deriving of conclusions from the foundations of theory, if it exists, should be looked for in Marx's other works.

So, where and how does Marx's scientific theory prove the thesis of the necessity and inevitability of a proletarian revolution, the thesis which underlies all prognoses on the future development of human society? What logical mistake, which leads to the striking disagreement between predictions and real life, is there in the proof and where is it? To answer these questions it is necessary to familiarize oneself with the fundamentals of the theory, i.e., with the first two statements of those listed on page 113.

The *Manifesto* starts with the following well-known words: "The history of all human society, past and present, has been the history of class struggles," and it ends with the prediction of the prospect of the proletarian revolution and the dictatorship of the proletariat. By this, Marx and Engels sort of hinted that teaching about revolution is a result of (some) general theory of social evolution. Such a theory was still to be created. Without it, as the "founders" well understood, the statement about class struggle would be of little meaning; moreover, it would not even be original. The vagueness of the notion "class" (its strict definition was not given until a half century later by Lenin) made the teaching even more indistinct. It took Marx eleven years to formulate his second thesis, the one about the dominant character of production in the evolution of human societies (*Critique of Political Economy*, 1859), and another eight years to substantiate it scientifically (*Das Kapital*, 1867). Together with the thesis about class struggle, they made up the foundation of the scientific theory of proletarian revolution and dictatorship of the proletariat, and of all prognoses about the future.

The essence of this theory, if to put it schematically using ideological slang, is the following. Production of material goods constitutes the basis, or foundation, of a social system, and it defines its character and its whole appearance. As the production is developed in a progressive manner, this defines the direction of a society's evolution. Further, production has two facets: forces of production and relationships of production, the first being a more mobile and revolutionary element, whereas the latter are more inert. Hence, changes in production starts with the first. Discordance, which originates at this point between the forces of production and relationships of production, promotes antagonistic contradictions between the classes and irreconcilable class struggle, i.e., revolution. Therefore, the inevitability of a proletarian revolution was derived from the principle of the inevitable delay in the development of the relationships of production. As for its necessity, it was derived from the opposite principle ("law") of them being of necessity in accord. It created an illusion of a logically non-contradictory scientific theory which not only explains the regularity of the whole historic development, but even predicts the time of future revolutions, based on the sharpness of the indicated conflict.

The question may arise: why an illusion? And where in such reasoning is the main error hidden (if to digress from the arbitrariness of the initial assertions)? In the Marxist terminology, a revolution, in general, means "a radical qualitative change, a leaping transition from one qualitative state to another." As for social revolution, it is a "coup in the public relations performed in a coercive manner" with the direct and active involvement of large masses of population in a concrete country. Therefore, a social revolution is a socio-psychic process because the human masses that participate in it are doing so not under the influence of some scientific theories, and not in the name of some remote goals, but in the name of justice, equality, some near goals, everyday demands, emotions, and passions. Of course, economic interests are present, too, but not only them, and often not to such a great degree. Therefore, it was also important to demonstrate a direct and unequivocal connection between economy (basis) and social and psychic processes. The latter do not lend themselves easily to being packed into a determinist pattern, unlike production of material goods and the material world in general.

A scientific theory looked convincing only when applied to the previous human history, in which, besides a primitive commune system two more systems could be distinguished: a slave-owning one and a feudal one. In some countries they orderly succeeded one another, in good accordance with the theory. Also, as Marx and his followers believed, the theory explained well the inevitability, necessity, and the eves of the past revolutions. But for these two systems, the connection between economics (basis) and social psychology is relatively simple: under slavery, a master physically coerced his slave to work and the slave hated him and protested in the attempt to get free. Similar situations existed under feudalism. It is far from being so for the capitalist system in the condition of democracy which guarantees basic rights and political freedom to an individual. It is even more challenging to attempt to prove that under capitalism the conflict between forces of production and relationships of production can be resolved only in a forcible manner, by means of revolutions, by a leap, or an explosion, rather than gradually, by means of compromises, concessions, agreements, or parliamentary struggles. If both ways are assumed as a possible pattern, than the whole theory of the proletarian revolution in its orthodox formulation collapses, and Bernstein and other revisionists were right.

To find a proof of a singular connection between economics and social psychology in a capitalist system, one has to address *Das Kapital*, which Marx himself called the major work of his life and the most destructive projectile ever launched in the head of a bourgeois (see Marx and Engels' *Letters on Das Kapital*, p. 111, Russian edition). Does *Das Kapital* really contain such a proof? Is it true that Marx succeeded in proving on its pages that economics (basis) is an "independent variable" of the whole social life, and that it totally defines the social psychology of the capitalist society? Did he succeed in scientifically proving the necessity, inevitability and regularity of a proletarian revolution? As soon as such a question is asked, it becomes evident that there cannot be a simple answer (yes or no) to it. If to assume that such a proof exists, then what is to be done to real life which not only disproved the conclusion about the inevitability of revolutions in the developed countries, but did not confirm many other predictions of the scientific theory either. If *Das Kapital* does not contain such a proof, then other, no less complex, questions arise.

The orthodox viewpoint holds that *Das Kapital* is devoted almost exclusively to the scientific validation of the fact that the essence of the capitalist system, which is based on free enterprise, lies in the unfair and arbitrary appropriation by a capitalist of a surplus value created by workers, and it creates conditions for an arbitrary and cruel exploitation. It is from here that the connection between economics and social psychology is derived, as well as the inevitability of a proletarian revolution. But in a contemporary capitalism the problem of a surplus value has become even more vague than one hundred fifty years ago, when it caused heated and endless discussions. For example, the scientific and technological revolution has convincingly demonstrated (when totally automated assembly-line factories were introduced) that goods can be created without workers and, consequently, without variable capital and surplus value in the Marxist meaning, without exploitation of the proletariat. At such factories, it is probably machinery that is exploited, and, in the final analysis, the work of its living and dead creators, i.e., factors which are commonly related to the general human culture. This tendency is predicted to be increasing. Of course, exploitation of conventional "labor" is also there, together with the distribution of the corresponding surplus value among all "classes" of a contemporary capitalist state in a conventional production with a variable capital and real workers. "Proletariat" in such a distribution is usually represented by strong trade unions, whose role Marx did not foresee, and who very often dictate their own conditions. Every "class" in a contemporary developed country is interested in obtaining a bigger share and it is fighting for it, but certainly it is not interested in revolutions or destruction of the system.

All these factors witness that *Das Kapital*, based in its analysis on capitalism as it was one hundred fifty years ago, is not, figuratively speaking, a *Das Kapital* of our own time, and no serious economist would use it to study economics of contemporary capitalism, or would refer to it to prove the necessity and inevitability of proletarian revolutions in developed countries. All economic parts of *Das Kapital* already belong to history, together with, therefore, all attempts to substantiate a direct connection between economics and politics as a common regulating law of the industrial society. Marx and Engels made a mistake in defining the tendencies in the development of capitalism of their days.

In the sensational book by Rostow, *Stages of Economic Growth* (1954), this viewpoint is related in the following manner:

In short, Marx belongs among the whole range of men of the West, who, in different ways, reacted against the social and human costs of the drive to maturity and sought a better and more humane balance in society. Driven on - in his father's phrase - by a 'demonic egoism', by an identification with the underdog and a hatred of those who were top-dog, but also <u>disciplined to a degree by a passion to be 'scientific' rather than sentimental</u>, Marx created his remarkable system: a system full of flaws but full also of legitimate partial insights, a great formal contribution to social science, a monstrous guide to public policy. One failure of Marx's system began to be revealed before he died; and he did not know how to cope with it. Some believe that his inner recognition of this failure is responsible for the fact that *Das Kapital* is an unfinished book.

Such a viewpoint looks convincing only at first glance. Its weakness lies in the underlined words. Marxism was not at all a failure, rather, slightly changed and converted into Marxism-Leninism, it continued to spread all over the world and define the face of the contemporary world, in spite of the erroneousness of economic and other concepts. The characterization of Marx is not correct either: scientific work implies a continual search of truth, therefore, a "passion to be scientific rather than sentimental" means a simple, ardent search for truth; devotion to it. Collapse of such a "passion" is usually extremely tragic for individuals, and it cannot but affect their work, and would not remain unnoticed by people around them. We would have to either accuse Engels - who was a co-author of many of Marx's works - of intentionally keeping silent about such a "collapse", or of being completely ignorant in Marxism. Because it was Engels who prepared three of the four volumes of *Das Kapital* for publication. Of little persuasiveness is the reserve attributed to Marx's works. Rather, they were the opposite. It was Marx who first invented a distinctive style in communist literature, characterized by emotional harshness, rudeness even towards former comrades in arms, and a lack of tolerance. Later on, this style was picked up and further perfected by Lenin. All this, together with many other facts, shows that when Marx wrote *Das Kapital*, his main goal was not an unbiased search for truth; rather, it was something else. For that reason *Das Kapital* includes neither scientific substantiation of the connection between economics and social psychology, nor scientific proof of the necessity and inevitability of a proletarian revolution. This is why it is not correct to speak about the collapse of Marxism as early as in Marx's lifetime. On the contrary, as it is clearly seen from the "vitality" of Marxism and its hundred-year evolution, which will be discussed below, Marx was right in his assertion that *Das Kapital* was the apex of his creative activity, his greatest success. Only this success is not related to political economics or any other branch of science usually meant when the word "scientific" is used.

To fully understand the main content of the four parts of *Das Kapital* and the goal pursued by Marx in writing it, it is useful to first consider Marx and Engels' predictions of the world revolution and their attitude to the socialist movement which originated in Europe in the mid-nineteenth century. This attitude was revealed, as it is well known, in the teaching on the two phases of communist society (socialism and communism), as well as in the sharp discussion on the two methods of capitalism reformation. Examination of these issues casts light on the essence of Marxism as a scientific theory.

c. Predictions of World Revolution

Marxism originated in the middle of the nineteenth century, when England was undoubtedly the most developed country in the capitalist world. Next were France and Italy. It was the study of British capitalism that laid the foundation for *Das Kapital*. For that reason, it would seem natural to assume that in England all contradictions and curses of capitalism would demonstrate themselves to their utmost, and that the pre-revolutionary situation would build up there first. Nevertheless, the *Manifesto* does not name England as the first candidate for the proletarian revolution, and not even France, or Italy, but it names Germany as such, a country considerably behind other European countries at that time. By the mid-nineteenth century, Germany had just rid itself of serfdom and it still held some feudalist features. Nevertheless, the *Manifesto* states the following:

> Communists pay special attention to Germany. There are two reasons for this. First of all, Germany is upon the eve of a bourgeois revolution. Secondly, this revolution will take place under comparatively advanced conditions as far as the general civilization of Europe is concerned, and with a more advanced proletariat than the British proletariat in the seventeenth century or the French proletariat in the eighteenth. Consequently, in nineteenth-century Germany, the bourgeois revolution can only be the immediate precursor of a proletarian revolution.

It is seen from this quotation, - and it is of a paramount importance - that Marx had an idea about revolution in a weaker link and even about its development into a proletarian one, even before the foundations of the scientific theory were formulated. Both of these ideas, it is known, were picked up by Lenin, Trotsky, and others.

However, the 1848 unrest in Europe did not bring about proletarian revolution in Germany, nor in any other country. The beginning of the world revolution was put off. Hence, two decades later, in his introduction to the 1867 German edition of the first volume of *Das Kapital*, Marx writes the following: "In England the process of revolution is becoming really tangible. Upon reaching a certain stage, it should spread to the continent. It will acquire there more brutal, or more mild forms, depending on the level of the working class itself." Three years later, in his letter to S. Meyer and A. Vogt, Marx explains: "England, being a metropolis of capital, a power until now dominant on the world market, is <u>so far</u> the most important country for the world revolution, and besides, it is the only country where material conditions for such a revolution has achieved a certain degree of ripeness. For that reason, the priority goal of the international comradeship of workers is <u>to accelerate</u> a social revolution in England." (underlined by the author). Marx does not mention, though, that more than twenty years ago he proclaimed that such conditions were ripening in Germany.

The First International did not succeed in the "acceleration" of revolution in England, and, contrary to all prognoses, it unexpectedly started in France only a year after the above pronouncement. The world revolution did not follow, though, and the International peacefully passed away in America, in 1876. Therefore, Marx turned his eye further East. One year after the First International disintegrated, in his letter to F. Sorge (1877), Marx predicted a revolution in Russia:

> This crisis [the beginning of the Russian-Turkish War] is a new turning-point in European history. Russia... has been on the brink of an upheaval for a long time; all the elements are ready... The upheaval will start, according to all rules of art, with constitutional flirting, and the <u>imbroglio will be grand</u>... <u>This time</u> the revolution is starting in the East, where the hitherto unshattered bastion, and the reserve army of counter-revolution are situated. (*Selected Work*, 1940, Vol. 2, p. 534, underlined by the author).

Five years later, in his introduction to the Russian edition of the *Manifesto*, Engels adds: "...Today he [the tsar] sits in his palace in Gatchina, a prisoner of revolution, and Russia has become a vanguard of the revolutionary movement in Europe."

The character of these and other analogous pronouncements shows that Marx and Engels were inclined to regard any political imbroglio in Europe as a beginning of a worldwide proletarian revolution. Russia was not considered an exception, even though serfdom had just been abolished there (early 70s), and it could boast neither proletariat nor revolutionary proletarian movements. The "revolution" of which they speak was, as is known, undertaken and engineered by a few dozen members of The People's Will who chased after the Tsar with bombs, while the masses remained indifferent and passive.

Nevertheless, eight years later (1890) - Marx was already dead by that time - in his preface to the German edition of the *Manifesto*, Engels wrote about the possibility for Russia to jump over capitalism right into socialism and possibly even into communism:

The question we have to answer is: Will the Russian peasant communes (a primitive form of communal ownership on land which is already on the down grade) become transformed into the superior form of communist ownership of land, or will they have to pass through the same process of decay we have witnessed in the course of the historical evolution of the West? There is only one possible answer to this question. If the Russian revolution sounds the signal for a workers' revolution in the West, so that each becomes the complement of the other, then the prevailing form of communal ownership of the land in Russia may serve as a starting-point for a communist course of development.

In 1894, just before his death, Engels went even further: "No revolution in West Europe can wholly conquer as long as Russian statehood exists nearby in its present state." ("On Social Relations in Russia"). Now we know that students and followers of Marx and Engels fully utilized all these hints and leaped, even without a revolution in the West - but leaped where?

All of these forecasts did not stop Engels from asserting in 1892 (in "On the Historic Materialism"):

> The victory of the European working class...can be guaranteed only by the collaborative efforts of England, France, and Germany. In the latter two countries the labor movement is well ahead of the British one. For Germany the time of its triumph is even predictable. Its success over the last twenty-five years is unprecedented. It progresses with increasing speed... Judging by its present state, is it not possible that Germany will become the arena of the first great victory of the European proletariat? (Marx and Engels, *Selected Works in Two Volumes*, 1949, Vol. 1, p. 379)

This quotation is of interest for the reason that the word "revolution" is not mentioned there at all; it deals with "victory" only. It is not hard to see in it the hint on the future "scientific" theory which will discriminate between the total victory and the ultimate one. It is also characteristic that Engels does not even mention their previous unsuccessful predictions concerning the beginning of the world revolution, the first of which was given half a century before. He escapes criticism by using the vague word "victory".

All of these, as well as many other, prophecies prove, first of all, that the founders did not have a clear understanding of the real political situation in Europe in the second half of the nineteenth century. They did not have a "feeling" for it, such, for example, as that enjoyed by Bismarck, who understood that Germany was going through the formation of a centralized national state in which some traits of totalitarianism were embedded, and who predicted national socialism there several decades before its actual appearance (Spencer, *Foundation of Sociology*, 1898, p. 697, Russian edition). All predictions of a world proletarian revolution, starting from the *Manifesto*, also confirm the supposition that their belief in the necessity and inevitability of such a revolution and the dictatorship of the proletariat preceded the creation of the "scientific theory", it defined their outlook, and guided all of the scientific activity of Marx and Engels. The first volume of *Das Kapital* carries the imprint of this faith. During the lengthy period of its creation (1845-67) Marx deviated - little by little - from the scientific impartiality, starting to appeal to the readers' hearts rather than to their heads. It is demonstrated, for example, in the artificially stressed conclusions about the moral justification of the laborers' struggle for their trampled rights, or about the irreconcilability of contradictions between a worker and a capitalist. The most characteristic in this respect is its last, the seventh part, dealing with the universal law of the capitalist accumulation (chapter 23). Law on the impoverishment of the proletariat acquires a grotesque character of the law on its brutalization: "Accumulation of wealth at one pole is...at the same time accumulation of misery, agony of toil, slavery, ignorance, brutality, mental degradation - on the opposite pole." (p. 464, 2nd Russian edition, 1905). Many other concepts also underwent a similar "stressing."

Gradually it changed the character of the teaching. If the *Manifesto* spoke about cultural growth, spiritual development, consciousness and solidarity of the working class, later on such features as slavery, ignorance, moral degradation and even brutality are highlighted as current tendencies demonstrating the emergent necessity and inevitability of the revolution. Therefore the degree of contradictions of capitalism and preparedness of the working class to revolution should be determined by these qualities now. They will also define the character of the proletarian revolution, as well as whether its form will be more brutal or more humane (as it is said in the preface to *Das Kapital*). But if to pose a question about the necessity and precondition of the world revolution, then why wait for the brutality and the moral degradation of the vanguard class in the developed capitalist countries? This "commodity" is plentiful in our world and actually the developed countries have less of it than any other place. This point is not far from the conclusion that the most revolutionary class is the one inclined to greater violence. And gradually the center of gravity of the teaching shifts to the nearer goal: the capture of political power in the "weak link". Now only one step separates it from Leninism.

d. To the Question About Two Phases of Communist Society

The best example that sheds light on the character of the scientific theory and on the process of its creation is Marx and Engels' attitude to the socialist movement which unfolded in the second half of the nineteenth century. Let us cast a brief glance at the way it originated. The first socialist organization, the All-German Working Men's Union, was born in 1863, that is before the first volume of *Das Kapital* was published. It was headed by F. Lassalle (1825-64), Marx's student and comrade-in-arms. Five years later, another (rivalrous) organization, headed by another of Marx's pupils, K. Liebknecht (1826-1900), was created. Both organizations merged in 1875 ("Gotha Program"), giving birth to the German Social Democratic Party, which, only two years later, won nearly a half million voices in the elections, and twelve mandates, to the Reichstag. In the early 90s, as many as two million voters cast their ballots for it (twenty-five percent), and it kept under its control more than sixty trade unions. The socialist movement, which started in Germany, rapidly spread over many European countries: the first, constituent congress of the Second International (1889), was represented by twenty-two countries.

What was Marx and Engels' attitude to such a new phenomenon in the international labor movement which was destined to have such a great future? The attitude was absolutely negative! Marx, in his long letter to L. Kugelmann (1865) writes: "While he [Lassalle] was engaged in agitation, relations between us were suspended: 1) because of his self-praise-exuding braggadocio to which he added the most shameless plagiarism from my writings and those of others; 2) because I <u>condemned</u> his political <u>tactics</u>..."

Two years later, in the preface to the first German publication of *Das Kapital*, Marx reiterates his accusations of plagiarism ("...even terminology of my own creation...")[62] and adds: "Of course, I do not speak about particulars, into which he plunges, neither about practical usages of theory - I have nothing in common with that..." Merciless criticism of the first socialist organizations, together with personal attacks on the leaders of the movement for their "betrayal" of the course of the proletariat (the priority task is revolution), continued thereafter[63] as well. Equally criticized was the newly born trade union movement.[64]

---

[62]Borrowed also were, as it turned out, "all general theoretical provisions... for example, about the historic character of capital, about the connection between relations of production and means of production, and so on, almost word by word..." From this and many other Marx pronouncements, it is seen that Lassalle, being Marx's student, was a true and consistent Marxist, the only thing he negated was the singularity of the revolutionary path and revolutionary tactics.

[63]This attitude towards Lassalle did not change after his death. Very characteristic in this respect is Engels' letter to Kautsky in February 1891.

[64]The sharpest criticism is probably the following: "As for the city laborers here (in England), one has to regret that the gang of leaders did not get into the Parliament. It would be the surest way to get rid of this riffraff." (letter to F. Sorge, August 4, 1874).

However, after the crushing defeat of the Paris Commune and the collapse of the First International, the labor movement in the developed countries was increasingly deviating from the pattern of the world proletarian revolution drawn by Marx and Engels towards a pattern of parliamentary struggle and gradual social reforms without revolutionary shocks. The number of socialists was growing, and the number of communists was decreasing; the labor movement became socialist and social democratic rather than communist. Therefore, to avoid isolation, Marx and Engels were forced to introduce some changes into their tactical precepts in the hopes of influencing the new movement from inside in the desired direction. In connection with such an alteration of tactics, which now allowed peaceful parliamentary struggle of the working class for their rights (see next paragraph), it became necessary to introduce certain changes into the foundations of the scientific theory. One such alteration was the admission of two phases of the future communist society, which did not interfere with the foundations of the teaching, and at the same time turned out very convenient and effective in political maneuvering.

In his critique of the Gotha Program section devoted to the distribution of earned income,[65] Marx explains why it is impossible to demand a "fair" distribution of income in a society which emerges from the capitalist system. After which his notorious words about two formations follow:

> But these defects are inevitable in the first phase of communist society as it is when it has just emerged after prolonged birth pangs from capitalist society... In a higher phase of communist society, after the enslaving subordination of the individual to the division of labor, and therewith also the antithesis between mental and physical labor, has vanished; after labor has become not only a means of life but life's prime want; after the productive forces have also increased with the all-round development of the individual, and all the springs of cooperative wealth flow more abundantly - only then can the narrow horizon of bourgeois right be crossed in its entirety and society inscribe on its banner: From each according to his ability, to each according to his needs!

---

[65]Specifically, these words: "The proceeds of labor belong undiminished with equal right to all members of society." Also: "At the fair distribution of the earned income..." (cited by 2nd Russian edition, Vol. 19, pp. 9 and 12).

So, this is all of the alteration!   The word "socialism" is not even mentioned, though it is evidently meant, and Engels has to repeatedly explain thereafter why he and Marx did not call the *Manifesto* a "socialist" one (see, for example, prefaces to the 1888 British or 1890 German editions).

More essential alterations are contained in another place of "The Critique", directly after the remark on the two phases. Marx writes:

> Quite apart from the analysis so far given, it was in general a mistake to make a fuss about so-called distribution and put the principal stress on it.[66]   Any distribution whatever of the means of consumption in only a consequence of the distribution of the conditions of production themselves.   The latter distribution, however, is a feature of the mode of production itself. The capitalist mode of production, for example, rests on the fact that the material conditions of production are in the hands of non-workers in the form of property in capital and land, while the masses are only owners of the personal condition of production of labor power. If the elements of production are so distributed, then the present-day distribution of the means of consumption results underline{automatically} [underlined by the author]. If the material conditions of production are the cooperative property of the workers themselves, then there likewise results a distribution of the means of consumption different from the present one.

This quotation does not even mention the words "revolution" and "dictatorship of the proletariat", and the habitual revolutionary polemic slang is changed to the neutral scientific one. Further, it follows from the above that communism as an ultimate goal should not be thought much about, rather, the attention should be concentrated on its first phase (meaning socialism). As the complete communism is still very far, all discussions about it should be terminated, since they can isolate revolutionaries from workers. Indeed, in the same place Marx explains:

---

[66]Why a mistake? Because distribution is a revolution with dictatorship.

I have dwelt more at length with the 'undiminished proceeds of labor', on the one hand, and with 'equal right' and 'fair distribution', on the other, in order to show what a crime it is to attempt, on the one hand, to force our Party again, as dogmas, ideas which in a certain period had some meaning but have now become obsolete verbal rubbish [underlined by the author], which it cost so much effort to instill into the Party but which has now taken root in it, by means of ideological nonsense about right and other trash so common among the democrats and French Socialists.

e. Question on Two Roads to Socialism

A considerable step towards "realistic understanding" was made by Engels in his sensational Introduction to Marx's *The Class Struggle in France From 1848 till 1850,* which was written shortly before his death and is therefore often considered as his testament. For the first time Engels recognizes and explains the reasons for the erroneous prediction by himself and Marx of the world proletarian revolution in 1848 (he does not mention other erroneous predictions). He writes:

History has shown us too to have been wrong, has revealed our point of view of that time to have been an illusion. It has done even more: it has not merely disposed of the erroneous notions we then held; it has also completely transformed the conditions under which the proletariat has to fight... History has proved us, and all who thought like us, wrong. It has made clear that the state of economical development on the Continent at that time was not, by a long way, ripe for the elimination of capitalist production... (Vol. 7, p. 9).

After that Engels points out a new historic factor: a rapid growth of socialist movement for gradual reforms and, particularly, that of the German Social Democratic Party, and a new weapon (one of the sharpest) - universal suffrage. Engels writes:

Together with this successful utilization of universal suffrage,
however, an entirely new method of proletarian struggle came into
operation... The time of surprise attacks, of revolutions carried
through by small conscious minorities at the head of unconscious
masses, is past...[67] The irony of the world history turns everything
upside down. We, the 'revolutionists', the 'overthrowers'[68] - we are
thriving far better on legal methods than on illegal methods and
overthrow. (2nd edition, Vol. 7, pp. 14, 15, 20).

Such a confession was evidently not easy for Engels, as it conflicted with
the whole of the teaching guidelines considered earlier. It is seen from the
heated polemics that unfolded among communists after the Introduction was
published, from Engels' accusations that Liebknecht distorted the Introduction,
as well as from Engels' attempts to take his assertions back. In his letter to
Lafargue (April 3, 1895) Engels wrote:

X [Liebknecht] played a bad joke on me. From my Introduction to
Marx's Articles on France in 1848-50, he took everything that could
serve him in his defense by all means of the peaceful and anti-violent
tactics... But I recommend such tactics only for Germany of today,
and even that with considerable reservation. To France, Belgium,
Italy, and Austria these tactics cannot be wholly applied, and they
can become inapplicable to Germany tomorrow.

As is well known, such reservations are not provided in the Introduction
itself. But the point is that Engels could not refuse and did not refuse totally
from the violent methods of the overthrowing of capitalism. It is important that
he was forced to recognize a possibility for other means, and further
development of the working movement in the developed capitalist countries
convincingly demonstrated the correctness of only one of them, namely the
peaceful parliamentary struggle. It is also important that by recognizing two
ways he made one more step in the direction of making the future communist
ideology even more flexible.

---

[67]Evidently he did not foresee Lenin.
[68]Even in quotation marks!

Undoubtedly, it is Bernstein who should be given credit for working out a theoretical substantiation for the peaceful transition from capitalism to socialism in the countries of developed capitalism. In the 1890s, he wrote:

> Is there any sense, for example, in repeating the phrase about dictatorship of the proletariat in the times when in a number of institutions representatives of social democracy are in fact embarking on a path of parliamentary struggle, proportional representation and public legislation - all these denying dictatorship? At present it has become so obsolete that it is impossible to reconcile it with the reality other then by depriving the word 'dictatorship' of its true meaning and attaching to it some softer interpretation...All practical activity of social democracy is reduced to creating such circumstances and conditions which would make possible and necessary a transition of the present social system into a higher one without convulsive upheavals. (*Conditions of Socialism Realization and the Tasks of Social Democracy*, 1901, Russian edition, pp. 158 and 159).

It is recognized that theoretical substantiation of the opposite, convulsive, method of transition from capitalism to socialism in backward countries should be credited to Lenin. So, by the beginning of the twentieth centennial, Marxism, so to speak, has split into two opposite and conflicting teachings, each of them considering itself a true, orthodox one. It is this seeming division of the teaching, which gives the illusion of two Marx's, that is used at present to validate the slogan "Back to Marx!" Though in reality only one of them is orthodox, that of Lenin, in accordance with the evolution of Marxism during its founders' lifetime, as it was considered above. As for Bernstein, he and his followers recognized - and even at that, only partially - only Marx's economic teaching, mostly its part on the surplus value, which they considered a moral justification for the workers' struggle for their rights thus substantiating the socialist worker's movement. All other parts of Marxism, especially its dialectics, they rejected as erroneous, and they proclaimed a slogan "Back to Kant!" As for Lenin, he accepted Marx as he was, together with all his contradictions. The remark on two stages on the road to communism he developed into a teaching on two phases (see next paragraph). Neither did he reject categorically the possibility of two ways and two forms of struggle, but he developed and implemented only one of them. Therefore it is Lenin who should be considered Marx and Engels' most faithful student, follower, and heir. For that reason, before summarizing this digression into Marxism as a scientific theory, it is important to briefly consider the Leninist stage of its evolution.

2. Leninism

a. Development of Teaching on Proletarian Revolution

In a certain sense the history of Bolshevism can be considered a pre-history of partocracy. There are two reasons to it: first, its ideological and organizational succession, and second, formation of partocracy took place at the same time as the decline and degradation of Bolshevism. The beginning of this dichotomous process can be conditionally assigned to 1920-21, and associated with the Tenth Congress. By that time it became clear that no hopes for world revolution could be held in any observable future. This fact predetermined the beginning of the ending of Bolshevism, because it was rigidly attached - ideologically and psychologically - to such a revolution, as a priority goal. The process of Bolshevism's withering lasted almost one and a half decades, when its last bearers were burnt in the crucible of the Stalinist purges, and slogans about world revolution quietly and unnoticeably disappeared from view. Stalinism took over. The crucial ideological, organizational, and practical achievements of classical (Leninist) Bolshevism did not dissipate, and they became a part of partocracy.

There is no doubt that the theoretical substantiation of Bolshevism belongs to Lenin. Before analyzing it, it is very important, though, to rid ourselves of two widely spread and still existing myths. One of them is claiming that Lenin is an absolute "genius", as if such a genius exists at all. From there it follows that whatever Lenin says, no matter in what field of human activity, is to be considered an insight of genius, a pronouncement of genius, or a teaching of genius. In reality, if such an epithet is justified at all, it is true only if applied to his political activity. This is the big myth. The small myth is that Lenin was an expert of Marxism. This one is worth deliberating in more detail. All Lenin's biographers said (and say) a number of times that Lenin, even in his young years (first half of the 90s), surprised everybody with his "deep knowledge of

Marxism." That is why his first and key work *What is To Be Done?* (1902), which has every right to be called Lenin's "*Communist Manifesto*" was the result, as it was declared, of a thorough and profound study of Marxism and its creative application to the Russian conditions. Was it really so? Which of Lenin's works demonstrate this deep knowledge of Marxism? Usually the following ones are named: *Three Sources and Components of Marxism* (1913), *Karl Marx* (1915), *Imperialism as the Ultimate Stage of Capitalism* (1916), and *Philosophical Notebooks* (1914-16). But all of these works are related to Lenin's late immigration period rather than to its beginning. Also, their character not in the least demonstrates a deep knowledge of all facets of the Marx-Engels teaching. The first of them is nothing but a brief note, the second one is a popular essay for the thesaurus *Granat* - and not only popular, but even non-critical and primitive, as by that time many weak sides of Marxism (like the surplus value) were already well known and thoroughly studied. Further, *Imperialism...* is a small popular brochure published under a pseudonym, Ilyin, written by contract with the publishing house *Parus*, in which even the size was specified - five pages. The publishers changed the name of the brochure and abridged it by half. The original text, as Lenin himself indicated, he was unable to restore. It was being "restored" already in the Stalinist period. It is common knowledge how documents were restored at that time. Therefore there are no good grounds to consider this work by Lenin a "direct continuation" of *Das Kapital* (see, for example, *Concise Dictionary on Philosophy*, ed. by Rozentahl and Judin, 1954). As for *Philosophical Notebooks*, they are nothing but draft copies, not designed for publication. Besides, they do not touch (or almost do not touch) the most important part of Marxism - its economic theory.

Hence, Lenin's key work, *What is To Be Done?*, which lays the organizational foundations of all varieties of Bolshevism, was written long before he was able to study (and did study) Marx's key works on economy (which laid the foundation for the two roads of the development of the workers' movement). From this it follows that the choice of one of these roads - the revolutionary one - is a choice of faith rather than knowledge. It means also that Lenin is not as much Marx's student or a continuer, rather he is his spiritual heir who shared his faith in the universality of violence. This is why he developed only the teaching on the proletarian revolution and dictatorship of the proletariat.

It is natural to start his analysis with the definition of Leninism as it was introduced in ideology:[69] "Leninism is the Marxism of the epoch of imperialism and the eve of the proletarian revolution. More precisely, Leninism is the theory and the tactics of a proletarian revolution in general, the theory and tactics of the dictatorship of the proletariat in particular." This definition highlights two parts on Leninism: the teaching on proletarian revolution, and the teaching on the dictatorship of the proletariat (power), and it indicates their connection with Marxism. Besides, it indicates that the first part is the expansion of Marxism (the phrase "in general"), and the second - the leading one - its further specification and deepening.

Let us first consider the first of these parts (expansion), i.e., teaching about proletarian revolution. It can be schematically formulated - in analogy with Marxism - in the form of the following interconnected statements:

1. Not capitalism in general, but its highest stage - imperialism - is the eve of the proletarian revolution.
2. Due to extremely uneven development of imperialism a proletarian socialist revolution can start and win in a single country, specifically where the front of capitalism is weaker.
3. Such a single country should not of necessity be an advanced, industrially developed one; the proletariat there should not of necessity compose a majority of the population (as it can have allies).
4. Revolution in this country will represent a beginning and prerequisite of the world proletarian revolution.

First, several remarks on the character and interconnection of these statements. The second and the third of them are, evidently, the substantiation of the applicability of Marxism to such a backward country as Russia (this is the "expansion"), whereas the first and the fourth ones establish the connection between this "expansion" and Marxism: without world proletarian revolution, Leninism secludes itself from Marxism. Further, the singularity of Leninism lies in the combination of all four statements into a single theory; three of them taken isolatedly from the first one would represent a mere progression of Marxism. In

---

[69]This definition is given by Stalin (*Foundations of Leninism*, 1924), and it has never been doubted or criticized in communist literature. Its first part is reproduced word for word in the *Big Soviet Encyclopedia*, 3rd edition, 1974 (without reference to Stalin, though).

the previous section it was indicated that Marx and Engels admitted that revolution can start and even win in one country, even an industrially backward one. Among possible candidates they mentioned Russia (see section 1, pages 122-123). Engels spoke of possible revolution in Russia as a "signal" and "prerequisite" of a proletarian revolution in Europe (page 123). As for the first statement, if isolated from the rest, it fixes only qualitative changes in capitalism in the three decades after Marx's death (a new phase) and the fact that in the nineteenth century, revolution did not happen anywhere. This somewhat rehabilitated Marxism, after all its unsuccessful predictions of a revolution.

In this particular outline, the elaboration of the Marx-Engels theory of a proletarian revolution has entered contemporary ideology. It is usually asserted that Lenin created this "elaboration" before the October revolution ("in general") which meant that he presumably foresaw, or even predicted its coming. In reality, Lenin had nothing to do with this formulation; it was carried out by Stalin, after Lenin's death, in his work *On the Foundations of Leninism* (1924). Also, it was Stalin who first used the term "Leninism" and then incorporated it into ideology and history.

When the origins of Lenin's theory of revolution in the weaker link are regarded, usually two of his pre-Revolutionary works are mentioned in this connection: *The United States of Europe Slogan* (1915) and *Military Program of the Proletarian Revolution* (1917). These two works, though, are dedicated to absolutely different questions, and revolution in the weaker link is mentioned in passing and very vaguely.[70] The word "revolution" is not even used, instead,

---

[70] At the end of *The United States of Europe Slogan*, Lenin writes: "Uneven economic and political development is an absolute law of capitalism. Hence, the victory of socialism is possible first in a few or even in one single country. The victorious proletariat of that country, having expropriated the capitalists and organized its own socialist production, would confront the rest of the capitalist world, attract to itself the oppressed classes of the other countries, raise revolts among them against the capitalists, and, in the event of necessity, come out even with armed force against the exploiting classes and their states." (underlined by the author). The article, "The War Program...", was published in German and was addressed to a Western reader. As one of the excuses of the future revolutionary wars ("thirdly") it declared: "The development of capitalism proceeds extremely unevenly in the various countries. It cannot be otherwise under the commodity production system. From this it follows irrefutably that socialism cannot achieve victory simultaneously *in all* countries. It will achieve victory first in one or several countries, while the other will remain bourgeois or pre-bourgeois for some time." (underlined by the author).

"victory of socialism" in the epoch of "violent political and economic cataclysms, the sharpest class struggle, civil war, revolutions and counter-revolutions" is referred to.

Therefore, it is not a political revolution (capture of power and destroying the old state machine) that is spoken about in these two "predicting" articles, but a social one, i.e., construction of socialism. For this reason it is impossible to conclude (based on them) about Lenin having predicted the October coup, as well as the delay of similar coups in other countries. However, the division of revolutions into social and political ones turned out to be very convenient for political maneuvering, which was masterfully proven by Stalin. Moreover, in the above quotations, the word "Russia" was never mentioned, and it is not indicated that a backward country can become a country of triumphant socialism. Only at the end of the second article, the word "pre-bourgeois" suggests that Lenin possibly meant Russia. Therefore, the above articles cannot serve as a foundation for the conclusion that the world proletarian revolution can start in an industrially backward country, such as Russia. Finally, at the same time, Lenin wrote two other voluminous works: *Imperialism* (1916), and *State and Revolution* (1917), the second being finished right before the October coup (August to September). It was the most appropriate place to discuss the possibility of a revolution in a backward country, or its possible delay in developed countries. This was not discussed in the least: neither there nor in other of Lenin's works, until the very time when such a revolution occurred, and this delay became a fact and a huge problem (see next section). That is why communist literature connects the development of the scientific theory of a proletarian revolution in the epoch of imperialism only with the articles mentioned above.

Here is a good place to mention one important circumstance for later development. Why was a phrase like "the victory of socialism" used in these "predictory" articles rather than the "victory of the revolution", as in Engels' (see page 122-23), or the "construction of socialism" (socialist society), as one might expect if the possibility of a delay is presumed? The first part of the question emerges in connection with the work *What is to Be Done?*, which was devoted to the principle of organization of a totalitarian "party of the proletariat". In it, Lenin considers political revolution as an act of capturing political power. The answer to the second part of this question is based on the fact that Lenin always viewed the building of socialism as a coercive construction of a social system by a totalitarian party that captured power (dictatorship), as a struggle for socialism.

Therefore, everything that is assumed to be Lenin's scientific theory on revolution in imperialism's weaker link, and the construction of socialism in a single country, was formulated much later, after the power in Russia was already captured. And it was not accomplished by Lenin himself, but rather by Stalin and his followers. Not a single one of Lenin's pre-Revolutionary works assumed and discussed the possibility of a revolution in a weaker link to remain the only revolution in the world for years and decades. The possibility, that later became a reality, that by the middle of the twentieth century all industrial countries would find themselves even farther from the proletarian revolution than in the times of the *Manifesto* was not admitted or even discussed. Lenin realized that such an assumption was equivalent to a total dissociation from Marxism. That is why he always maintained that Europe was on the brink of a proletarian revolution. He said that before the 1905 revolution, before the October revolution, before the above articles, and after them. In the previous section it was shown that Marx and Engels did exactly the same for over a half century. These predictions of Lenin are very important for understanding the entire character of Leninism. We will dwell on them in more detail.

b. Predictions of the World Proletarian Revolution

The difference between a revolutionary-practitioner and a reformist-theoretician is, as everybody knows, that the first one consistently and invariably proves and substantiates the necessity and inevitability of a revolution and predicts its coming in the near future in general. How realistic he is and how well he understands the current political situation can be assessed by the successfulness of his predictions of a concrete revolution. It was shown above that Marx's faith in the necessity and inevitability of a coercive restructuring of human societies which guided the whole of his scientific activity, hampered his understanding of the real situation in the world, and this was constantly revealed in his multiple erroneous predictions of the downfall of the existing system. Now, what about Lenin? Did he foresee the February Revolution in Russia, without which there undoubtedly would not have been the October one? All facts prove that the February Revolution in Russia, as well as the First Imperialist War, turned out to be a full surprise for Lenin and caught him unaware: the War - in Austria, from where he hardly managed to find his way out of, and the Revolution - in Switzerland, at the height of his fight against the Second International, which consumed all of his forces and attention and was aimed at accelerating that very same world revolution in a European country.

Evidences of it are numerous, and there is no point in analyzing them. I will only cite two of his pronouncements in the period directly preceding February 1917. In the article "Tasks of the Zimmerwald Left in the Swiss Social Democratic Party", which was sent to the left members of the party in the form of theses in December 1916, Lenin called on the Swiss proletariat for the revolution with the aims of overthrowing the rule of the bourgeoisie, of capturing political power, and of administering a socialist system. He wrote:

> Either the Swiss people will starve, and starve more and more severely with each week, and every day be subjected to the danger of being pulled into the imperialist war, i.e., to be killed for the interests of capitalists, or it will follow the advice of the better part of its proletariat, gather all its strength, and implement the socialist revolution. (4th edition, Vol. 23, p. 101).

And this prophecy was addressed to the state which had been very far from any revolutions for hundreds of years and which did not participate in any offensive wars since the proclamation of the "infinite neutrality" in 1815! The dilemma of "either-or" was invented by Lenin, and this fact proves how he misunderstood a concrete political and social situation.

The second quotation is about Russia. In his report at the meeting in Zurich, dedicated to the twelfth anniversary of the 1905 revolution, Lenin said:

> We must not be deceived by the present deathly silence in Europe. Europe is fraught with revolution... We, old people, may not live to see the decisive battles of this coming revolution. But I think I can express hope, with great certainty, that young people, who work so excellently in the socialist movement of Switzerland and all the world, these young people will have the chance not only to fight, but also to win in the future proletarian revolution (Ibid., p. 245).

He did not mention that Russia was at the brink of a new revolution. The February Revolution took place only a month later, and as for revolution in Europe, it has not happened until now.

Upon his return two months after the February Revolution, Lenin assessed the situation and put the capture of political power on the agenda. He declared that the world revolution would immediately follow the Russian one. For example, in his report at the April conference about the current period he said:

> When discussing imperialism from the point of view of Marxism, it is absurd to dwell on the conditions in one single country, when all the capitalist countries are so closely bound together. And this bond is immeasurably stronger now, during the war. All humanity has been kneaded into the bloody lump, and there is no escape from it separately. Although there are countries more and less advanced, the present war has bound them all together by so many threads that for any one separate country to try to escape from the tangle is impossible and futile.

Lenin did not seem to care that his assertion directly contradicted his earlier remark about the possibility of socialist victory in a single country. He did not mention either that he did not hope to live until the epoch of future fights. His main goal was to push his comrades-in-arms to capturing power in Russia.

Another three months later, in July 1917, he held that the world revolution had in fact already started:

> From the very beginning the Russian proletariat understood that for the Russian revolution to succeed, for the course of peace, for the course of freedom, mutual support of the workers of all countries is needed, an international insurrection of the bleeding European proletarians is needed. Its war cry will be 'Long live the world revolution!'... All over the world the petrels have started their flight. In England workers have already started an open fight to curtail the capital, in France soldiers agitate for peace and revolution, Germany witnesses a continuous ferment and strikes, in America the bourgeoisie turns to executing by fire the socialists who lift the banner of the fight against the war. Spain is inflamed in the

revolutionary skirmish of classes (see *Manifesto at the Sixth Congress of the RSDRP*, June 26 - July 3, 1917).

Here, to prepare the party to capture power, Lenin was explicitly exaggerating and even telling lies.   It is known that direct calls for capturing power were pronounced at the meeting of TsK RSDRP (Central Committee of the Russian Social Democratic Labor Party) in October. The decisions of this plenum said:

> TsK recognizes that the international state of the Russian revolution (mutiny in the fleet in Germany, as an extreme demonstration of the world socialist revolution in Europe gaining pace), as well as winning by the proletarian party of the majority in the Soviets... all this puts on top of the agenda an armed insurrection... From the political analysis of the class struggle in Russia and Europe follows the necessity of the most resolute, most active policy, which can be only the armed insurrection (Lenin and Stalin, *Collected Works on the History of VKP* (b), Vol. 1, p. 964, 1933).

On October 20, directly before the coup, Lenin said: "Bolsheviks do not have the right to wait for the congress of soviets, they must take power immediately. By doing so they save both the world revolution and the Russian revolution." (5th edition, Vol. 34, p. 340).

The utterly successful and rapid capture of power, together with the delay of the revolution in Europe, was a surprise to the majority of the party members. It is seen from heated discussions that engulfed the party in 1918. Discussions on almost any question were invariably deadlocked by the problem of the delaying world revolution, and for more than a year[71] Lenin had to resort to various trickery as a means to pay for his erroneous predictions. It was vividly demonstrated for the first time at the 7th Congress of the Party (March 6, 1918) during the discussion of peace with Germany. How stunning the three-month delay of the world revolution was can be judged by the following words from Lenin:

---

[71]Serious unrest started in Europe only at the end of 1918, with riots in Germany, in the city of Kiel. After that Lenin's tone changes drastically.

The revolution will not come as quickly as we expected. History has proved it [same as Engels: instead of recognizing his mistake he blames history], and we must be able to take this as a fact, we must be able to reckon with the fact that the world socialist revolution cannot begin as easily in the advanced countries as the revolution began in Russia - the land of Nicholas and Rasputin, the land in which the overwhelming majority of the population were quite indifferent to the conditions of life of the people in the outlying regions. In such a country it was quite easy to start a revolution, as easy as lifting a feather. But it is wrong, absurd, without preparation to start a revolution in a country in which capitalism is developed, which has produced a democratic culture and has organized every man [where is the crisis of capitalism then? - author[72]]. We are only just approaching the painful period of the beginning of socialist revolution... We do not know, no one knows; perhaps - it is quite possible - it will conquer within a few weeks, even within a few days, but we cannot stake everything on that [they already did!]. We must be prepared for extraordinary difficulties, for extraordinarily severe defeats, which are inevitable, because the revolution in Europe has not yet begun, although it may begin tomorrow. (5th edition, Vol. 36, pp. 15, 16).

---

[72]One cannot but recall here the edification of Lenin's predecessor, Tkachev, to Engels, in his open letter in 1874: "We do not have a city proletariat, this is true, of course. But then, we do not have a bourgeoisie at all. Between the suffering people and the despotism of the state that oppresses it we do not have any middle class: our workers will have to fight the political force only - force of capital is still in the bud... Our people are ignorant - this is also a fact. But then, its vast majority is fathomed with the principles of communal ownership of land; it is, so to speak, a communist by instinct, by tradition... (the) Russian people is tirelessly protesting... Therefore it can be called a revolutionist by instinct. It is needed only to simultaneously and in many places waken up the accumulated feeling of discontent and anger, which is always boiling in the hearts of our people... Our state looks strong only at a distance... Little is needed to dispel this illusion. Two or three military defeats, simultaneous uprising of peasant in many areas, an open uprising in the residency in the peaceful time, and the government will find itself lonely and abandoned by everybody." (Cited by D. Shub, *Political Activists of Russia*, 1969, p. 68).

In this connection the form in which Lenin encourages the disheartened and dismayed party members and deputies of the congress is interesting and significant:

> Since the European revolution has been delayed severe defeats await us because we lack an army, because we lack organization, because, at the moment, we cannot solve these two problems. If you are not able to adapt yourself, if you are not a revolutionary but a chatterbox; and I propose this not because I like it, but because we have no other road, because history has not turned out to be so pleasant as to make the revolution ripen everywhere simultaneously. (Ibid., p. 18).

Again, history is at fault rather than the scientific theory! In the political account before the same congress, Lenin makes another, even more striking pronouncement: "Yes, we will see the international world revolution, but for the time being, it is a very good fairy tale, a very beautiful fairy tale - I quite understand children liking beautiful fairy tales. But I ask: is it becoming for a serious revolutionary to believe fairy tales?" (*Complete Works*, Vol. 36, p. 19).

Here it would be appropriate to ask: did Lenin himself believe in the forthcoming world revolution, or were all his pronouncements (given above as well as many others) prompted by the motives of intra-party struggle and other, purely political considerations? Many facts, indeed, argue in favor of his faith, and show that he himself was perplexed by the delay of a revolution in the West. It looks like that after three months of this delay he still believed in its coming. Continuing to underline the necessity of the world revolution ("Without revolution in Germany we will perish...") he declares however: "Having learned this lesson we shall overcome our split, our crisis, however severe the disease may be, because an immeasurably more reliable ally will come to our assistance, viz., the world revolution." (Ibid., p. 20). This unshakable faith somewhat justifies Lenin in his mistakes, and raises him even higher as a sturdy revolutionary, ready for any unpleasant surprise and any blow of fate. However, such a viewpoint cannot be supported by any evidence.

Question about faith is of importance only for the personality characteristics of Lenin. To study the character of his scientific theory more significant is the question about what was the goal that guided all his activity, including the creation of his scientific theory.   What was Lenin's goal: revolution in Russia, or world revolution through revolution in Europe? Neither one. First of all, Lenin was a consistent revolutionary, i.e., destructor. Since any revolution, as he was convinced, starts with the capture of political power, the whole of his theoretical and practical activity was mainly concentrated on the substantiation and creation of a centralized organization aimed at capturing political power, as well as on the preparation for such a capture. Then, where: in Russia, or in Europe? Wherever the favorable conditions would be created. Until the February Revolution, Lenin probably thought that such conditions would emerge in a European country. In favor of it stood his immigration at the age of thirty, his permanent residency in Europe until 1917 (he stayed in Finland only briefly in 1905-06), his attitude towards the 1905 revolution, and also the fact that in immigration, most of his effort was aimed at arguing within the Second International. This is why the World War and the February Revolutions turned out as a surprise to him. After the February Revolution, he quickly understood though that the situation had changed, and without hesitation, he returned to Russia as soon as a chance presented itself.

Very characteristic in this respect are his words at the Third Comintern Congress on July 5, 1921 (Vol. 26, p. 451, 3rd edition):

> When we started the <u>international</u> revolution [underlined by the author], we did so not because we could forecast its development, but because a number of circumstances compelled us to start it. We thought: either the international revolution comes to our assistance, and in that case our victory will be fully assured, or we shall do our modest revolutionary work in the conviction that even in the event of defeat, we shall have served the cause of the revolution and that our experience will benefit other revolutions. It was clear to us that without the support of the international world revolution the victory of the proletarian revolution was impossible... In actual fact, however, events did not proceed along as straight a line as we expected. In the other big capitalistically more developed countries the revolution has not broken out to this day.

Further, Lenin said that the Soviet power was a "miracle" and the October Coup was a "miracle." And when this miracle took place, they succeeded in firmly establishing their power. But the second "miracle," namely the world revolution, was late, and then, post factum, the creation of a "scientific theory" about the weaker link started. Long forgotten articles were pulled out into the light, together with forgotten quotations about the division of revolutions into political and economic ones. They were edited, refined and (under Stalin) falsified, to become a coherent scientific theory which allegedly possessed a predictive power.

c. Teaching on Power (Dictatorship of the Proletariat)

Now let us consider the second and the main part of Leninism - his teaching about the dictatorship of the proletariat or an unlimited power (concretization and deepening of Marxism, see pages 133-34). It was created by Lenin - the main features - one-and-one-half decades before the teaching on the weaker link. And he "deepened" Marx, not only by creating a finished theory of universal organization for capturing and holding state power, but by succeeding in proving its correctness in practice in Russia after the February Revolution as well, when conditions were favorable. This second part of Leninism, unlike the first, enjoys predictive quality. It is this part that comprises the essence of Leninism.

This teaching was first described, as it is well known, in Lenin's work *What is To Be Done?* (1902). In this work, Lenin for the first time formulated the organizational principle of the communist party's construction, now known as "democratic centralism" and incarnated in all communist parties of our time without exception, independent of whether they already hold power or just strive to it. He did not invent it (as this principle was known since time immemorial); rather he formulated it as it applied to political and social conditions in such a country as Russia, where the struggle of a political party for power was developing in the absence (or insufficiency) of political and social freedoms and where democratic traditions were lacking. The "gene" of totalitarianism is contained in this principle itself, and the totalitarian structure is created by incorporating this principle of organization into all spheres of the political, social, and economic activity of the state power. The Leninist teaching on power is a theory, a strategy, and a tactic of such an incorporation before and after the power is seized.

In this teaching, it is important to regard the origins of ideology. To do that we have to return to *What is To Be Done?*; to that part of it where the possibility of combining conspiracy with democracy is substantiated (it was discussed in detail in the beginning of section 2 of Chapter 1). Lenin agrees with his critics (see the quotation on page 15) that democracy (he uses the term "broad democratic principle") is incompatible with conspiracy as a principle of construction of all social democratic parties. From here it seems to follow that the Bolshevik Party is not democratic, and that conditions in Russia were not ripe enough for creating a social democratic party capable of performing a proletarian revolution. A lengthy preparation to it is still ahead, and for the time being, Russia is able to have only a *coup d'etat*, performed by a conspiratorial organization, i.e., by a minority.[73] But such conclusions are made in science rather than in politics. As for Lenin, he is a politician first of all. Therefore, he is sounding out ways to avoid these conclusions that could prove harmful for the set goal (capture of power). He works out a new understanding of hierarchical democracy (centralization of leadership and decentralization of responsibility - see chapter 2), as well as new argumentation to be used in all arguments about democracy, party, and revolution. This argumentation is based on dialectical rather than regular logic, and Lenin all the time is contrasting between "either-or" (you are either with the proletariat or with the bourgeoisie, you are either a revolutionary, or a reformist - meaning filth). Also, in all his ideological articles he never forgets that he addresses only those who share his faith in the necessity and inevitability of the violent way of restructuring human societies. Only for them is such argumentation convincing. In the final analysis, this argumentation was reduced to the introduction of the double meanings of the terms "democracy", "openness", and "elections". Thereby, the scientific theory starts to gradually transform into ideology. This is where its origins are to be looked for (see Chapter 7).

---

[73]This conclusion is known to be made by Tkachev and his predecessors Zainchevski and Nechaev: "Revolutionary minority, after ridding the people of the yoke of the oppressive fear and horror of the powers that be, opens up before it an opportunity to exercise its destructive revolutionary power, and, by leaning on this power and skilfully directing it towards the destruction of the immediate enemies of the revolution, it destroys all strongholds that protect them and thus deprives them of all means to resistance. Then, using its power and authority it introduces new progressive communist elements in the conditions of the people's lives; shifts this life from its age-old basis, enlivens its numb and callous forms." (P.N. *Tkachev, Selected Works*, in 2 volumes, Vol. 2, pp 167 and 169).

Ideology plays an exceptional role in the system of power of "dictatorship of the proletariat." Its formation, according to Lenin, is inseparable from the practical activities of the organization, i.e., of the ruling party. Therefore, all its statements, laws, axioms, and paradigms, are continually changed, clarified, and polished, in accordance with the current tasks of the organization. This process of formation is studied in detail in Chapter 8. Here it is enough to underline only that according to Lenin's teaching on power, ideology acquires real meaning and power only in direct association with the organization that created it. In *What is to Be Done?*, Lenin even declares that only such an association makes the workers struggle a "truly class" one. Lenin emphasizes all the time that in political struggles, ideas become a real force only when combined with power. Immediately after the historic split (1903), Lenin wrote: "Formerly our party was not a formally organized whole, rather it was a sum of individual groups, therefore no other relations among these groups were possible except ideological influence. Now we have become an organized party, and this means the creation of power, conversion of authority of ideas into authority of power." (Vol. 6, p. 291). Conversion of "authority of ideas into authority of power," means exactly the process of amalgamation of the teaching and organization which transforms the scientific theory into ideology, and theoretical struggle into the ideological one.

3. Scientific Theory of Power Capture

a. Marxism-Leninism as a Teaching on Capturing and Keeping Political Power

Now let us cast a brief glance at the scientific theory of proletarian revolution and emphasize its most characteristic features. One of these features was repeatedly highlighted earlier, and it means that formulation of all key provisions of the theory are based on the concrete social and political situation in the world, which implies that they are changing all the time as the situation changes.

For example, let us consider the question about the organization of the communist party. In the middle of the nineteenth century, capitalism became international. On these grounds, Marx and Engels thought that proletarian revolution should also be international. Therefore, the communist organization should be of the same character as well. They viewed it as a professional, democratically centralized and conspiratorial one, however, they did not succeed in creating such an organization. That is why neither the 1848 European Revolution, nor the 1871 French one, were turned into world proletarian revolutions. Furthermore, the communists' membership and influence in industrial countries started to decline, and the working man's movement assumed explicitly socialist, or reformist, character. So, although their scientific theory was formulated by that time (formulated as applied to the conditions of the first half of the nineteenth century), practice dictated corrections. Taking all this into account, together with some final remarks by Marx and Engels, Lenin introduced these corrections.

Lenin proceeded on the assumption that any revolution starts with the seizing of concrete political power in an individual country. The worldwide political power was non-existent as of yet. Therefore, the revolutionary organization should also be national rather than worldwide. Hence, practical activity should start with the creation of national organizations, and theoretical activity should be dedicated to answering such questions as how to build an organization of revolutionaries, what should be its strategy and tactics, and so on. The scientific theory for the organization aimed at capturing power is described in his "manifesto", his work *What is to Be Done?* It was written when Lenin was approximately the same age as Marx was when he wrote *Communist Manifesto.* Lenin had to introduce some corrections into the teaching, which he did, naturally, in consideration of the political and social conditions in Russia. This is how the theory of combining legal and illegal struggle was born, teaching about the proletariat's allies and about escalation.

Still, the existence of effective organization is only one of many necessary conditions for seizing power; corresponding social and political conditions are needed, too. The 1905 Revolution demonstrated that such conditions were not yet ripe in Russia. So, Lenin concentrated all his attention on the fight in the Second International, where he performed on behalf of a new party created by himself in Russia, whose goal was to prepare for revolution in industrial European countries, according to Marx's teaching. The beginning of the First World War seemed to favor this goal. But life again had it its own way: the February Revolution took place, which created extremely good conditions for capturing power, but the three worldwide revolutions did not follow after that, nor after the October Coup, nor after the Civil War... New, more radical reformulations of the foundations of the scientific theory were needed. Lenin started working on them, and Stalin, Trotsky and Mao Tse-Tung completed them.

Marxism connected the beginning of a revolution in an individual country with the level of production. More precisely, with the degree of contradictions between productive forces and the relations of production which reveal themselves in the sharpening of class struggle. This key provision was not confirmed by practice. Lenin's teaching on imperialism and its uneven development, and on revolution in its weaker link, weakened the rigid connection between the level of capitalist development and the probability of a revolution. Moving the eve of revolution to the highest phase of capitalism accounted for the failure of Marx and Engels' predictions about the timing of revolution, thus reconciling theory and practice. Further, as long as now the whole world is announced to be the arena of revolutions, then conclusions about the global split into two hostile camps, about the destitution of the proletariat and the degeneration of the bourgeoisie did not look so absurd any longer, as they were in Marx's teaching regarding developed countries. An opportunity presented itself to interpret the terms "proletariat" and "bourgeoisie" more broadly, and together with them, the term "proletarian revolution" in industrially undeveloped countries as well. It became possible to explain a revolutionary situation in a concrete country, especially an undeveloped one, by sharpened conflict between forces of production and productive relations in some other country.

Still, in Lenin's formulation of the scientific theory, a national revolution in a separate country was regarded as a "beginning and prerequisite of the world revolution." It did not agree with either the national tasks of the Bolshevik Party as a national organization, nor the general situation in the world at that time, which became quite clear shortly after the Civil War. Once more, life corrected scientific theory. Consequently, Stalin's "manifesto"[74] formulates the theory of world revolution in a different manner:

> World revolution will develop by revolutionary secession of more
> and more countries from the system of imperialist states... The
> stronger the development of socialism in the first country, the faster

---

[74]Namely, his three works: *On the Foundations of Leninism* (1924), *October Revolution and Tactics of Russian Communists* (1924), and *On Leninism* (1926).

this country transforms into the basis for the further unfolding of the world revolution, into the lever of the decomposition of imperialism, the faster and more thoroughly the world revolution, and the process of secession from imperialism of new countries will unfold. (*On Leninism*, 11th edition, p. 104).

Linked to this main proviso of the theory, its other statements had to be reformulated too. For example, the teaching about the construction of socialism in one country became also different: not only socialism, but even communism can be built in "one, separately taken, country", even if it is economically underdeveloped, like Russia. Moreover, provided that such an underdeveloped country of the "victorious proletariat" exists, other seceding countries, even if those at the stage of the decomposing tribal system, like Mongolia, can transfer to building socialism and communism, even bypassing capitalism (see reference to Engels, page 122). These and many other statements of the same nature do not make any new theory that could be called Stalinism, rather, they are a logical development of Leninism in accordance with ""practice".

As another example, let us consider the question about the withering of the state. The corresponding statement in Marx and Engels' scientific theory is formulated in the most clear form by Engels in his work *Socialism: Utopian and Scientific* (1880):

The proletariat seizes political power and turns the means of production into state property. But, in doing this, it abolishes itself as a proletariat, abolishes all class distinctions and class antagonism, abolishes also the state as state... The first act by virtue of which the state really constitutes itself the representative of the whole of society - the taking possession of the means of production in the name of society - this is, at the same time, its last independent act as a state. State interference in social relations becomes, in one domain after another, superfluous, and then dies out of itself; the government of persons is replaced by the administration of things, and by the conduct of processes of production. The state is not abolished. It *dies out.*

Lenin, in his work *State and Revolution*, written directly before the October Coup, comments on this and other like pronouncements about the dying out of states in great detail, and he totally agrees with the author's viewpoint. But *coup d'etat* took place, the Civil War ended, the "hierarchically centralized organization of professional" strengthened its position at the top of power and established the dictatorship, and life again started to introduce corrections of the theory. All processes connected with the dying out of the state were actually opposite to what had been predicted: all outer and inner attributes of the state were strengthening, the numerical value of secret and open police was growing, the judicial system was hurriedly created, centralization of rule was enforced, GULAG was created and began to spread all over the country, and so on, and so forth. Only by the end of the 1930s, after the process of power consolidation was completed and it transformed into a totalitarian one, the corrections were introduced into the theory of the state's dying out. In his report to the Eighteenth Party Congress in 1939, in its part called "Some Theoretical Questions", Stalin cites the same quotation from Engels and asks: "Is Engels' statement true?" He answers himself that it is true only under two conditions: if the international factor is disregarded, and if socialism has won in the majority of countries. Otherwise, dying out is impossible even if socialism is completely built (the 1936 Constitution). The state will have to exist even when communism is completely built, "unless the capitalist surrounding is liquidated, unless the threat of offense from outside is eradicated..." (*On Leninism*, 11th edition, p. 606).

This example vividly demonstrates how a scientific theory was being built to justify the accomplished fact, namely, an unexpectedly revealed tendency of the evolution of organization. The dying out of the state meant the dying out or the "falling asleep" of the ruling organization. But this organization, which, by the end of the Civil War, amounted to millions of members, did not wish to "die" or to "fall asleep". Neither did it wish to share power with anyone. Stalin understood it and used it for his own goals. After his death, however, still no signs of "dying out", or at least weakening of any state functions, were observable. Nor did it happen after the state surrounded itself with a continuous ring of "socialist" states, when there was no longer any sense in speaking about capitalist surroundings. New scientific concepts appeared to satisfy new demands and goals of the ingrained system of power.

So, all in all, the most important feature of the "scientific theory of proletarian revolution" is that all its key provisions are formulated on the basis of practice. If to divide this practice conventionally into six stages: creation of organization, a coup, the destruction of the existing system of power, creation of a new system of totalitarian power, construction of socialism, construction of communism - then, the scientific theory ends at the fourth stage, that of creation of the absolute state power. After which, the power evolves according to its own laws. These laws are not well studied yet, since the corresponding practice does not lend itself easily to generalizations (there are only two countries, Russia and China, where all stages of practice were evolving independently), and also because after the fourth stage is achieved, the society becomes closed, and the inner mechanisms of the evolution of organization, and all processes involved in it, become secret. Therefore, the scientific theory can only be regarded either conditionally or ironically.[75]   Marxism-Leninism as a scientific theory of proletarian revolution is concluded at the capture of power, and the establishment of the dictatorship of the proletariat, after which it is forced out by ideology.

It is worth noticing that all of these theoretical statements, like the whole of Leninism in general, are the consequences of Marx's scientific theory (see above, pages 112-13). Now let us see how matters stand with the basic statements. At this point we come across the second distinguishing feature of Marxism-Leninism: all its main conclusions are not - and cannot be - derived from these basic economic statements. Moreover, as the scientific theory developed, these consequences were increasingly separated from the basis, and, in particular, revolutionary Marxism separated from economic Marxism, and Leninism from Marxism. The *necessity* of proletarian revolution cannot be deduced from *Das Kapital* logically, since *Das Kapital* admits the alternative: revolutionary or peaceful solution of conflicts between labor and capital. This fact was recognized by the founders by the end of their life, and it was practice that influenced it (see section 5), but it not in the least shattered their faith in the universality of violence as a means to change human societies. Any

---

[75] As an example, one can consider Stalin's theoretical exercises at the end of his rule on topics such as the problems of linguistics and economic laws of socialism, and the similar exercises of Khruschev, about which it is preferred to keep silence. They demonstrate that totalitarian power is unable to distinguish between theory and practice, since it loses the understanding of its own limits.

revolutionary who shares this faith will not be inclined to put a serious value on the peaceful alternative, and he will close *Das Kapital* with the conviction that the existing capitalist system should be destroyed by force.   As for the *inevitability* of the proletarian revolution, it is "proven" in the scientific theory by referring to dialectics (solving antagonistic contradictions by explosion). This proof does not rely upon scientific logic, but again upon faith. The point is that the domain of Gegel's laws of dialectics was a sphere of thought, or spirit. Marx, by "turning Gegel's dialectics upside down" ascribed its laws to nature. And if "leaps" and "contradictions" are akin to both nature and thought, then "practice" indeed becomes the only criterion of truth. And as laws of dialectics are not related to any real scale of time, then the timing of the resolution of social conflicts is set arbitrarily.

In the same manner, matters stand with all other conclusions of the scientific theory.   Above it was demonstrated with the example of Lenin's teaching on revolution in the "weaker link" of imperialism, which was presented as a consequence of an uneven and "jumpy" character of development. However, it was derived, as it was underlined, after the fact, i.e., after the revolution in Russia happened. The consequence of the delay of the state's dying out until the complete construction of communism was concluded in the same manner. In passing, Stalin also "concluded" the consequence about the sharpening of class struggle with the advancement of socialism in one country in a capitalist surrounding.

b. *Marxism-Leninism and Exact Sciences*

The scientific theory of class struggle, proletarian revolution and dictatorship of proletariat is undoubtedly the pivotal part of Marxism-Leninism, without which it would have lost all its militant spirit and practical value, and revolutionary Leninism would have separated from economic Marxism. At this point it would be natural to ask: does this part of Marxism-Leninism bear the character of a scientific theory: even if not the theory of social development (which was shown above), then at least the theory of capturing and holding political power?   Or is it to be considered only a "teaching", as some critics claim, or, finally, as a false teaching, as opponents - anti-communists - declare? Marxism-Leninism itself firmly and decisively answers the question of its classification as a science. This answer is not a later interpretation of Marx and

Engels' students and followers: the founders paralleled their teaching not with any sciences, but with exact sciences, mostly with biology and physics. It is discussed, for example, in Marx's preface to the first German edition of *Das Kapital*, in Engels' preface to the British 1888 edition of *The Communist Manifesto*, and also in Engels' brochure, *Socialism: Utopian and Scientific*. During the epoch of the cult, pretentiousness of Marxism-Leninism increased, and it even placed itself above exact sciences.

We will answer the question about the scientific character of Marxism-Leninism at the end of the section. At this point, let us confine ourselves to a more narrow problem of whether it is possible to speak about any similarity between Marxism-Leninism and such sciences as physics and biology. What is the similarity, if any? Or, if there are no similarities, what are the radical differences?

First, a few words about the investigation method in exact sciences. These sciences are divided into fundamental and applied (practical) ones. Fundamental sciences study general laws of living (biology) and non-living (physics and math) nature. Their method of study can be schematically represented in the form of the following chain:

experiment 1 (observations) $\rightarrow$ formulation of the problem $\rightarrow$ hypothesis (guess) $\rightarrow$ experiment 2 (preliminary verification) $\rightarrow$ theory $\rightarrow$ consequences $\rightarrow$ experiment 3 (confirmation of regularity)

Consequences of a theory should be derived from its main statements logically by some non-contradictory method (by no means with the help of dialectical logic!), and experiment 3 should be "clean", i.e., free of uncontrolled influences and contradictory interpretations.

For applied sciences, such as radio-electronics, automatics, energetics, agricultural sciences, medicine and so on., as well as such narrow fields as genetic engineering, and some others, the method of study differs from the first one:

goal $\rightarrow$ hypothesis $\rightarrow$ experiment 1 (preliminary verification of hypothesis) $\rightarrow$ theory $\rightarrow$ experiment 2 (goal achieved, practice)

The major difference lies in the presence of a concrete goal, brought from the outside, which is usually linked to one of the consequences of the fundamental science. But there exists a more essential connection between applied and fundamental sciences, it is that theory in applied sciences uses method and results of a fundamental theory and is organically attached to it.

Therefore, if we regard method of study only, then Marxism-Leninism can be related to applied (practical) exact sciences only, and not to fundamental ones: the scientific theory is founded on a pre-set goal: coercive restructuring of human societies, and practice is considered as the only criterion of its correctness and achievability. Also, this goal is included into theory organically, as, first, it preceded the creation of the theory chronologically, and second, it unites all individual goals of particular stages of practice (see above, pages 149-51).

This goal was first formulated by twenty-seven-year-old Marx in his "Theses on Feuerbach" (1845), which was long before *Communist Manifesto*, *Das Kapital*, and other fundamental works containing formulation of the scientific theory. Its eleventh thesis runs: "The philosophers have only interpreted the world, in various ways; the point is to change it." The contents of the theses clearly indicates that not a slow, gradual restructuring of the world was meant, but a revolutionary, coercive one. Further, if to disregard Marxism-Leninism's groundless pretensions to be above all sciences, then in this thesis the "world" means the social world, i.e., human society. But attempts were made to establish social laws not only by philosophers, but by historians, economists, and politicians as well. Merciless critique by Marx and Engels of all social sciences of their time indicates that they were deeply convinced that all such attempts were futile and all laws formulated by that time were erroneous. Therefore, the true meaning of the eleventh thesis is that all sciences studying human society did not succeed in establishing true laws of its evolution; but the main goal is not this, but the reconstruction of the society. True laws will be understood and found in the process of its practical restructuring. Therefore, the word "practice" is contained in seven out of the eleven theses, and is used more than a dozen times. It releases a true revolutionist from the necessity of studying theoretical sciences and referring to them in his practical activity.

The indicated similarity of the study method in Marxism and applied sciences, however, is merely a formal, seeming one. In the applied exact sciences, the goal, as it was underlined, is formulated as the result of a fundamental science, and in Marxism-Leninism, it is based on faith alone. The proofs used are in reality imitations of science, connected with the specific character of the contemporary epoch - that of scientific and technological progress. Also, practice in applied exact sciences is not at all the only criterion of truth, as in the case of Marxism-Leninism. There are other criteria, for example, the agreement between the applied and the fundamental theories, and between applied science and other consequences of fundamental science, and the experiment.

Is it possible, then, that the teaching on class struggle, proletarian revolution, and dictatorship of proletariat can be referred to as a specific variety of applied sciences or a specific stage of their formation? Such varieties do exist, as well as specific stages. Applied sciences often originate before the corresponding fundamental science is created or completed. In such cases, the original goal is not a consequence of the fundamental theory, rather it is based on a guess, on a scientist's intuition, or his belief. Then starts the construction of an empirical or semi-empirical theory, whose main content is the substantiation of the shortest way to achieve the pre-set goal. Such a "temporary" theory can stimulate a fundamental theory, and later be included fully or partially into the fundamental science. But until then, such sciences, which are usually called empirical or semi-empirical, are developed independently, autonomously, as their goals and hypotheses are in their turn drawn from practice and experience (the system of feedback). In such applied sciences, practice (experience) represents the only criterion by which to verify the correctness (achievability) of the goal, and, consequently, the correctness of the theory.

Another variety of applied exact sciences originates when a correct (achievable) but premature goal is set, when the general theoretical and experimental level of science is not adequate for its achievement. In this case, construction usually begins of a specific, pseudo-scientific theory and pseudo-scientific experimental method, specially designed to achieve the particular goal. Finally, if the goal is not achievable (wrong), then the corresponding "scientific" theory, as well as the corresponding experimental method, will always be anti-scientific and fallacious. Such sciences are usually called false sciences. Alchemy is a good example.[76] At its early stage (when the main goal was to

---

[76]Chemistry was born in ancient times. The idea to turn metals into gold is equally ancient, although the Arabic prefix "al-" appeared much later. An idea to produce the "philosopher's stone" appeared still later, and it predetermined the decline of alchemy as a science. A

transform metals into gold), it was a pseudo-science, but later (when it busied itself attempting to create a so-called "philosopher's stone" that would prolong human life), it became a false science. Another example of a pseudo-science is Lysenko's teaching about the influence of phenotype on genotype, before the mechanism of heredity was discovered. An example of a false science would be the multiple theories of the "*perpetuum mobile*".

Then, to what applied sciences should Marxism-Leninism - or, specifically, its teaching on class struggle, proletarian revolution, and the dictatorship of the proletariat - be linked? As soon as this question is asked, it becomes clear that such a comparison is void of sense, not only in regard to empirical and semi-empirical exact applied sciences, but pseudo-sciences as well. It becomes evident that in all known social sciences, i.e., sciences created by man to study human society, the terms "correct" and "achievable" goals are not synonyms any longer (as well as "incorrect" and "unachievable"). Therefore, when combined with the terms "untimely" and "timely", they produce a number of new combinations, such as "incorrect, but achievable goal", or "incorrect, but timely one", and so on, a situation absolutely foreign to exact sciences. Further, the assessment of the correctness of the goal already acquires an ethical character, and the assessments of untimeliness or timeliness become subjective, and "willful impulses" of individual persons and human masses have to be taken into account, because the cognition itself of social laws is "intertwined inseparably with his [the one who is cognizant] actions and desires" (K. Manhaim, *Ideology and Utopia*, Frankfurt-on-Main, 1969, pp. 148-49).

As an illustration, let us consider the scientific theory of a proletarian revolution. Its ultimate goal is the construction of an ideal communist society free of wars, violence, poverty, and exploitation. Scientific theory claims that it outlines the shortest way to accomplish this goal: it is the creation of organization, a coup, destruction of the existing state structure, creation of a new system of power (dictatorship of proletariat), construction of socialism and,

---

detailed history is described, for example, in F. Soddi's *History of Atomic Energy*. He writes: "Looking into the history of alchemy from the early days, we come to the conclusion that it embraced a considerable amount of very useful practical knowledge (which has not lost its value even now), which, in some peculiar manner, blended with an absolutely perverted theoretical approach, and with the faith (natural in those times) in a magic influence of the stars, and good and evil spirits upon the result of chemical reactions." (cited from the Russian translation, 2nd edition, 1979, p. 28).

finally, communism (see page 149). Hence, the achievement of the ultimate goal depends on the timely achievement of intermediate goals corresponding to each of these stages. In other words, the ultimate goal will be achieved if an effective organization will be successfully created, if by the end of this period favorable conditions for the coup will emerge (like a war, or economic ruin, as it was in Russia), if by means of propaganda and political agitation it will become possible to weaken the existing system of power, if, after the coup, the power will be successfully retained, and so on. All this chain of "ifs" must contain one more of them: if the organization will not start to degenerate after the power is seized, because this is what we observe all the time. Then it will disintegrate into a ruling top and a subjugated mass of rank-and-file members, as it was shown in previous chapters. At this point, progress towards the achievement of the goal discontinues. And, since the achievement of each of the above listed stages depends not only on the goal-driven and effective activity of a large organization, but on even larger masses of people (resistance), then it is most doubtful that such an exact science can exist which would be able to predict the results objectively, and to assess the achievability and timeliness of the ultimate goal. Only faith can determine the general direction of such a movement. The point is: what kind of faith is it? (see the next section).

Thus, one can speak only of some formal and remote similarity between Marxism-Leninism and certain applied sciences, based exclusively on the primacy of the goal. As for the exact sciences in general, Marxism-Leninism has nothing to do with them; at least, with their method. Therefore, any attempts to compare it with Darwinism or any exact science, and even, to put it above them, are void of any sense.

c. Marxism-Leninism and Military Sciences

Now let us return to the question put at the beginning of the previous section, i.e., whether Marxism-Leninism and, in particular, its main part - teaching on revolution - can be considered science in general, or is it just a teaching whose claims to being scientific are not justified. As it is known, there are a great many sciences, and they differ from one another by their goals, structure, character, and method. There is even a science on "classifying sciences",[77] which is more than one hundred years old, and according to which, all known and even yet unknown sciences can be classified in a variety of orders and systems by any of their different properties. Therefore, it would be more correct to ask what place Marxism-Leninism occupies in a definite system. Since Marxism-Leninism claims to be a cause-determinant description of "laws of nature, society and thought" (see, for example, *Concise Philosophical Dictionary*, ed. by Rozentahl and Yudin, 1954), then it is logical to use the degree of correspondence between theoretical predictions and real facts as a major factor for classification. Then all sciences (known and unknown) can be lined up successively, first physics and mathematical sciences, then biological, and so on, somewhere in the middle social sciences, and at the end such sciences as "science to win".[78] Still further will be extrasensory sciences, occultism, and yoga. Then, to find out how scientific Marxism-Leninism is, we must find its place in this classification.

With this purpose in mind, let us consider the similarities between Marxism-Leninism and the military sciences. Common for them is a goal set from the outside. For military sciences, such a universal goal is the destruction or suppression of an enemy. And this goal is not derived from any science. For Marxism-Leninism, its nearest and key goal (which defines its essence) is to seize political power and establish a dictatorship of a small group. The whole of the contents of military science and its character is reduced to the effort to achieve this goal in the most effective and quick manner in concrete situations. This is why it first answers such questions as "how?", and only then explains "why". Since large masses of people are usually involved in a war battle, and it is impossible to predict the behavior of each person or each group, then all scientific theories are created for idealized or average conditions. Therefore,

---

[77]It originated thanks to works by Sent-Simon (1760-1825), O. Conte (1798-1857), and Ampere (1775-1836). Conte considered that the task of philosophy was to construct a system of sciences (*A Course in Positive Philosophy*, 1830-42). Ampere classified all then existing and possible future sciences (*Practice in Philosophy of Sciences and Analytical Description of the Natural Classification of Human Knowledge*).

[78]This is how the instruction by the famous Russian military leader Suvorov was called, which was published in 1806. It consisted of two parts, the first one for military commanders, and the second one for rank-and-file soldiers. "Sciences to win" are mostly military sciences (though there are others as well). Constituent parts of military sciences are theory of military art (strategy, operative art and tactics), theory of the armed forces construction, theory of military economy, and military history (see *Big Soviet Encyclopedia*, 3rd edition, 1971).

every lost battle, i.e., disagreement between theory and practice, never disproves theory, but is used for making it more precise (feedback). Hence, military sciences are always empirical sciences, and for them, practice is really the only criterion of verifiability, whereas various theoretical constructions are of a very restricted character. All these features, as it was shown above, are fully enjoyed by Marxism-Leninism, particularly its main part - the teaching on class struggle, proletarian revolution, and dictatorship of the proletariat.

And this is not all. Similar to military sciences, Marxism-Leninism, when substantiating its goal and shortcuts to achieve it, also analyzes (and is in fact based on) the behavior of large masses of people, works out ways to purposefully influence them. This includes maneuvering (military and political) in concrete situations, and it contains (and is based on) teaching about the structure, functions and character of the most effective organization. To complete the likeness, it is worth recalling that a hierarchically centralized and conspiratory organization of professionals - party - is in essence analogous to a military organization. Further, there exists an ideology of war, in general, able to change and transform when applied to a concrete war, which can also be viewed as a similarity between military science and Marxism-Leninism. Irreconcilability with the inner enemies (even greater than with the external ones), many ways to ignite hatred - these are features akin to both of them. And the famous quote, "Here all mistrust must be abandoned, And here must perish every craven thought", which Marx offered to post at the entrance to science (just like at the entrance to hell) highlights the likeness of these sciences, because applied to regular exact sciences it looks absurd.

All this resemblance between Marxism-Leninism and the military sciences shows that, in the above classification, its place would be somewhere between social and military sciences. This proximity of Marxism-Leninism to the "sciences of how to win" has never been negated in communist literature. Let us look again at the definition of military science in the latest edition of the *Big Soviet Encyclopedia*: "System of knowledge on the preparation and conducting of a war by states, coalitions of states, or <u>classes</u> to achieve political goals." (here and below underlined by the author). In this definition, class struggle is not even discriminated from regular war, which accords with the following definition: "War is a social phenomenon inherent to a <u>class antagonistic</u> society. War is an organized armed struggle between different <u>social classes</u> and states in the name of definite economic and political goals. In its essence, it is the continuation of the policy of this or that <u>class</u> by different, namely, violent means." In the 1951 edition, this definition was supplemented by the addition: "Only Soviet military science is a true military science." The 1971 edition echoes: "The radical difference of bourgeois military science is its reactionary ideological basis and class essence."

Therefore, it is not accidental that all creators of contemporary communist ideology (Marx, Engels, Lenin, Stalin) were at the same time the creators of Soviet military science.[79] Moreover, "general theoretical and practical precepts that form the foundation of the Soviet military science were laid in the period of the First Russian Revolution (1905-1907) when Lenin and Stalin developed Marx and Engels' principles on the art of armed insurrection, and then, on this basis, they created a new political strategy" (*Big Soviet Encyclopedia*, 1951). So, Marxism-Leninism fertilizes military science, and vice versa. Also, it is not accidental that the social system after the October coup was called a "military communism",[80] and supreme leaders who had never been in the military and never in combat, often dressed up in military uniforms and awarded themselves the highest military decorations, ranks and medals. It is no doubt that the army's task is much simpler, narrower and more limited compared to the tasks of a political party, whose goal is the coercive creation of a totalitarian society. For that reason, Marxism-Leninism is much broader and more sophisticated than all the military sciences taken together. The similarities listed above merely serve to prove their proximity in the system of classification of the sciences, and they are given here for illustration, to highlight some features of Marxism-Leninism as a scientific theory of the seizing of power by a small group of people and the establishment of a dictatorship. The elements of this theory existed even before

---

[79]In the second edition of the *Big Soviet Encyclopedia* (1951), seven out of eleven columns are devoted to Stalin, thus distinguishing his exceptional contribution in the development of the Soviet military science. In the next (1971) edition, all of it was omitted, and, besides Lenin, Frunze, Tukhachevsky, Shaposhnikov, and several others were named its creators.
Nevertheless, military terminology introduced into Marxism-Leninism by Stalin is left in, and it continues Stalin's cause.

[80]It would be far-fetched to consider accidental, when Morgan's term "military democracy" was picked up by Marx and Engels. As it is indicated in the 3rd edition of the *Big Soviet Encyclopedia*, "Marx and Engels attached to it (the term) a universally historical meaning, and started to describe with this term the "final stage of the decomposition of the primitive communal society, and its transformation into a class society." Later Lenin disguised "military democracy" with the help of the term "democratic centralism."

Marx and Engels. But compared with Marx, Engels, Lenin, Stalin and Mao, Plato is an idealist, Machiavelli is narrow-minded, Jesuits are too preoccupied by their religious notions, Nietzsche is a poseur, and Hitler is a maniac. Only Marxism-Leninism succeeded in incorporating all the isolated and odd pieces of this ancient science into a single scientific theory of how to capture power, and how to keep it and use it for the coercive restructuring of the social structure of the society - and all this as applied to contemporary epoch, with all its scientific and technological achievements taken into account.

4. Founders and Their Faith

Throughout all this chapter it was emphasized more than once that faith in the necessity and inevitability of violence as the only way to restructure human society guided all the scientific activity of the founders of Marxism-Leninism, and it preceded the creation of the scientific theory. The study of the latter will not be complete if we do not consider briefly the nature of this faith itself.

The faith of a scientist is usually formed as a result of lengthy observations and thinking over facts and actual events; it is formed as a quintessence of his life and professional experience as the result of a conscious attitude towards the outside world. The faith of prophets is different. They, one can say, are born with faith as it guides all their deeds, words, and teachings. The Bible is filled with the teachings and the pronouncements of prophets. In natural sciences, the role of such a faith, if it plays any role at all, is not a leading one, and most often it is negative. Besides, there is faith aimed at creation, and there is faith aimed at destruction. What kind of faith did the founding fathers have?

To answer this question, let us use a historic parallel between Marx and Plato, without forgetting, however, that any historic parallels are very conditional. The possibility of such a comparison lies in the fact that they both believed that an ideal human society could be created only by coercive means. One can also find some resemblance in their views of communism, and in some of their statements on class struggle and economics.[81] The influence of Plato can also be traced in the formulation of the second thesis on Feuerbach. Nevertheless, contrary to these similarities, the faith of Marx and the faith of Plato belong to diametrically opposed types.

---

[81]Marx was well acquainted with Plato's teaching and he cited him a number of times (see, for example, his commentary to the second volume of Plato's work).

Plato was born in the year of Pericle's death (428 B.C.), in the epoch of the highest might and flowering of the state of Athens, his motherland. He survived a fierce twenty-seven-year-long Peloponnesian War (433-404), which resulted in the capture of his home city, Athens; then, a nine-year-long Corinthian War (395-386); the origination, apex, and decay of the Second Athenian Maritime Alliance (378-355); the origination, apex, and decay of Thebes; and many other events that gave evidence of the beginning decay of the Greek civilization. His last years coincided with the gradual, but steady, pressure of a backward Macedonia, which later, ten years after his death, took over the whole of Greece. All of these factors affected the evolution of Plato's social convictions, from a zealous defender of freedom and democracy, to a convinced proponent of a coercive communist system. This evolution, which was the consequence of his disappointment in people, was seen by Plato as a tragedy of life.

At the beginning of his life, Plato was a brilliant gifted youth, a descendant of the last Athenian King, Kodras (on his father's side), and of the greatest Greek lawmaker, Solone (on his mother's side). He was on the one hand - a gymnast, wrestler, horseman, two-time winner at the Olympiad - and, on the other - a musician, poet, artist, and playwright. Meeting with Socrates at the age of nineteen completely changed his whole world outlook. For seven years, he was his student and a follower in his search for truth. The execution of his teacher in 399 had a tremendous impact on Plato. He fled from Athens, and for twelve years, he traveled within the limits of the world known to him, studying the life of other nations. The results of this study were evidently depressing; according to various witnesses, Plato's character changed drastically over that time. Upon returning to Athens at the age of thirty-nine, Plato founded his famous Academy, and wrote the first chapter of his *Republic*. Before he finished it, he traveled twice to Syracuse in the hopes of bringing reason to the Cicilian tyrant, and convincing him of the necessity to restructure the state on different principles. The first of his visits, as it is known, ended up in his enslavement. But that was not all. At the age of sixty-six, he undertook one more trip with the same goal, and this resulted in his flight. All these personal failures, together with the decline of the Greek civilization, predetermined his views and his faith that an ideal human society could only be brought about by means of coercion, and that democracy, which was the basis of Greek society, did not lead to anything good. His *Republic* and *Laws*, where Plato relates his social views, sort of sum up this process, which anyone can easily understand. (*Laws*, to which he devoted the last seven years of his life, was not finished).

Marx's epoch was of a very different character. He lived in a period of so-called industrial revolution, when the foundations of contemporary society were laid. Using his own terminology, the epoch of the establishment of capitalism undoubtedly demonstrated many negative facets, vices and curses, from our contemporary viewpoint. But it does not seem very probable that this particular circumstance had played a decisive role in the formation of Marx's faith, as it is sometimes asserted. After all, the shortcomings of the preceding medieval society were perhaps even more significant than those of capitalism; and Marx himself never denied the progressive character of the new society. To understand Marx's faith, it is very important to note that he did not notice the domineering tendency of his epoch, or that he did not even want to notice it. And the tendency was: the capitalist system at that time was painfully working out - within each European state - ways of deterring the centrifugal forces of uncontrolled free enterprise, it was laying foundations for the future technological revolution and, linked to it, an unprecedented raise of the living standards and unprecedented democratic freedoms. During Marx's lifetime, his motherland, Germany, became one of the most powerful states in Europe, and also a homeland of socialist movement, whose impact on the structure of the contemporary world it is difficult to overestimate. Over the same period, in Great Britain, the trade union movement was born, which has prospered ever since all over the world. In the next century, the trade union and socialist movements changed the social face of all developed countries by defining its evolution by way of gradual and slow reforms, rather than revolutions.

Marx's faith, unlike that of Plato, was developing independently of this social background, and even, as it was shown above, in defiance of it - in defiance of the main trend of his epoch, which did not remain unnoticed by many of his followers. Marx and Engels saw the events around them as distorted through the prism of their faith. Any political bustle, they greeted as the beginning of the long-awaited world proletarian revolution, as the beginning of the crash of the existing system. Their faith had nothing in common with the faith of a scientist, and Plato's faith was in essence that of a scientist.

The founders enjoyed their faith in the universality of violence for solving major social problems all their life, which can be supported by a large body of evidence. For example, as early as in 1843, a twenty-three-year-old Engels wrote in his article, "Achievements of the Movement for Social Restructuring on the Continent": "...Political freedom is a pseudo-freedom, the worst variety of slavery..." A year later, while studying the British Constitution, and happily predicting a forthcoming wreck of the British social system, he again declared that "...democratic equality is chimera." (see *Complete Work*, 1st edition, Vol. 2, pp. 369, 394). As it was mentioned above, Marx formulated his credo on the restructuring of the world at age twenty-seven ("Theses on Feuerbach", 1845), long before his major economic and philosophical works were written. Three years after *The Communist Manifesto*, in a letter to his friend Engels, he writes with a shade of regret: "Under universal suffrage, there is no point even thinking about revolution..." (October 19, 1851). Quite a few similar pronouncements can be found in his later articles, too, in spite of the "censorship" of his followers. And though in Marx and Engels' early years, they are interspersed with opposite pronouncements (for example, *On Censorship*, *On the Freedom of the Press*, and so on), later on their faith in violence gradually subjugated all other trends and became the pivot of their scientific theory.[82] And we can trace how their disappointment was growing after each erroneous prediction of the world revolution. So, by the character of their faith, Marx and Engels are more like prophets who decide, according to the trends of their epoch, to impart a pseudo-scientific shell to their prophecies about revolution.

Another difference is linked to the character of teaching. Plato lived in a cruel police state, where people were considered pawns or toys, and their interests were totally subjugated to the interests of the state. Democratic freedoms, democratic organizations, and unalienable rights were out of the question in such a state. In such a state, human life is totally regulated, beginning from state affairs and ending with family matters, and even leisure, this regulation being supported by a system of very severe and brutal punishments. Physical coercion in it was supplemented by a spiritual one, a coercive ideology, this ideology being worked out like Marxism-Leninism was "worked out" by a small group of rulers and then "incorporated" into masses. Just like in Marxism-

---

[82]This faith was not void of ambitious desires and craving for personal power. Marx's letter to Engels, written two years after the First International was created (September 11, 1867), can serve as a good example: "Things are going on... And when the revolution, which might be nearer than it seems, comes, then we (that is you and me) will have this whole mighty machine in our hands... We might be very pleased..."

Leninism, this ideology was filled with hatred of democracy in any from. Further, politics in that state were put above economics and above laws, and all "means of production" were in the hands of the state. To complete the similarity with the contemporary communist regimes, it is worth noting that Plato's state should have been totally isolated from other countries (in Plato's particular case, by the sea), that in such a state, universal espionage and universal informing were legalized, and severe punishment was given not only for deeds, but for intentions as well.

Anyway, all these striking similarities should not obscure the radical difference between Plato's teaching about a communist state and the Marxist-Leninist scientific theory. Plato is an idealist, and for him reality is a mere shadow of the world of ideas. Further, in Plato's teaching, the motif of coercive restructuring of society is altogether lacking, also lacking are calls for revolution, or violence. He considered that persuasion was the main method of social restructuring, and he meant to convince all people, including tyrants. Construction of an ideal state out of a tyrannical, i.e., obviously bad and cruel, one, he probably considered as the easiest achievable version of creating an ideal communist society. In his teaching about state, Plato concentrates all his attention on the state itself - its character, structure, laws, rather than on the ways to reconstruct it. Now let us see how matters stand with Marx. They stand the other way around! He did not concentrate his attention on the character of the future society, which he avoided describing altogether, but on the ways of violently restructuring the society, restructuring by way of a murderous revolution and the establishing of a dictatorship, and he meant to restructure not at all a tyrannical or totalitarian society, but the most democratic one by those times. Therefore, Plato's faith bears some positive features, whereas Marx's faith is destructive.

What can be said about the faith of other founders of Marxism-Leninism? In the process of development of the scientific theory, figures of the founders gradually lose their human features, and their spiritual life becomes progressively poorer. Oppositely, their faith in the necessity, inevitability, and regularity of violence becomes stronger, more consistent, and it rids itself of any hesitations or doubts. Already in Lenin's works, it its very hard to distinguish any period of searches, hesitations and uncertainty, like the one we can easily trace in early Marx and Engels. His democratic pronouncement and emphasized democratic behavior bear a trace of showing off and posing. Stalin was organically unable to exercise any doubts or hesitations, as all his spiritual aspirations were aimed at getting absolute power. Nothing is known about Mao Tse-Tung's hesitations and doubts. This process of spiritual impoverishment, or "petrifying" ("dehumanization") which started with Lenin, is, as it was shown above, a consequence of the evolution of organization.

CHAPTER 7
ORGANIZATION AND IDEOLOGY

1. Pre-history of Bolshevism

The process of the transformation of Marx's teaching on the proletarian revolution into ideology started, as it was shown above, straight after the publication of *The Communist Manifesto*. Lenin only completed it. On the other hand, contemporary communist ideology in its orthodox form is the ideology of Bolshevism. From this it follows that we can speak about a pre-history of the bolshevist organization covering the period, during which the ideology of Bolshevism was organically growing out of Marxism. A brief account of this pre-history will be given in this section, the main attention being paid to the connection between scientific theory, ideology, and organization, and also to those aspects of the pre-history which communist orthodoxy prefers to keep silent about.

The "Communist Manifesto" was the program of a small conspiratorial organization called the "Communist League",[83] which can be considered a prototype of the Bolshevik Party. Article 1 of its charter defined the goals of the League in the following way: "Overthrow of bourgeoisie, domination of proletariat, abolition of the old bourgeois society based on the antagonism of classes, and construction of a new society without classes and private property." Article 2 defined the conditions for membership: a) lifestyle in agreement with this goal; b) revolutionary energy and zeal in propaganda; c) profession of communism; d) abstension from participation in any anti-communist, political or national society, and informing the leading committee about such a participation.

The organizational structure of the League was defined rather vaguely. Nevertheless, all four elements of the future Leninist "democratic centralism" can be traced there, namely, professionalism, hierarchy, centralization, and conspiracy. For example, Article 5 read: "The League consists of communes, districts, leading districts, the central committee and the congress." Article 2E demanded "subordination to the orders of the League", and Article 2F required

---

[83] 1847-52. In his article "History of the Communist League", Engels points out that this organization was preceded by two other conspiratorial societies: "League of the Outcasts" and "League of the Just". Marx and Engels were connected with the latter from its origination (1836) until its reorganization into the "Communist League" in 1847. Only two of its representative congresses took place: the constituent one (which failed to adopt the "Communist Manifesto" as its program) and the closing one which formalized the split.

members "to keep secret all internal affairs of the League". To this, Article 4 added: "Members of the League are given special nicknames" (cited by the *Complete Work*, 2nd edition, Vol. 5). Still, of all these elements of "democratic centralism" are formulated vaguely, intangibly, and in a number of cases, inconsistently.

The history of the Communist League sheds some light on the founders' characters and their attitude to the future theory of the proletarian revolution, which was still to be created. The immediate reason for this split was the demand by the minority (the Schapper-Willich group) to start the revolution straight away ("We must reach the dominance right now, or there will be nothing for us to do", Ibid., Vol. 7). But the majority, headed by Marx, thought that the revolution would be premature (i.e., Marx showed himself to be a "Bolshevik" with "Menshevik" views). Nevertheless, in March 1850, it was Marx himself who called for an immediate armed struggle and declared that "a new revolution is in the offing". Several months later, it did not prevent him, though, from again denying this call and announcing: "At such a universal prosperity at which productive forces of the bourgeois society develop as luxuriantly as it is possible at all within the frames of the bourgeois relationships, a genuine revolution is out of the question." (Ibid., Vol. 21, p. 211). Several years later in his letter to Engels (April 16, 1856) he again asserts: "The whole thing in Germany will depend on the possibility of backing the proletarian revolution by some second edition of the Peasants' war. Then the affair will be splendid..." (Ibid., Vol. 29, p. 34).

The history of the League also discloses the founders' notions about the tactics of the intra-party struggle. After the split, Marx, on the one hand, was stigmatizing his "Mensheviks" for their plot-making activity and calling for a broad open discussion and open propaganda of the ideals of revolutionary struggle; and on the other - in 1850, together with Engels, he secretly conspired with the Blanckists and signed, with them, a secret agreement concerning the creation of the "International Association of Communists-Revolutionaries" with the goal of "toppling all privileged classes, and subordinating these classes to the dictatorship of proletariat". Although this agreement was annulled by the end of the same year, the very fact that it was concluded is very indicative. Later on, such agreements become a routine practice.

The First International (International Working Men's Association) was created in 1866, two decades after the *Manifesto*. By that time Marx's scientific theory was largely completed (*Das Kapital* was published in 1867), and industrially developed countries witnessed the origination and strengthening of the socialist movement in a variety of shades. The underlying idea was that the International would unite all different socialist trends: British trade unionists, French Prudonians, German Lassalians, anarchists (Bakunin), Blanckists, and so on. However, they did not succeed in working out a common platform. For this reason the International as a single organization did not take part in the French Revolution. Just like the Communist League, the International managed to survive in Europe for about six years. Only five of its representative congresses took place, and it disintegrated shortly after its permanent charter was adopted (the Hague, 1872), at which time its General Council migrated to the USA. In the USA, it succeeded in convening only one conference (1876) which sanctioned the dismissal of the International.

Such is the formal history of the International. In the orthodoxy, the First International is considered a very important stage of the communist founders' struggle for the creation of the proletarian party, a continuation of the course started by the Communist League. To confirm this assessment, the following words of Lenin are usually cited:

By uniting the labor movement of different countries, and trying to converge different forms of pre-Marx socialism (Mazzini, Proudhon, Bakunin, British liberal trade-unionists, and Lassalian right-wing sways in Germany) towards united operation, fighting with theories of all these sects and small schools, Marx carved out a single tactic of the proletarian struggle of the working class in different countries. (Ibid., 4th edition, Vol. 21, p. 33).

However, such an orthodox evaluation sins by holding back a number of essentials. Let us look at them. Usually, the readiness with which Marx and Engels made considerable theoretical concessions is not highlighted (sometimes not even mentioned), and these concessions are always considered as temporary, dictated by the interests of organization. This readiness, which was demonstrated in the activity of both the Union of Communists and the First International is very characteristic of all founders and is pivotal in understanding the process of transformation of scientific theory into ideology.

When the International was created, its "Constituent Manifesto" said that "gaining political power has become the greatest duty of the working class", whereas the preamble to the charter said that "the economic emancipation of the working classes is therefore the great end to which every political movement ought to be subordinate as a means." (Ibid., 2nd Edition, Vol. 16, pp. 10,24). In this concession the political struggle looks to be subdued to the interests and tasks of the economic struggle. Further, neither the "Constituent Manifesto", nor the charter mention the world proletarian revolution, nor armed struggle, nor dictatorship of the proletariat. Such a compromise with the new socialist movement is very noticeable in all documents of the International.

However, almost at once Marx and Engels plunge into a consistent struggle for reversing all these concessions, or, as the orthodoxy puts it, struggle for the purity of the scientific theory. The history of this struggle is well-known and there is no need to get into it again. The greatest success was achieved after the beginning of the Franco-Prussian War and the Paris Commune, at the last two congresses. At the 1871 London (the one before the last) conference, a resolution was adopted which summarized a lengthy struggle around the question of the political tasks of the working class. It still bears some remnants of the old compromise (for example, it refers to a "social", rather than a "proletarian" revolution). The formulation of the "famous" 7th paragraph of the charter adopted at the last (Hague 1872) Congress, demonstrates a further elimination of such remnants.[84]

It is important to remember that this theoretical maneuvering was secondary to the organizational struggle within the International. This struggle started immediately after the General Council was established. It was aimed at introducing the principle of democratic centralism and getting a ruling position in the General Council and the whole of the International. The last congress marked the greatest success of this organizational struggle: the rights of the General Council were considerably broadened (for example, it was given the right of cooptation), and the Bakunin alliance, which had been seeking a special role in the International, was liquidated. Two years before, Engels, the closest

---

[84]"In its struggle against the collective power of the possessing classes, the proletariat can act as a class only by constituting itself as a distinct political party, opposed to all the old parties formed by the possessing classes... The coalition of the forces of the working class, already achieved by the economic struggle, must also serve as a lever in its struggle against the political power of its exploiters." (Ibid., Vol. 18, p. 143).

of Marx's comrades-in-arms, had been introduced into the General Council. As for the leading activists of the International, many of them either perished or were fugitives. A year after that, another important decision concerning the simplification of the organizational structure was adopted: all national organizations and parties were declared sections of the International. Marx became a recognized leader of the International, though he occupied an insignificant position in the General Council, that of a corresponding member on German affairs. And finally, by that time, the numerical value of communists in the industrially developed countries reached its maximum, and nothing seemed to portend the collapse of the International. Nevertheless, the congress in the Hague turned out to be the last one. After that the Council was moved to the USA - to the country where the communist movement did not exist (and never developed even in the later years), and where even social-deomocratic parties never originated. In other words, the International was stealthily buried in the place where the ground for its activities was the least favorable.

Why? What is it that the orthodoxy holds back? It is holding back the fact that the First International became a crushing defeat of Marx's attempt to create a revolutionary party of working class men dedicated to a proletarian revolution in the industrially developed European countries. Above, a line from Marx's letter to Engels written a year after the constituent congress was cited (see footnote on page 164), which ran: "...we (that is you and me) will have this whole mighty machine in our hands...". A year after the last congress, though, Engels in his letter to Babel (June 20, 1873) wrote the following:

> After the Commune, it [the International] had a colossal success...
> We know very well that the bubble *must* burst. All the riff-raff
> attached themselves to the International. The sectarians within it
> began to flourish and misused the International in the hope that the
> meanest and most stupid actions would be permitted them. We did
> not allow that. Knowing well that the bubble must burst some time,
> our concern was not to delay the catastrophe, but to take care that
> the International emerged from it pure and unadulterated. The
> bubble burst in the Hague [and it is after the theoretical and
> organizational victory!], and you know that the majority of the
> Congress members went home sick with disappointment.

The reason for this failure was the ultimate forcing out of an independent communist movement from the industrial European countries by the socialist one. When Marx and Engels created the First International, they hoped to influence that latter from inside, to channel it in the desired direction. They understood that it could be accomplished only by a means of a single centralized organization similar to the Union of Communists. And they were close to success. However, together with the strengthening of their authority and power in the International's leadership another process unfolded, that of the dropping out of an increasing number of sects, which gradually switched to the struggle for economic rights, better working conditions, social reforms, and democratic freedoms - all within the frames of the existing social system. The number of true communist-revolutionaries among the workers began to drop and it achieved its natural minimum (see below).

By the end of the nineteenth century, socialism forced out communism together with the First International from the industrial European countries. It returned half a century later though, and only after Marxism was fertilized by Leninism. This communism, which changed into Bolshevism, turned out to be very different; it was implanted by the East, rather than naturally spreading from there. This return, however, was preceded by an almost fifteen-year-long struggle by Lenin against the socialist movement in the Second International, which in many features repeated the struggle of his predecessor in the First one, and had the same result. Over this whole period, as well as afterwards, Lenin's theoretical and ideological struggle was aimed at, and almost totally reduced to, a struggle with the ideology of socialists and social democrats rather than with that of the bourgeoisie.

2. Formation of Ideology

To study and understand science, some minimum abilities, commitment, and free time, are required. Therefore, science is available to few. On the contrary, ideology is devised for human masses. For that reason, the scientific theory should first be simplified, and some of its parts and statements should be supplied with commentaries. Further, Marx and Engels created their scientific theory using the European, and first of all, British, example, whereas communist ideology is spreading all over the world irrespective of the degree of capitalist development, of culture, or of democracy; it is even more effective in those places where capitalism is lacking or just starting. Hence, the indicated simplification of the scientific theory should be supplemented by the universalization, broadening, and stretching of its main principles, laws and dogmas. All this should also account for the level of understanding of those masses to which it is addressed. And finally, it is not scientific theories that influence the behavior of human masses, but their own feelings, emotions, traditions, and passions. This element should also be accounted for in ideology, while it is absolutely foreign to science. Together with a simplification of the teaching, it leads to its vulgarization. These three elements will be considered in this section.

Broadening and universalization take place mainly at the right ideological border. In communist ideology, this border separates orthodox communists from their more right comrades in the labor movement: socialists, social democrats, Christian socialists, national socialists, and so on. One of the characteristic signs of the transformation of the scientific theory into ideology is the shifting of this border and its blurring. In Marx's scientific theory, such a boundary, and a very distinct one, did exist; this is why Marx and Engels were so hostile to the socialist movement which originated in Europe in the second half of the nineteenth century (see Chapter 6, section1). This border was defined by the recognition of communism as an ultimate goal, by the recognition that the revolutionary way of restructuring the capitalist society was the only possible way, and by the recognition that the dictatorship of the proletariat was an inevitable statehood form after the revolution. The border was also preserved in Leninism. However, in the future, especially after the appearance of Eurocommunism, this border in the labor movement of the industrially developed countries became very vague.

This process started, as it was pointed out in Chapters 1 and 6, during Marx and Engels' lifetimes, with the split of the ultimate goal. After the socialist movement had originated, and especially after the Paris Commune, communists began to lose ground in the labor movement, and their relative numbers started to shrink, while the number of socialists was growing. This is why the "Critique of the Gotha Program" (1875) divided the ultimate goal of communism into two stages and alleged that the question of the ultimate goal is not that important (see pages 127-28). In this connection, Engels had to repeatedly explain why the *Manifesto* was called "Communist" rather than "Socialist".

The second concession was made by Engels when he admitted - under the pressure of circumstances - that capitalist society could be restructured by both peaceful and violent means. Contemporary Eurocommunism goes even farther in this respect, as it denies both the revolutionary way and the dictatorship of the proletariat. None of the founders ever allowed any concessions with regard to the question of the dictatorship of the proletariat. But this is not all: demands of polycentrism, independence for individual communist parties, reconciliation with religion, and many other things are being put forward.

What are the reasons of such a friendliness of communists towards their adversaries? We can indicate two of them. Preserving both their unity and firmness of the organizational principle, communists, in such a maneuvering at the right ideological border, obtain an overwhelming advantage over all other parties which allows them to achieve astounding results at a considerably smaller numerical value. Such a hierarchically centralized and conspiratory organization creates good grounds for a sharp and unexpected change of course, strategy, or tactics by way of a behind-the-scenes collusion among its leading top and sending the corresponding orders down to all branches. Such turns can hardly be accomplished by their ideological adversaries, socialists and social democrats, with their openness and intra-party democracy. The second reason for the right border blurring, lies in the communist ideology's striving to expand, to become universal and be able to insinuate itself into various social layers in different countries. This expansion does not threaten the organization as long as it manages to preserve its unity, and does not affect the effectiveness of its "practice" as long as the principle of "democratic centralism" stays intact: after all, all these concessions are only verbal.

Now let us look at the simplification and vulgarization of the scientific theory, one of whose tools is the ousting of scientific logic by means of deliberate introduction of an ambiguous and vague terminology, which is then used in the ideological struggle. The splitting of the three main notions, which was considered earlier, is a particular case of a more general process. Below we will provide some examples of how theoretical notions were deformed and vulgarized by way of introducing ambiguous terms, with the help of which theoretical ideas are converted into ideological ones, controlled by the interests of the organization's struggle for power in a concrete period of time (for more detail, see Chapter 8).

In the foundation of Marx's theory of the proletarian revolution lies the concept of class struggle as the driving force of history leading to the dictatorship of the proletariat. Marx, though, did not give an exact definition of the term "class". For that reason, many concepts of his scientific theory that contain this term are of little content and easily lend themselves to stretching. Let us see how the concept of class struggle and proletarian revolution was changed in the formulation of the ideology. Lenin was the first to give the exact definition of the term "class" (in his work *A Great Beginning*, 1919). It happened after the revolution, at the height of the Civil War, when the interests of the organization in power demanded more specific discrimination between enemies and allies. Besides, it was necessary to justify a proletarian revolution in a peasant country, due to the delay of the world revolution (the working class man is a mere "hegemon"). Nevertheless, the introduction of a "strict" definition did not confer any content and meaning to the concept of the class struggle and proletarian revolution. To the contrary, Lenin interpreted the terms "proletariat" and "bourgeoisie" very loosely and even introduced one more vague term - "masses", which turned out very convenient in the ideological struggle (see Chapter 2, section 2).

Now, the Marxist concept of class struggle became flexible enough to substantiate other important theoretical (in reality ideological) ideas. Using this concept, Lenin devised a new notion of sharpening class struggle. Unlike Marx, however, he considered it, not under the capitalism, but under a higher stage - imperialism; and from this new notion he derived another one, after the fact, about the necessity and inevitability of a proletarian revolution in an industrially undeveloped country with a negligible percent of proletariat (in Russia). Stalin simplified this concept still further and made it "understandable" for the party "masses". The interests of the power gaining strength in the country, and the consolidation of the organization, demanded that the class struggle ought to sharpen, not only under capitalism and imperialism, but under socialism in "one, separately taken country" as well, in the conditions of the capitalist surrounding. And Stalin successfully substantiated this idea, knowing too well that he would be much more convincing once he had punitive organs and GULAG at his disposal.

The formulation of the class struggle theory was ultimately completed by Mao. The Marxist thesis that the history of human kind is a history of class struggle sounds different in Mao's treatment: "From the very beginning of its existence, human society moves forward through shocks and changes. No revolutionary changes and achievements are possible without big shocks. Therefore, no leap into developed society is possible." (cited from F. Burlatski, *Maoism or Marxism*, Moscow, 1967, p. 80). It is characteristic that Mao relates the meaning of the dogma fairly precisely without using the word "class" which says nothing to the majority of Chinese people. In his teaching, the notion of "revolutionary war", or simply "war", which is more familiar to Chinese people, little by little takes the place of the class struggle. He says: "War is the bridge which humankind will have to cross in order to get in to a new epoch without wars. We are for the elimination of war, we do not need war, but war can be eliminated only through war." (Ibid., p. 388).

This example demonstrates too well how ideological doctrines were formed. The thesis on class struggle was further simplified and adjusted to the understanding of the general masses; these masses being quite concrete each time: Russians, Chinese, Vietnamese, or Mongols, etc. The term "revolution" itself undergoes a blurring as there appear "peaceful" revolutions and "not peaceful" ones. The same happens with the term "proletariat". All of the terminology used gradually becomes more vague, but at the same time more universal; applicable in a wide variety of situations. As for the ideological doctrines themselves, they acquired such a shape and such a character that the question about their correctness or falseness became meaningless: they were not derived logically from any other well substantiated statements. Ideological statements can only be effective or not effective in a given moment of time and under given conditions. Once conditions change, their formulation changes too, as well as the meaning of the terms within them.

All of this makes ideology anti-scientific, because in it an inner logical structure typical of any science gradually disappears. But ideology is not designed for knowledge. This shortcoming becomes a virtue in a so-called "ideological struggle", which will be considered in the following section. Lack of logical structure makes some ideological statements invulnerable for such a criticism, just as some dogmas of faith are invulnerable. Therefore, ideology is more universal, and more adjustable to the ever-changing conditions of political struggle for power than any scientific theory.

3. Ideological Struggle and Formation of Composition

In the orthodoxy, the communist ideology is considered the main factor uniting all communists of the world. However, everything that was said above about ideology seems to prove the opposite: ideology is only able to separate rather than unite. This does not mean though that the orthodoxy is lying; it, as usual, tells a semi-truth. Ideology is indeed a uniting factor, but not the main one and only for a definite portion of communists. The main uniting factor for communists is organization, which unites a certain part of them ("ideological contingent") with the help of ideology. Such a unification takes place in the process of the ideological struggle. This is exactly what Lenin meant with the following famous quotation: "Before we unite and in order to unite, we must first decisively and definitely separate." (Ibid., Vol. 4, p. 378).

The number of communists and their distribution throughout countries can be judged only by the official communist sources, which often knowingly provide overstated figures. The reference book *Political Parties of Foreign Countries* (Moscow, 1967) informs its readers that by 1967, out of 45 million communists (without Indonesia, whose Communist Party was crushed in 1966), so-called socialist countries accounted for 41 million, or 85% (averaging 4% of their 1 billion population). Out of the remaining 4 million communists, industrially developed capitalist countries accounted for 2.4 million (0.35% of their total population of 670 million), and underdeveloped countries accounted for 1.6 million (0.09% of their 1.8 billion population).[85]

Therefore, all countries can be divided into three groups. A minimal extent of communism is enjoyed by the underdeveloped countries, and it can conditionally be taken as 0.05% or their population. Then the corresponding figure for the industrially developed countries (twenty-six of them) will be one order higher, and for the socialist countries it will be another ten times higher.[86]

---

[85]The 1974 reference book gives close figures. If we use them, we will get 4.6%, 0.37%, and 0.06% respectively for socialist, developed and underdeveloped countries; i.e., approximately the same values in spite of the general increase in the number of Communists by 13 million (according to the communist press) over the seven-year period.

[86]These are the figures given in 1974: Albania - 90,000 (4%), Bulgaria - 700,000 (8%), Hungary - 750,000 (7.2%), East Germany - 1.9 million (11.2%), Poland - 2.2 million (6.8%), Romania - 2.4 million (11.4%), Czechoslovakia - 1.2 million (8.5%), Yugoslavia - 1.1 million (5.2%), Vietnam - 1.1 million (5.2%), China - 28 million (3.5%), Korea - 1.6 million (10%), Mongolia - 64,100 (4.5%), Cuba - 170,000 (1.9%), CPSU - 14 million (5.7%).

In view of such a distinct division of the three groups, it would be reasonable to assume that the role of ideology as a uniting factor will be different in each of them.

From this viewpoint, of the greatest interest will be the group of the industrially developed countries, for this is where Marxism itself came from, and the role of ideology could be expected to be the greatest in them. If we compare data from different sources, then at the beginning of the 1970s, the greatest number of communists was possessed by Italy, France and Japan (2.3 million out of the total 2.4 million) - countries that suffered defeat in the Second World War, which was connected with severe social shocks. Next goes Finland, for the same reason and for the reason of the "Finlandization". These four countries excluded, the average percent of communists in the remaining countries (twenty-two) again does not exceed the minimum value given above.

So, the value of 0.05% of the population can be conditionally considered the minimum of communists in the contemporary world, independent of levels of production, or levels of cultural development, or traditions or any other factors. One can also assume that an increase above that minimum takes place, mainly, thanks to those who are dissatisfied and actively protest in periods of social disorders and cataclysms. Not only do the above four countries confirm that, but also the fact that in the majority of European countries (except Italy at the beginning of the 1970s) the numerical value of communists has not achieved the maximum level of a hundred years ago (for example, in Great Britain it is about 90,000, in France - 450,000, in Germany - 150,000), and is, as a rule, lower than that of Socialists and Social Democrats. Russia is not an exception from this rule either: the number of Communists (Bolsheviks) in it before the February revolution did not exceed the indicated minimum (about 30,000 - approximately 0.02% of the population), but already in April it almost tripled, and by March 1918, it increases more than ten-fold (more than 300,000).

The minimum world level of communists (0.105%) does not surpass the majority of demographic anomalies such as schizophrenics (0.5%), drug addicts, quacks, and spiritualists, and in a number of cases it is even lower. But its influence upon various social and political processes in many countries and in the world as a whole is by far disproportional to the number of communists. This can be explained by the existence of a centralized and conspiratorial organization, and until recently, by the role of the CPSU and the CPC in the international labor movement. This is why the analysis of the composition of this minimum, together with factors of unification, and also of its role in the contemporary world, is of great interest.

It seems natural to assume that it is the commonality of the goal rather than ideology that works as a uniting factor in this case. Therefore, the minimum of communism ought to contain at least two layers (groupings), one of which lays stress on the near goal - seizure of political power, and the other on the ultimate goal of constructing an ideal society (communism). A common method - violence - can keep them together and even unite them, especially before seizing state power. They are fanatics of power and fanatics of the idea of equality (see Chapter 8). Such individuals have always been there: in any society, in any nation, in any state. Due to their exceptional activity these "passionaries" (L.N. Gumilev's term) have left a noticeable mark in human history. For the first ones power is a goal in itself, for the second ones it is a means. That is why their alliances are always temporary, and their mutual fight often defines the major direction of the intra-party ideological struggle.

In the industrially developed countries, in the periods of social disorders, the number of communists increases above the minimum in the process of a sharp ideological struggle, and usually at the expense of socialists. The corresponding contingent can be called "ideological". Only in such states, can the problem of the unity of communists be considered purely ideological, and ideology can be viewed as the main unifying factor. This assumption is confirmed by a number of facts, and, in particular, by the fluctuations of the numerical value depending on the social and political situation. The decrease of the number of communists (and the corresponding increase in the number of socialists) in Austria by 45%, in Belgium by 21%, in Great Britain by 12%, that was observed after the occupation of Czechoslovakia by Warsaw Pact troops in 1968, serves as a good example of such fluctuations.

In what manner does the hierarchically centralized and conspiratory organization of professional politicians transform ideology into the uniting factor? The point is that at any concrete moment of time, and in any party the right ideological border, which divides communists and socialists, is established by the ruling party apparatus in accordance with the concrete social and political situation. This border is established after the behind-the-scenes collusion and then it is decreed from the top down as an obligatory party law. Since then, all the key ideological concepts are formulated according to this decision, and this is what the huge ideological hierarchies of communist parties are occupied with.

Revisionists, opportunists, and splitters are those party members who violate this generally accepted element of "democratic centralism" by starting to independently discuss and doubt the adopted law. This is why in any communist party there always exists a definite border that separates "insiders" and "outsiders". It is at this border that the non-stop ideological struggle takes place, whose aim is to unite "insiders" and oppose groupings of "outsiders".

In industrial states, ideological struggle is almost completely reduced to the fight between communists and socialists. How to explain the peculiar combination of an extreme sharpness of this struggle with the readiness to make very far-reaching concessions by way of shifting the right ideological border? It can be explained by the character of this fight itself and its goals. This fight is aimed, not as much at the unification or separation with socialists, as against unification of socialists of different shades among themselves. Temporary unions are almost always aimed at dividing socialists, as the main task is to force them out of the labor movement, including trade unions. This is the fight for the contingent; for the number of voices. The most advantageous position of the right border even lends itself to the quantitative estimation. In this struggle communists have been relying on their most dependable and committed conspiratorial organization which facilitated their political maneuvering, and, until recently, on the support of the Soviet and Chinese Communist Parties.

After they seize power, the number of communists increases by another order not because the number of fanatics of power or fanatics of ideas grows, but because there appears a new contingent, the one that considers power as a means to acquire material well-being or other similar things. Ideological struggle also changes: instead of inter-organizational (between the organizations) it becomes intra-organizational. At sharp and unexpected turns of the political course, which usually follow the behind-the-scenes collusion, a normal member of the party, due to his natural conservatism, is unable to keep up with such turns. Therefore, a considerable portion of communists from time to time find themselves either to the right or to the left of the "general line". Many of them are thrown overboard in the periodical "purges" or renewals of membership cards. This is usually called a fight for the "cleanness" of the party composition. In reality, it is a struggle for a homogenous composition. Such a fight enhances the effectiveness of the hierarchical selection, as it makes it more purposeful.

Let us recall some of the most evident turns. In Russia, the Mensheviks headed by Plekhanov are known to have become the first ideological victims, and then followed the social-revolutionaries, who were the Bolsheviks' allies in the October coup. After that, followed an enormous wave composed mostly of fanatics of equality, since it became impossible to excuse inequality and violence by the severe conditions of the Civil War, and because hopes for the world revolution did not come true. It is very difficult to assess the size of this wave, as at that time there was no one to take care of statistics. Whatever was left of the fanatics of the world revolution and international communism, were finished by Stalin in the 1930s. But it was already the result of several turns (war communism, a new economic policy, industrialization, collectivization), and of many purges, that such people as Molotov, Kaganovich, Kalinin and Beria not only survived, but also obtained a good opportunity for rapid promotion to the apex of power.

The next gigantic wave of thrown-away communists was observed much later, after the Twentieth Party Congress, and it embraced mostly foreign communists. Thrown out of their habitual and convenient ideological world by this other turn, they joined their former colleagues who had earlier refused to follow Stalin, and together they took up a fortified position along the joint defensive line, namely Marx-Lenin. These "fathers and sons" who had been so irreconcilable towards each other in the recent past, united under a common slogan: not a step back! But this defense line of the former communists also turned out to be short-lived. A few less severe tremors, such as the Berlin, Polish, Hungarian and Czechoslovakian events, were sufficient for this defense to collapse. A new slogan emerged: back to Marx! Searches for a new intermediate line between communism and socialism started; "convergence", socialism "with a human face", and Eurocommunism were spoken about. This barrier also collapsed. These are the examples of big and sharp alterations on the "general line". An analogous process of the "self-cleansing" of communist parties takes place at a routine political maneuvering as well, though at a smaller scale, not too noticeably, but, nevertheless, no less effectively, as such turns take place all the time.

In each of those developments, a hierarchically centralized and conspiratory organization of professional politicians serves, not just as a filter of individuals, which was discussed previously, but also as a machine that processes human material ideologically. After all, these waves, accompanied by purges, changes of documents, and weedings, also result in new elections, so that the numerical value of a communist party always increases much faster than the population, economics and other social characteristics (the Soviet Communist Party increased several hundred-fold over seventy years!). Only those survive such a processing who are best adjusted, and this is how the uniform composition is achieved, which was discussed in detail in the previous chapters. Here we will underline only, that it is the same minimum of communism with a considerably rarefied layer of the fanatics of equality, but supplemented by a more numerous and united population of proprietors, i.e., those who consider power as a means of material well-being.

CHAPTER 8
IDEOLOGY AND IDEOCRACY

1. Introduction

Characteristic features of a contemporary totalitarian state are well-known. They are listed in Chapter 1 (see page 7), and this is how they are defined in the *Big Soviet Encyclopedia*:

> Totalitarian states and regimes are characterized by the state control over all legal organizations, discretional (not limited by law) authority of the power, prohibition of democratic organizations, eradication of the constitutional rights and freedoms, militarization of public life, repressions towards progressive forces and dissidence in general. (3rd edition)

All of these characteristics follow from the combination of two elements: a single ruling political party and a single and obligatory state ideology. Such a combination leads to the total, physical and spiritual, enslavement of an individual by the state, and consequently it defines a dead end in the societal evolution.

In this connection we face a problem of studying the interconnection of these two elements (or bases) of contemporary totalitarianism. Which of them is the leading, or dominant one? An answer to this question, which comprises the contents of section 1 of this chapter, leads to some important practical conclusions. If ideology dominates, then, for the most part, it is responsible for ugly inhuman practices. Then ideology must be improved and corrected. For example, it can reject the dictatorship of the proletariat, the reduction of all social causes to the class struggle, or reject communism as an ultimate goal, and stop at its first stage; socialism. Many other alterations can be introduced, for in the final analysis, ideology is just a system of verbal constructions. It is this type of retreat that we now observe in the East European countries. It is dictated first of all by the interests of organizations; such a retreat is very beneficial to leaders, because they can be viewed as victims of an erroneous ideology. On the other hand, if organization is a dominant element in totalitarianism, and ideology is a mere means, then the organization is liable to dismissal and its top leaders to trial, at least to the trial of history.

Exaggeration of the role of ideology is very characteristic of the social and political discussions of our times. The term "ideology" does not leave the pages of books, journals, and newspapers. It is all over banners, it is loudly vocalized by the speakers from their rostrums, and it is disseminated by media all over the world, among all people and all continents. Combined with other words, this term gives rise to some very unexpected combinations, and it is instilled in all languages. It turns out that there exists a "scientific" and a "non-scientific" ideology, a bourgeois and a proletarian ideology, as well as a petty bourgeois and a peasant one. There also is an "ideological work", and such varieties of it as agitation and propaganda. Also, there is an "ideological war" which, unlike other wars, never ends and sometimes even turns into "psychological" war. Other, rather sinister combinations originated, such as "ideological subversion" and "ideological inculcation" and so on, up to "ideological narcotic". It is impossible to list all the existing combinations.

The concerted propaganda of dozens of communist parties, conducted from a single center, was very effective until recently, as it managed to make an impression that ideology in the contemporary world began to take the place which, not long ago, was occupied by religion in the social life of society. This viewpoint, very advantageous to the communist parties, was even successfully imposed upon their opponents. Beginning with Berdiaev, many attempts have been made to pin the repulsive practices, innumerable victims, unrestrained militancy, aggressiveness, and expansion of the contemporary totalitarian communism on the communist (Marxist-Leninist) ideology.

Let us look at some examples. The first serious investigation of contemporary totalitarianism says: "Totalitarianism's aggressiveness does not originate from its craving for power. If it is fervently looking for expansion, it is not for the sake of expansion itself, not for material benefits, but only for ideological reasons." (H. Arendt, *Origination of Totalitarianism*, 1951). And further: "Authority of ideology (what is called ideocracy) and the construction of a fictitious world linked to it, which is artificially lifted out of the context of reality, this is what shapes the nature of totalitarianism. It is an absolutely new phenomenon in the history of mankind and it cannot be reduced to one or another stage of European history." (Ibid.)

Here, for the first time, Soviet and fascist totalitarianisms are not separated. And this is what Solzhenitsyn says about the connection between ideology and the practice of Soviet totalitarianism:

Ideology twists our souls like floor cloths. It corrupts us, our children, it stoops us lower than animals. Is it of no significance then? Is there anything more disgusting in the Soviet Union? If nobody believes but everybody obeys, it is indicative not of ideology's weakness, but of its brutal, inhuman strength. With the same powerful grip it leads our rulers... And today these rulers, poisoned by the venom of this ideology, unavoidably, as buffoons, repeat over and over again by a crib (even without believing what they are repeating, only understanding power! They are slaves of ideology too) and trying thoughtlessly to set on fire the whole world and to capture it. Even though it will destroy and crush them, even though they would have been more comfortable contenting themselves with what they have already seized. But this is how ideology drives them! (Cited from *Kontinent*, 1975, Vol. 2, p. 350.)

The weakness of all such statements is that ideology, considered in isolation, without its connection with other facets of communism, its organization, strategy, and tactics, appears under a scrutinizing eye as a meaningless, disorderly pile of laws, orders, dogmas, and consequences. Many of them are constantly changed and often contradict each other. Due to the ambiguity of terminology one constantly encounters double meanings. It also appears as an "expedient absurdity" or "oath of fidelity, cemented by a collective responsibility for a common sin and hypocrisy." (A. Sakharov). Or, finally, as a mere pile of lies ("Mont Blanc of Lies", P. Grigorenko). Further, if we accept ideology as a dominant factor of totalitarianism, then how can an evident similarity between the "practices" of Hitlerism and Stalinism be explained, in spite of their very different ideologies?

All discussions about ideology do not take into account two factors, connected with the understanding of the term. The term was revived by Marxists[87] on the brink of our century, and it was they who also introduced the term "ideological struggle", as a variety of political struggle, and it was they who performed this struggle most actively against all of their political adversaries.

---

[87]Marx, as is known, rejected the legitimacy of introducing the term and never used it as applied to his teaching (see *Complete Work*, 3rd edition, Vol. 3, p. 16, and Vol. 39, p. 83). It was revived by A. Labriola, G. Plekhanov, and V. Lenin.

Secondly, it is important that today the term "ideology" (as well as "ideological struggle") is first and foremost applicable to the communist ideology only.

If the discussants are asked what types and varieties of ideology exist in the world, the answer will be very instructive. First of all, contemporary communist (Marxist-Leninist) ideology will be named, then its varieties (Stalinism, Maoism, Trotskyism, Eurocommunism, and so on) and its main concepts will be described. Then they will name the fascist ideology, but difficulties will arise in naming its varieties and dogmas. The difficulties and disagreements will be further increasing. A Marxist-Leninist will also name a bourgeois ideology, but its characteristic will be very obscure and vague. The main ideas ascribed to it will turn out to be so different and form such a broad spectrum, that using the term will look altogether doubtful. A socialist ideology will also be named, however, its spectrum will also be very broad. This is so because both communists (socialism is their first stage) and fascists (national socialism) consider themselves socialists, as well as several dozens of other parties with very different strategies, tactics and practices. Many of them occupy the ruling position.

Therefore, it is natural to apply the term "ideology" to situations where it does not transform into an empty label used in a political struggle, i.e., for communism and fascism in the first place. In this connection, it is reasonable to accept the definition of this term used in the communist literature: "Ideology is a system of views and ideas which assess the attitude of people to reality and towards each other, to social problems and conflicts as well as it contains goals (programs) of social activity aimed at changing (development) the given public relations" (*Big Soviet Encyclopedia*, 3rd edition, 1972, underlined by the author).[88]

Critical literature provides numerous commentaries to the second part of the definition (underlined). We will not dwell on them, as it is important here to clarify the meaning put into the term "ideology" by communists themselves. Hence, let us look at some explanations given in the same edition of the *Big Soviet Encyclopedia*. It turns out that "it is not ideology that originates out of

---

[88]The underlined words are a later insertion. They are lacking, for example, in the 2nd edition of the *Small Soviet Encyclopedia* (1936): "Ideology is a system of images and notions on nature and society, i.e., a world outlook. In this sense, for example, a proletarian or a bourgeois ideology is spoken about. Individual forms of public consciousness - science, philosophy, arts, morale, law and religion, make up types of ideology."

conditions of the class living but a public psychology of a given class which creates a certain grounds for dissemination and digestion of its ideology." The class itself is unable to work out its own ideology; social democracy must do that (teaching on the party). After that "by spreading in the society and adjusting to the level of mass consciousness, ideology acts upon it and influences public psychology." This is about ideology in general. As for communist (Marxist-Leninist) ideology, this is what the *Big Soviet Encyclopedia* says about it: "Systems preceding Marxism bore some elements of science, but only Marxism is a scientific ideology in its true meaning."

First, let us emphasize the difference between ideology and world outlook. It is assumed that world outlook is being worked out by individuals independently over their lifetime. This process is affected by their families, community, or even the whole society, and coercion is not excluded. On the other hand, such parts of the outlook as ideals, values, principles, and convictions are worked out as a result of an inner, spiritual life of an individual. Goals, programs and deeds in general can follow from the world outlook, but are not contained in it at the outset. As for ideology, it is <u>worked out</u> by a political party (i.e., organization) and then, in the ready-made form, is <u>incorporated</u> into a definite social layer (class), goals and programs being contained in it at the outset. World outlook is in general conservative, as for ideology, it can be mobile, dynamic, flexible.

Consequently, in contemporary communist literature ideology is essentially understood as the social and political outlook of a political party, which includes its program, charter, strategy and tactics. Communist ideology is an outlook of the Communist Party, and Marxism-Leninism is its core. It means that behind ideological formulations stand concrete interests and goals of an organization of a current moment. The latter change all the time as the political and social situation changes. Therefore, ideological positions should also be constantly corrected, reformulated, correlated. It also means that there should exist a direct association between the inner structure of ideology and the character of the corresponding organization.

Communist parties are, as is known, closed, extremely centralized and conspiratorial organizations aimed at a coercive capture of the entire power in a state. It is reflected in the character of ideology and in the process of its formation. For example, the words "worked out" and "incorporated" in the above explanation of ideology can be re-interpreted and change their meaning at the alteration of the inner or outer situation. The greatest alteration ought to take place right after the capture of power and establishment of the dictatorship of the proletariat. All of their accumulated experience shows that after that, agitation and propaganda ("incorporation") were supplemented by the "education" of the masses in the conditions of the dictatorship and isolation of the society (this is already an "instillation"), which, using conventional language, has always meant that physical coercion is supplemented by a spiritual one, i.e., that totalitarianism is established. In so doing, ideology transforms into ideocracy.

The totalitarian character of contemporary communism is embedded in its organization rather than its ideology, and specifically in its organizational principle; ideology just disguises it. Since the time of *The Communist Manifesto*, the scientific theory was being created, elaborated, developed, and supplemented; ideology was being formed and altered under the pressure of practice; but the organizational principle, that of "democratic centralism", remained unshakable. Over the century and a half that has passed since the *Manifesto*, quite a number of varieties of communist ideology appeared, but there was not a single communist party that refused the principle of "democratic centralism". This principle always was - and still is - unshakable, refusing it would be equal to refusing communism. This is why communist ideocracy is in fact the power of a communist organization through ideology by means of its coercive instillment in the outlook of individuals.

Consequently, in contemporary totalitarianism, organization is primary and ideology is secondary. Or, using Marxist-Leninist jargon, organization pertains to the basis and ideology to the superstructure, and they both are closely interconnected. Is it possible then to extend this conclusion to other contemporary ideologies, for example, fascism? If so, the similarity of organizations must somehow be revealed in the similarity of ideologies. Is it really so? Many other questions arise too. If ideocracy is coercively instilled in the world outlook of individuals, in what particular manner is this instillment effected? It is not easy to answer these questions because, in totalitarianism, functions of ideology are not reduced to a simple concealment of the totalitarian essence of the organization, and the inner structure of the latter is not homogeneous and it reflects the history of its functioning.

2. Axiomatics of Ideology

Let us make a distinction between the main structure of ideology, which is defined by the inner structure of organization, and a supplementing structure of the second order, which depends mainly on the outer and inner conditions of the organization's functioning; on the history of the country, its culture, traditions, and so on. The main structure of ideology can be defined with the help of several interconnected statements which the word "axiom" seems to fit best. To describe structures of the second order the word "paradigms" is used below.[89] All political organizations whose goal is to seize and hold power in a contemporary state have much in common in the axiomatics of their ideologies, i.e., in the formulation of axioms and their interconnection.

To illustrate, let us look at the contemporary communist ideology and compare it with other ideologies. In its axiomatic, the central place is occupied by the first two axioms, which will be later referred to as the "split" axiom and the "irreconcilability" axiom. First, let us consider the former: the "split" of any society into classes. In it the "split" is important rather than the classes, the latter being a vague and indefinite term. Before Lenin, and after him, none of the founders tried to define or clarify it. It was not only needless, but even disadvantageous, as it could obscure the main thing in the axiom, that is the "split" between "us" and "them". Such a division, though, ("us" and "them") can be traced in any contemporary ideology. In fascism, it is "select" and "not select" races, in socialism - working men and capitalists. In the latter case the split is not so definite and sharp as in communism and fascism. Neither is its organization as well arranged as a communist or a fascist one; even a unified charter and a unified program are lacking, and besides there are so many varieties of socialists. Correspondingly, there are many shades of "split". A similar feature is observed in the contemporary bourgeois ideology and its petty bourgeois variety. Nevertheless, in each of the three ideologies, a division into "us" and "them" can easily be traced. Even a religious organization which originated in the Middle Ages on the basis of Christianity and laid the foundation

---

[89]Paradigm literally means example, or pattern. In the wider sense, it is (according to Kuhn) "an original conceptual schema, a mode of stating a problem and solving it, and of the investigation methods dominant in the scientific community in a definite historic period." (*Structure of Scientific Revolutions*, Moscow, 1962). In the text, this term is used in the sense of ideological stereotypes and is applied to political organizations.

for the Spanish Inquisition, worked out its own ideology, which similarly divided people into true and untrue believers.

The second axiom asserts the hostility and irreconcilability of "them" and the irremovability of the "split". The harder the organizational structure, and the more definite and sharp the split, the more hostile and aggressive "they" are in respect to "us". The greatest aggressiveness is naturally demonstrated by communist and fascist ideologies, as well as by their Middle-Age predecessor, the medieval ideology of the Spanish Inquisition. On the other hand, the least aggressiveness is found in the organizations where the structure is less rigid, the centralization is weaker, and the unity and cohesion within the organization are less pronounced.

Not a single contemporary ideology aimed at seizing and keeping political power exists without the third axiom: "We" will win. In this case the same regularity is again revealed: the stronger the organization, the sharper the "split", the greater is its confidence in the ultimate victory and the louder are the wordy claims that this confidence is justified "scientifically". In reality this postulate is needed to attract more supporters into the organization and to demoralize the adversary.

The fourth axiom is the promise of a reward after the "victory". The necessity of such an axiom is evident, because entering any organization restricts an individual's freedom to a certain degree, narrows down his choices and demands additional work and efforts, very often without any real compensation. The axiom moves this compensation into the future. In the communist ideology it is communism, with its "to each according to his demands"; in the fascist ideology it is a thousand-year-long reich with the domination of the select race; in the socialist one it is social justice ("to each according to his labor"); in the bourgeois one it is freedom of enterprise; in the medieval-inquisitional one it is paradise for the faithful; and so on. The illusory character of such promises is in particular revealed in the fact that the "reward" moves farther away as one tries to approach it.

The axioms are tied together by other verbal constructions/paradigms. Formulation of paradigms, their inter-relation and combination define the "pattern of thinking" (Kuhn), its style, and the key ideological stereotypes. All of them are extracted from the corresponding teaching. For example, the Marxist-Leninist teaching on classes contains a substantiation of all paradigms linked to the first axiom. Substantiation of the second axiom and adjacent paradigms is extracted from the teaching on class struggle and proletarian revolution. Substantiation of the paradigms of the remaining axioms is contained in the dialectical and historical materialism, and also in the teaching on two phases, i.e., socialism and communism. Examples of the corresponding paradigms will be given in the next paragraph. Fascism is not elaborated in such detail, and it is more difficult to distinguish its corresponding parts. This is understandable, though, because the organization behind this teaching did not exist longer than a couple of decades, and it only enjoyed power for twelve years. But there is little doubt that, if not for its destruction, a corresponding ideology would have been worked out and included all four axioms with detailed paradigmatics.

It is important to note one particular feature of axiomatics: the first two axioms are related to the present, and the last two to the future. Such symmetry is also preserved in paradigmatics and it reflects the symmetry of the organization itself, aimed at seizing and holding state power (see the next section). This feature introduces an element of unreality into ideology and gives an impression of its duality, which will be discussed in more detail below.

Any questions about the falseness or the truthfulness of axioms of one or another ideology or its individual paradigms are meaningless. Only questions about their effectiveness and persuasiveness are meaningful and legitimate, because they will be different even for different sub-systems of the same organization, leaving alone different layers of population, different countries, and different periods. Effectiveness and persuasiveness also change with time. The question about the scientific character of ideologies is more complex: all contemporary ideologies are as much scientific as the political sciences. In the broad spectrum of contemporary sciences, their place is, as was discussed earlier, somewhere between social and military sciences (see Chapter 6, section 3). Their degree of scientific character is also proportional to the effectiveness of their impact upon human masses and human individuals separately. In the final analysis, both effectiveness and persuasiveness are measured by the effectiveness of the organization itself.

In conclusion, let us touch upon a possible objection concerning the understanding of ideology as a social and political outlook of political parties in a pluralistic society. Are there not too many ideologies in such a society? And is it always possible to discriminate among them? For example, consider republicans and democrats in the United States. According to the assumed definition of the term, the general character of ideology and its key features are defined for the most part by the goals, character and structure of the organization. The assertion about similarity of ideologies is justified to the same extent as it is justified to apply the term "ideology" to the tasks, programs, strategies, tactics and corresponding paradigmatics of these organizations. The above two parties are of the same type, therefore, their ideological differences are minor.

3. Paradigmatics

Axiomatics is not even a frame of ideology, rather it is its incomplete skeleton deprived of all its joints (connection of axioms). When the ideology of commandocracy ("commandology") is formed, it is supplemented by a complex system of paradigms, which make up its "live tissue" - a system which is constantly changing, depending on the current task and on a concrete inner and outer situation. Who forms such a system of paradigms and how is it formed? The answer to the first question is evident: the whole organization does, mostly its middle and upper levels. The key role there is played by a special ideological hierarchy, which starts from the numerous army of propagandists and agitators relieved from all other responsibilities (ideological "termites") and ends with the chief ideologist. The answer to the second question ("How?") is not that evident, because the process of formation and its result are defined not only by the character of the inner structure of the commandocracy, and its concrete goals and tasks, but also by the inner and outer conditions of its functioning, which constantly change. Thereby, paradigmatics comprises the reflection of the organization's evolution, of its history.

The orthodoxy assumes that Marxism-Leninism is simultaneously a teaching ("a scientific theory of public evolution") and an ideology. In reality - and it was discussed in detail earlier - they are essentially different, simply because it is an author (or a group of authors) that stands behind a teaching, and an organization that stands behind an ideology (see Chapter 6). But this is not the only difference. The fourth chapter of the *Concise Course of the CPSU* provides a brief presentation of the Marxist-Leninist ideology which guided the CPSU activities over almost half a century, and which was instilled by it in all strata of society. This version of ideology was undoubtedly formulated on the basis of Marxist-Leninist teaching, but it differs noticeably from both Marxism and Leninism. What is the difference? First, it is an element of vulgarization. Besides, the accents are shifted and the logical connection between the key positions of the teaching is lost. The same features can be traced in the transformation of Marxism-Leninism into Trotskyism and Maoism. All of this means that when an ideology is formulated on the basis of some teaching, first the latter is "disassembled" into parts, then it is reformulated with the help of paradigms, after which the parts are "assembled" and tied up with axioms. It is in the process of "assembling" that the accents are shifted.

Let us give an example of the ten key paradigms which are extracted from Marxism, indicating only their succinct names. The corresponding quotations will be provided in those cases only when they are deliberately distorted. 1. paradigm of class struggle; 2. paradigm of basis and superstructure; 3. paradigm of existence (social existence determines social consciousness, the word "social" is often omitted); 4. paradigm of practice (practice is the criterion of truth, meaning the "only" criterion); 5. paradigm of violence (violence is a midwife of history, the corresponding quotation is "Violence is a midwife of any old society when it is pregnant with a new one."); 6. paradigm of restructuring the world (11th thesis on Feuerbach: "The philosophers have only interpreted the world, in various ways; the point is to change it."); 7. paradigm of communism and socialism as two phases; 8. paradigm of freedom (freedom is a realized necessity); 9. paradigm of dialectical contradictions; 10. paradigm of proletarian internationalism.[90]

The corresponding quotations, on the basis of which paradigms are built, are generally known. The founders pronounced them at different times, for different reasons, often to clarify or highlight certain thoughts. Torn out of their context, they lose their direct connection with the teaching. In the hands of ideologists, though, they acquire a new life and unexpected power at solving practical problems. Often, by forming bizarre combinations in ideology, they

---

[90]Let us list the most characteristic paradigms of Leninism: 1. paradigm of masses; 2. of ideological opposition ("This is how the question stands: either bourgeois or socialist ideology. There is no middle here, for no 'third' ideology has been worked out by mankind..." (*What is to Be Done?*)); 3. of partyism; 4. of delimitation ("Before uniting, and in order to unite we must first decisively and definitely separate"); 5. of morality ("We say that our morality is completely subordinate to the class interests of the proletarian struggle. Our morality is deduced from the interests of the class struggle of the proletariat." (Vol. 41, p. 309).

obtain the meaning opposite to what the founders meant. For example, Stalin's doctrine about the sharpening of class struggle in the course of the socialist development was formulated on the basis of paradigms of violence, practice, and existence, and Brezhnev's doctrine about limited sovereignty of socialist countries - on the basis of paradigms of violence and proletarian internationalism. Whereas, in the teaching they are tied together by a conventional logic, in ideology it is the logic of political struggle. In the multi-million party mass they are used in different combinations or individually in the form of precepts and ideological stereotypes, selectively affecting different party layers and various categories of non-party citizens. Ideological work is mainly reduced to the re-formulation of paradigms, the re-establishment of their interconnection, and their connection with axioms as well as to the accommodation of the whole ideology to the practical activities of the organization, its current goals, strategies, and tactics. On this field, thousands and tens of thousands of ideological "termites" are playing Among them are quite a few outstanding experts of their trade. It can be very dangerous to underestimate the results of their collective work even in the periods of "*perestroikas*" and the temporary defeat of organizations.

It was pointed out earlier (see Chapter 5), commandocracy has some features of self-organized systems. Any system of this type works out a specific mechanism of feedback in its interaction with the environment which secures its wholeness. In what manner does this feature of commandocracy affect the process of its ideological formation? First of all, it affects the formulation of axioms and paradigms of separation. The key separation into "us" (the system) and "them" (environment) should run though the whole ideology as a defining thread. And it would have been the case if the pyramid of power and socium as a whole were homogeneous; such an ideology could have been called partology. In reality (and it was shown earlier in Chapter 5) all commandocracy, as well as the ruling party, disintegrates vertically in time and with the growth of its numerical value into several sub-systems due to inner causes of its evolution, whose demands, interests and goals are not always compatible. Besides, horizontal inhomogeneities (departments) are formed as well. After such a fragmentation, the wholeness of the system can be preserved only under a serious threat from the outside, when an outside enemy smooths over all contradictions, intrinsic frictions, and mutual discontent within the organization. This is why expansionism is embedded in the commandocracy structure itself.

For this reason, ideology has to be militant, has to constantly point out a real or imaginary enemy and inspire hatred of him. And indeed, inner and outer enemies are permanent companions of any commandocracy since the moment of its origination.

Though power in a commandocracy is spread all over its structure, to the greatest degree it is localized in the separated special bureaucracy. Therefore, the key separation into "us" and "them" is defined by the barrier that secludes it. Self-preservation, by means of parasitism on society, is the major uniting goal of the ruling top. What opposes it and who are its true enemies ("they")? Everything and everybody that, and who, tries to remove the isolating barrier and, together with it, their privileges. First of all, it is those from the intermediate layer (the pacing ones, or a dynamic sub-system) for whom this barrier is an obstacle to get into the *nomenclatura* and a cause for the sharpening of competition near it. Secondly, it is a considerable portion of the lower sub-system, characterized by the mass psychology of equality and brotherhood which experiences a natural antagonism to all the privileged and selected. They also back up the uniformity of the whole social hierarchy. And finally, it is all society. This is why it is in the interests of the ruling top to deny and disguise a real separation and substitute it by the ideological one.

In this connection, the paradigmatics of commandology are formulated in such a manner that they disguise a real separation and channel inner tensions and inner antagonism onto outside enemies. These enemies can be - depending on current tasks - either capitalists, or imperialists, or just bourgeoisie, or a concrete country, for example. Accordingly, "we" can be either laborers, or the whole working man's class, all socialist camp, or just people, or a class, or its party. As for the inner enemies, commandology views them again as outer enemies appearing in the form of the fifth column, or the legacy of capitalism, its machinations, and so on.

The efforts of the ruling top to substitute goals is a way of hiding behind this substitution of the real separation by an unreal (ideological) one. In ideology such a substitution is performed with the help of the paradigm of partyism: the ruling party acts "on behalf" of the ruling class and the latter one - "on behalf" of the working people. In its turn, the leadership of the party acts "on behalf" of the whole party, and leaders - "on behalf" of the leadership. The same order is observed all along the whole pyramid of power. Another formulation of the same paradigm exploits "in the interests of formula. In reality (and it was discussed in Chapter 5), the road to the *nomenclatura* means clambering along the steps of the pyramid of power, individually up to the boundary of special bureaucracy, and collectively after it is crossed. Hierarchical selection has nothing in common either with delegating, or nominating, electing or representing. This is why protecting any interests except for individual, corporative or those of a clan, is out of the question.

This major unreality in the axioms and paradigms of separation entails unreality of all other axioms and paradigms. For example, the axiom "we will win" has a real meaning only for a representative of the commandocracy's top, i.e., when the opposition is real. Even then, it is so only until the state power is seized and the ruling layer is consolidated. After that it acquires the meaning of "we have won". In this connection the ultimate goal, that of communism, is moved into the past for the special bureaucracy. Uncontrollably doing with all state riches, special bureaucracy is already satisfied "according to demands", and no other social system is able to give it more. On the other hand, if under "us" it is understood as the whole ruling party, then for it the ultimate goal becomes unreal and is moved farther away as it is approached. The same thing happens to many other paradigms. And as ideology permeates all political, economic, and social spheres of society, then the shade of unreality is present in each of them, Moreover, even the language itself becomes somewhat unreal because many works have two or even more meanings.

This duality creates an impression of two ideologies: the ideology of the ruling top and the ideology of the lower strata subordinated to it. The first one reflects the interests and goals of the hierarchy's dome, and it bears a justifying connotation. For example, in it such paradigms are accented as "(hierarchical) existence determines (ideological) consciousness"; "practice (of ruling) is criterion of truth (of subordination)"; or "violence is a midwife". In the second, the paradigms of class struggle, of restructuring the world, and of two phases are emphasized. In fact they are the two ends (poles) of a single ideology, which is worked out in the upper layers and hurled down onto the middle and lower ones. In other words, ideology gets some features of a vector. In the final analysis, the fact that it has a direction is a reflection of the properties of organization: the command links a superior who gives orders, with a subordinate who carries them out.

Any ideology is a means to subordinate and even enslave people spiritually in addition to their physical subjugation or enslavement by the organization.

Moreover, all contemporary ideologies use a common method for such an enslavement: the goals of an individual are substituted by the goals of the organization. In hierarchical organizations, the impact of ideology becomes even more effective when the coercion is masked and an illusion of the voluntariness of such a substitution is created. In doing so, ideology inevitably intrudes into the world outlook of an individual, affecting the process of its formation.

4. Ideology and World Outlook

Briefly, the social outlook of an individual is an approximate model of the social world surrounding the individual within the horizons of his interests. Ideology is also an approximate model of the social world as it follows from the similarity of the definitions of these two notions.[91] As the interests and goals of an organization and an individual are often incompatible, how is it possible then that these two models can be combined and co-exist in the head of one person?

Let us first consider the similarities and differences in the way these two models are formed. Formation of both a world outlook and an ideology is a collective process, but the first one is guided by organization; the second one - by the social environment, whose borders are determined by the horizon of a person's interests. Different are the mechanisms of formation as well. The most characteristic quality of individuals is the ability and possibility to exercise moral choices, without which formation of their outlook (convictions, values, and so on) is impossible.[92] Personality exists while this possibility and ability exists; if

---

[91]The definition of ideology was given above, on p. 186. The same source (*Big Soviet Encyclopedia*) defines the world outlook in the following manner: "System of summarized views on the objective world and a man's place in it, on relations between people and surrounding reality and among themselves, as well as their convictions, ideals, principles of cognition and activity, their values, determined by these views." Comparing the two definitions, one can easily see that their first parts (up to the words "as well as") coincide in essence.

[92]The author shares the view expressed and substantiated by B. Porshnev in his work *Function of Choice as Foundation of Personality* (in Russian): "A man as a personality is a being that makes choices... Choosing is an elementary mechanism out of whose products a personality is made up and by means of which it is developed. The mystery of choosing lies in the fact that it is preceded by co-existence, in one individual, of two mutually excluding tendencies. Choosing is the removal, throwing away of one of the alternatives. Stimuli for it are

they lack, only an individual exists. On the other hand, the distinguishing feature of an organization is hierarchical centralization which directly or indirectly (through ideology, as was shown in the previous paragraph) restricts the possibility of a moral choice and weakens the ability to perform it, which cannot but deform a personality. The higher the degree of centralization and the longer the exposure to ideology, the more intense is the deformation.

A person has a natural desire to expand the sphere of free choice within the whole horizon of its interests (a road to total freedom). This is impossible to do in the society. A totalitarian organization has a natural desire to subordinate a person, to deprive it of its sphere of free choices. However, this leads to psychic deformations and psychic abnormalities, which will be considered in detail in the next section. The compromise between these two incompatible demands acquires shape of the simultaneous co-existence of the sphere of free choice, and an ideological sphere. In the final analysis it is reduced to the compromise between an individual's goals and those of the organization and the deformation of the world outlook. How is this compromise achieved and what kind of deformations are they. These are the questions considered below.

Contemporary organizations are usually very complicated and therefore they need a qualified and effective leadership. This is possible, though, only if their members "want" to be ruled, when they do not exercise an active or a passive resistance, or, at least if this resistance is localized in some acceptable boundaries. If this factor is lacking then members of the organization can only be coerced, and the effect of organization (organizational gain) is neutralized by the effect of disorganization, which is first revealed in such spheres of activity that demand initiative, enterprise, and energy, i.e., in those difficult to control. Supervision gradually transforms into coercion. And the higher the degree of the necessary coercion, the greater is the disorganization. This is how matters stand in reality. This is why an effective substitution of individual goals by the ideological ones must be very gradual and should maintain at least an illusion of voluntariness. Hence, the ideological effect on a person's world outlook should also be performed in the same manner. Creation of such a gradualness and such an illusion is the main ideological problem. And not only is it the main problem, but also one of the most complicated ones, which is confirmed by the enormous

---

numerous, previous choices being the decisive one though. It is their set that makes up the core of a personality. A personality has its history - it is a history of rejected alternatives." ("Problems of Personality", materials of 1969 Symposium, 1969, Vol. 1, pp. 344-46).

sizes of ideological departments (hierarchies) in the contemporary communist parties and other like organizations.

How is this problem solved? Today's world witnesses an unprecedented broadening of the horizons of an individual's interest. Now the whole world is united in an unprecedented manner, and wherever important events occur, mass media and propaganda make them known all over the world in no time. So such events may very rapidly affect some facets of life in many countries. Such interconnection and interdependence of the whole world is comprehended by the majority of people and it gives rise to a permanent need for information, which creates a state of informational "hunger" if it is lacking or not sufficient. On the other hand, a personal social experience remains very limited for the majority of people because of state borders, limitations imposed on movement, or simply due to hostility and alienation. For this reason a person's picture of the outer social world ("model of the world"), which plays such an important role in the formation of the world outlook, is created by way of extrapolations, conclusions using analogy, stereotype deductions, and so on. These two factors create a unique opportunity for a state and any totalitarian organization to manipulate the flux of information and thus instill ideology in the outlook by narrowing and deforming the horizon of personal interests.

The first goal of the ideological indoctrination is to create at least a small ideological sphere inside the horizon of interests of a developing personality. It can be very small at first and partially overlap with the rest of the outlook without restricting, noticeably, the sphere of free choice. Later on, especially after a person enters the organization and starts ascension along the hierarchy, it will inevitably expand and gain autonomy. The initial stage of indoctrination is reminiscent of an inoculation ("vaccination"), of an ideological narcotic. It is even reflected in the ideological stereotypes: "to inoculate the Marxist-Leninist attitude", "to form a revolutionary conviction", and so on. As with any vaccination, the earlier it is administered, the more effective it is. This is why the initial ideological treatment starts in childhood, very often at the kindergarten level, by making kids senselessly memorize ideological slogans, sing revolutionary hymns, and repeat ideological stereotypes without understanding their meaning. Then it is continued in the same manner in elementary and secondary school. Gradually the narcotic effect creates the illusion of voluntariness, and the ideological sphere of the outlook starts to oust the personal one.

The main stage of ideological indoctrination starts with the beginning of the ascension along the steps of one of the hierarchies, and it is performed in the process of practical participation in fulfilling purely organizational tasks. The act itself of entering a totalitarian organization becomes irreversible. It immediately and drastically narrows the sphere of free choice; correspondingly, the ideological sphere broadens, and gradually interests and goals of organization starts to dominate in it. As the functionary ascends, the organization narrows the sphere of free choice still further by using purely organizational measures, and it also lowers his ability to make a free choice by deliberately shaping his demands and interests.

The latter is achieved in the following manner. In any totalitarian hierarchical organization, power and material benefits (e.g., salaries, extra material privileges, awards) are distributed in strict accordance with the hierarchical level. Therefore, the degree of satisfaction of the material demands that has already been formed is almost totally defined by the hierarchical position; and of those that are growing (and it is well known that they always are) - by the upward promotion. Whatever demands, interests and goals a functionary has when he enters the pyramid of power, later on, for the majority of functionaries, they transform in such a manner as to become almost totally focused on upward movement. In other words, promotion becomes a so-called "actualized" (dominant) demand. Therefore, behavior of a regular, average functionary (and the majority of them are like that) will be defined mainly by his assessment of the probability of promotion. Such a deformation of demands starts from the field of his official activity and then it spreads to other spheres as well. Gradually it affects the scale of moral values, and consequently deforms the world outlook.

This deformation is enhanced by the general influence of the totalitarian organization. To survive in such an organization for any considerable period of time, and moreover, to succeed in it, one needs to train specific qualities, such as unconditional devotion to the leadership, loyalty, adaptability to one's surroundings, and a mere respect towards the superiors. Very often this is not enough, and abilities to play the hypocrite, to maneuver, to conceal one's feelings and goals, to pretend, are needed too. When all these qualities are developing, one of the most specific abilities of the human brain as a means to survive in complex social conditions, as an organ of adjustability and adaptation to them is demonstrated to its fullest.[93]

How do all of these things affect the process of the ideological formation? In the course of promotion, as was shown in the previous section, the meaning of some paradigms changes, also the accents are shifted, and an element of justification strengthens. Now an element of vulgarization and cynicism is added to it too, as ideology is being "pulled" on the actualized demand. And the demand is to keep and guard the achieved level; accordingly, consolidation and fortification of the "special socium" ("us") against any danger ("them") becomes an actualized goal. Especially so after the border of special bureaucracy is crossed, when a functionary finds himself either directly at power, or in the zone of special privileges. This is where he utilizes the ability of his brain as an organ of survival to justify them! For him, revolutions are now just slow "leaps" and they always occur from above. The principle "according to work" means "according to the hierarchical position" and therefore his hierarchical existence begins to determine his ideological consciousness. Lenin's paradigm of morality, deduced from the class struggle of the proletariat, was especially convenient for him as it helped lull the annoying conscience. Ideological ideals (communism, socialism, equality and brotherhood) are little by little forced out by real interests of survival and promotion, transforming ideology into commandology, and ethics into "special ethics", containing elements of deliberate deception, lies and falsehood.

Ideological cynicism inside the socium and ideological orthodoxy for the rest of commandocracy and the world amplify the illusion of two ideologies, which was discussed in the previous section. It makes leaders of commandocracy and the majority of higher functionaries two faced: one thing is said from the rostrums (outward ideology) and different, often opposite things are said among themselves (inward ideology). This duality of commandology

---

[93]In confirmation, this is what one of the founders of bioenergetics said: "The brain is not an organ of thinking, rather it is an organ of survival, just like fangs and claws. It is constructed in such a manner that it perceives as the truth what is nothing but an advantage, and those who are able to see their thoughts through to the end completely ignoring the consequences must possess almost pathological constitution. Such people make martyrs, apostles, or scientists, and the majority of them end up in a fire or in the chair, electric or academic." (Albert Saint-Dieurdix, quoted from G. Zopf, "Relation and Context", in the collection *Principles of Self-Organization*, Moscow, 1966, p. 419). This is true especially for the functionaries of a totalitarian organization.

often requires outstanding diplomatic abilities and even artistry.[94] In reality it is a mere demonstration of the two spheres of consciousness: a personal and an ideological one, which function in different fields of existence. If such a functionary reads an original source, he learns only those things that correspond to his actualized demand and serve his changing goals. On the other hand, artistry and diplomatic skills which are so important for survival in a totalitarian organization gradually become traits of his character. Both these "acquisition" gradually "grow into the personality" and impart in it a two-faced character. A huge ideological apparatus channels this process in a desired direction. Its bit-by-bit character creates an illusion of voluntariness, an illusion of freedom of choice and even an illusion of the personal development. But in fact only an ideological sphere of consciousness is developing, which little by little forces out and deforms the personal one. At a certain stage of this process the two can even separate. In the next section it will be shown that it brings an individual to the brink of a psychiatric disease - sociophrenia.

5. Organization and Personality

A personality of any individual is formed under the influence of a concrete social environment. Changes in the environment inevitably exert pressure on a mature personality. When an individual is included in a goal-oriented organization such pressure can be especially strong as it acts upon a person purposefully. If, above that, the organization is hierarchically centralized and partially isolated (department) then the deformation of psyche can become

---

[94]The following words by Khruschev about Stalin serve as a good illustration: "Stalin is really great, even now I confirm that he was far ahead of all! But he was an actor, he was a Jesuit. He was able to act in order to show himself in a definite quality." (*Memoirs*, Ogoniok, 1989, No. 27, p. 31). Duality was akin to Khruschev himself as well, and this fact is reflected in his tomb at the *Novodevichevo* cemetery. And this is what Charlie Chaplin said about Hitler, according to his son's evidence: "While working with this scenario ["The Great Inquisitor"] father was studying his character. He got all the newsreels he could about Hitler and was watching them for hours, at home and in the studio. Among them were scenes in which Hitler, for example, talks with children, caresses babies, visits sick people in the hospitals, demonstrates his oratorical talent at every opportunity. Father memoriz.:d all poses of the dictator, copied his manners and was utterly carried away by it. 'This person is a first-class actor' - he used to say in admiration - 'We are far below him!'" (quoted from "*Inostrannaya Literatura*", 1976, No. 7, p. 144).

irreversible. Conditions of a totalitarian regime enhance these deformations and their irreversibility. What kind of deformations are they? How do they originate and develop in the process of hierarchical ascension? Under what conditions do they turn into irreversible psychic anomalies? These are the questions considered below. As they are very complicated and poorly studied, only some general considerations which follow from the previous analysis of commandocracy and its ideology will be presented.

To explain the inevitability of psychic deformations let us take note of the fact that all organizations inside commandocracy bear many features of so-called totalitarian organizations. It is such organizations as, for example, labor camps, labor colonies, monasteries, psychiatric hospitals, jails and many others. They are all characterized by a strict regulation of work, rest, and leisure, by strict limitations on movement, weakening or total loss of contacts with the outside world, narrowing of the sphere of personal choices, as well as special measures of suppression by way of humiliation. A lengthy stay in such organizations produces a characteristic anomaly which has a number of names, such as: a syndrome of social disorder, hospital and jail psychosis, and reactive psychosis. For a weaker form of psychic deformation which appears in lengthy isolated expeditions, terms "expeditional fury", "arctic psychosis" and "desert sickness" are used. Their main cause lies in the destruction of barriers which in normal conditions separate three spheres of life: night rest, work, and leisure.

Ordinary organizations within commandocracy are certainly not so totalitarian as the ones listed above, and they do not destroy all barriers between the three spheres of life. Still, in them - though to a smaller degree - a similar conflict between what a man wants and is able to do and what he is allowed to do is present. In other words, fields of demands, abilities, and possibilities do not intersect (see Appendix, Section 4). This is exactly what constitutes one of the key reasons of "syndrome of social disorder" and other like deformations. In addition to this perpetual conflict, created by organizational measures, there also exists a permanent ideological influence described earlier. This imparts a special form to the syndrome of social disorder.

Let us consider how these processes evolve in the lowest level of commandocracy. This layer differs very little from regular citizens and its most characteristic feature is a maximum degree of informational isolation and physical restraint. A complex system of coercive attachment to a certain residence area (residency permit) and place of employment, to a certain collective, restricts free socialization and free access to information. Alienation is further enhanced by a purposeful instillment of psychosis of secrecy and by a constant ideological propaganda of vigilance against "intrigues". Shortage of information cultivates social ignorance. Also, amalgamation of repressive and safeguarding organs makes people aware of their total defenselessness. On the other hand, a universal literacy, universal secondary education, availability of a higher education - all this leads to an extraordinary broadening of the horizon of interests of an individual. Resulting is a painful discrepancy between knowledge, education, wishes, ambitions, and abilities of an individual on the one hand, and the reality on the other. The lower layer of commandocracy is also characterized by the fact that, for it, the ideological unreality is maximized.[95] Formation of a personality under such conditions is known to lead to the development of the inferiority complex (below - inferiority syndrome).

Widely spread, inferiority syndrome is the most characteristic feature of the population of the lowest level of commandocracy. The key reason for such a syndrome is a discrepancy between the broadening horizon of a developing personality and the real possibilities. This discrepancy is viewed as a conflict as the illusion of voluntariness gradually fades under the blows of real facts and the coerciveness of outer restrictions and ideology becomes more and more evident. Coercions stimulate the defensive mechanisms of a person[96] and shifts interests to areas not affected by it. Such a process is always painful. The greater the narrowing of the sphere of free choice, the greater are the tensions accumulating in the central core of an individual, and the more desperately he defends himself and fights for his right of choice in the remaining small area of demands - interests.[97]

---

[95]See pp. 189-90. Unreality in the "us" and "them" interpretation inevitably leads to the unreality of "me", because "me" is nothing but an individual case of "us", its derivative. (B. Porshnev, "'Us' and 'Them' as a constituent Sign of a Psychic Community", *Materials of the 3rd All-Union Congress of the Society of Soviet Psychologists*, 1968, Vol. 3, p. 275).

[96]Forcing out (of contradictions, conflicts, and so on), suppression (by an opposite reaction), projection (re-addressing), rationalization and sublimation (switching over), and others. If they fail to operate, then such typical reactions of a person such as alienation, humility, autism (self-absorption, withdrawal from reality), deprivation, moral devastation and others emerge.

[97]Total formalization of behavior is impossible even in the most totalitarianized organization. It would mean a complete causative prediction of human actions. And this is impossible for the simple reason that psychic break-down happens before it can ever be performed resulting in a psychiatric disease.

The ability to resist and methods of self-defense depend on the innate qualities of individuals and their experience. Direct and active social protest is the destiny of very few. The majority would rather choose "peaceful co-existence" bordering with psychic breakdown,[98] or a flight in the broadest meaning: outward (immigration), inward (inner immigration or alienation), upward (ascension to power). Waves of outward immigration accompany all commandocratic regimes of our time, regardless of their location. Inner immigration is supplemented by a passive resistance and a boycott of all constructive efforts of the power.

If all attempts of a developing person to find an autonomous field of free choice turn out fruitless, then in the lowest level suppression of development, i.e., social infantilism of personality, becomes an alternative to a "peaceful co-existence" bordering with psychic breakdown. Inborn talents remain unclaimed and they die out. It is in this direction that totalitarian organization pushes all the processes. This is what it uses to instill ideology under the guise of a freely formed outlook. The "secret" of a narcotic effect of ideology lies in the illusion of free formation, because in the sphere of ideology there is no freedom of choice of alternatives. Remaining infantile, a personality just obtains some additional qualities of a "man of the masses". A man of the masses suffers neither reflexy nor inferiority syndrome; his spiritual demands are reduced or lacking altogether, and his social demands are severely deformed. Such people compose the majority of the inner environment of commandocracy and at the same time a "reserve army" to replenish its contingent. This is one of the reasons for the extraordinary success of a contemporary communist ideology.

Now let us consider commandocracy's intermediate layer. A direct road to power is ascension in one of the three major hierarchies: the party, the KGB, or the military. Choosing one of professional hierarchies is a road to knowledge. But it is also a road to power, as all hierarchies intertwine at the upper levels and ascension on any of them may end up on the ruling top. At some point, an ascending functionary obtains his own subordinates, he becomes a superior, and enters commandocracy proper. As he ascends, some measures of physical coercion become weaker, quantity and quality of the information received

---

[98]The border of the psychic abnormality has a conditional character. Sometimes a zone close to the border is separated and special terms are introduced to describe it, such as: pre-psychopathy, or psychic inferiorities. These questions are for example considered in P. Gannushkin, *Clinics of Minor Psychiatry*, Moscow, 1964).

increases, and ideological <u>unreality</u> decreases. Correspondingly, the horizon of interests and a sphere of free choice broaden. Oppositely, successful promotion in the conditions of severe competition requires a purposeful limitation of demands and interest, their total subordination to the actualized demand of promotion; it is necessary to observe strict discipline, to be loyal to the power, and so on. Besides, and this is the most important, it is necessary not only to voluntarily accept all ideological dogmas and paradigms in their formulation at a given moment in time, but to participate actively in their instillment in the lower layers of the commandocracy and the population in general. It cannot but lead to the broadening of the ideological sphere and the narrowing of the personal one.   Two new psychic deformations originate: ideological and party syndromes.

The party syndrome is characteristic of a dynamic sub-system of an intermediate layer (so-called "pacing ones" - see Chapter 4, section 3, and Chapter 5, section 2).   It originates when the demand for advancement dominates and is rooted in the organizational structure, whose characteristic feature is an impossibility to separate an individual contribution of a functionary in the general outcome of the organization's activity, which was underlined above. The sphere of free choice narrows to the utmost and a person, as if dissolved in the party, becomes "a sum total of intra-party relationships."[99] Individual will is suppressed by a collectivist will.

Cited below is Trotsky's pronouncement at the Thirteenth Party Congress in May 1924, which serves as a good example: "I know that one cannot be right against the party. One can be right only with the party and through the party, because no other ways to achieve the rightness were created by history." (Cited from Avtorkhanov, *Origination of Partocracy*, 1973, Vol. 2, p. 178). Even more characteristic is Piatakov's pronouncement:

> ...But true Bolsheviks/Communists are people of a singular cast. We are unlike anybody else, we, the party, consisting of people who make impossible things possible. Imbued with the idea of violence, we direct it against ourselves , and if the party demands, if it is needed to or important for it, then, by a willful act, in a matter of 24

---

[99]In complete accordance with Marx's definition: "Essence of man is not an abstraction, inherent in a concrete individual. In its reality, it is a sum total of social relationships" (Vol. 3, p. 3). In our case, it is intra-party relationships.

hours, we will be able to throw out of our heads the ideas which we were fussing about for years.   You are absolutely unable to understand that, you are unable to get rid of your narrow 'I' and to subordinate to a harsh discipline of a collective.   But a true Bolshevik is able to do it.   His personality is not bound by the boundaries of 'I', but it is spread all over the collective. (Conversation with I. Valentinov in Paris at the beginning of the 1930s, journal "*Slovo*", 1989, No. 11, p. 24).

It is characteristic that in the quoted pronouncements the word "ideology" is not even mentioned, which makes this syndrome different from the ideological one.

An ideological syndrome, unlike the party one, is rooted in the hypertrophied growth of the ideological sphere with its subsequent separation from the personal one.   In its boundary case it can transform into fanaticism.   Also, ideological unreality leads to the loss of ability to choose alternatives, because the possibility of choice becomes very narrow or is excluded almost altogether in the ideological sphere.   Reduction of the personal sphere relieves a functionary from a painful state connected with the pressure of organization; at the same time it relieves him of pangs of conscience.

Thus, at the middle levels of the hierarchy of power, individuals with two characteristic psychic deformation will, little-by-little, accumulate: the party and the ideological ones.   Superimposing, they produce various combinations and give rise to moral and psychic monsters, a whole gallery of them is reflected in literature.   Now what about the top of the pyramid?   What is the ultimate result of ascension to the apex of power for the personalities of those ascending?   In other words, who are they, the leaders of commandocracy possessing the total of political, economic and social power in the state?

When such a question is asked, first one thinks about a gallery of figures of the first rank: Hitler, Stalin, Mao.   Then go smaller characters: Ho-Shih-ming, Khruschev, Brezhnev, Castro.   Then go figures of the third rank, even more numerous.   Each of them is surrounded by numerous comrades-in-arms.   From the viewpoint of a normal ordinary person, they are all very weird characters, this weirdness should be inherent in both leaders and comrades-in-arms, and also in the environment that produced them.   What is so strange about them?   Very often it is said that they are fanatics of ideology, i.e., an extreme case of ideological syndrome. It means, though, that they are psychopaths, as fanaticism is a variety of psychopathy connected with lack of criticism. It is very doubtful that it is their common feature. For example, it cannot be said about Brezhnev. Another opinion is that they are fanatics of power. Again fanaticism, and again a doubt: it is hardly their common feature either. What to do with ideology then, which becomes a means to achieve power for many of them: pragmaticists of ideology and fanatics of power?

It is very difficult to answer these and other questions, first of all because in all known varieties of commandocracy, lives and activities of their tops have been a complete secret until recently. In some of them, they are a secret even now. And not only the party and state activities, but private lives as well, which could have shed some light on the spiritual world of the top and on how its concrete representatives achieve the supreme power. Secondly, it is difficult to answer them because these representatives themselves tell very little about it, even in those rare cases when they are dismissed and find themselves out of office (e.g., Molotov, Kaganovich and others). Even in such exceptional cases they do not write memoirs, do not give interviews, abstain from any frank pronouncements which would reflect their personal standpoint about past and present events.[100] This is why assumptions and guesswork become inevitable.

First, let us pay attention to the fact that neither Stalin, nor Mao can belong to either party or ideological fanatics. The same can be said about Hitler or any other second-rank figures, though with a smaller degree of probability. All of them possess elements of political pragmatism to this or that extent, while pure party or ideological fanatics can be met only at lower levels of the hierarchy of power. It follows then that in the process of ascension special conditions are created that slow down the development of both party and ideological syndromes and at the same time promote political pragmatism. What are these conditions and how are they displayed?

Speed of promotion is one of the evident conditions: neither syndrome has enough time to develop into fanaticism at a rapid upward movement, or, oppositely, they both can be forced out by political the pragmatism inherent in all bureaucrats at a slow ascension. What does the speed of promotion depend on?

---

[100]The only exception is Khruschev's memoirs. But even in them one clearly sees the helplessness of the author's attempts to somehow reconcile the ideological and personal approach to the described events (see, for example, footnotes to p. 202). Even more characteristic is the poverty of such attempts in the memoirs of A. Gromyko.

First, on the individual qualities of a functionary, which will be discussed below. Also, on rapid restructurings of commandocracy, which are usually connected with repressions, purges, and displacements. Usually it takes place in the process of the ideological struggle, in which it is fanatics who are weeded out first because of their stiffness, rigidity and clumsiness; as for political pragmatists, they enjoy all advantages in the competitive struggle and they use all of the weaknesses of the first ones in full measure. Still, no matter what advantages the pragmatists have, they are revealed selectively in the process of hierarchical selection. It is then that the bureaucratic essence of commandocracy is demonstrated, especially of its intermediate layer which plays the key role in the hierarchical filtering out.

To understand it better, let us recall the main features of this layer: the existence of two sub-systems - a dynamic and a conservative one, as well as the multiplicity of avenues to the apex of the pyramid of power (Chapter 5, section 2). The party and ideological syndromes, turning into fanaticism, are for the most part characteristic of the dynamic sub-system (so-called "pacing" ones), and on the contrary, bureaucratic pragmatism is characteristic of the conservative sub-system. However, a bureaucrat in a commandocracy ("commandocrat") possesses many new features which the conventional bureaucracy of a democratic society does not have. A single pyramid of power transforms any functionary in a commandocracy, at any level, into a protege of a ruling top, and it increases his independence of his subordinates and, in the final analysis, his general irresponsibility. Further, a typical commandocrat is not free of either the party or the ideological syndromes, but he uses them pragmatically, in his own interests, which makes him different from the party and ideological fanatics. Finally, a commandocrat is originally from the lowest level and therefore he is not free, at least at the beginning of his ascension, from either inferiority syndrome, or the psychology of a man from the mass with his uncontrollable vital cravings (Jose Ortega y Gasset).

So, in such a complicated environment, with hardly compatible features, leaders of commandocracy are formed and their hierarchical selection is performed. It was shown above (Chapter 4), that in a ruling centralized hierarchy, the highest speed of upward movement, all other conditions being equal, is enjoyed by three psychic types which, for the sake of brevity, can be called careerists, rulers, and possessors. Hierarchical selection increases their relative number already at the middle levels as they are subjected to inferiority syndrome, as well as to the ideological or party syndrome, to a lesser degree than the rest. It is so for the first two types thanks to their innate qualities that help them unfold additional means of defense against the pressure of their hierarchical surrounding. As for the third one, which is a more numerous and more important category, it works out the defense system against fanaticism gradually, in the course of ascension. For this category of functionaries, who consider their hierarchical position as their property, the slower the ascension, the lesser is the personality deformation as in this case they can develop their new territories in the sphere of acquisition, within which they are able to exercise their natural right to choose alternatives and bear responsibility for the consequences, gradually, little-by-little.

Corruption is a particular case of a much broader phenomenon, which does not have a general term yet and which comprises using office position in egoistic and personal interests; bribery, forgery, cronyism, and patronage. As this phenomenon is inseparable from bureaucratic hierarchy (Chapter 4) and is, in fact, a deformed variety of pragmatism, then we have some grounds to call it a hierarchical syndrome. And whatever is said about this bureaucratic "disease" in scientific, satirical, or humorous literature, in the considered context it is not deprived of some positive role. In a totalitarian society, in which a complete physical enslavement is supplemented with a spiritual one, under which an independent value of an individual is negated, hierarchical syndrome becomes almost the only alternative to the party and ideological fanaticism in the apparatus of power. It is one of few semi-legal forms of protest against suffocating totalitarianism. If not for it, the nightmare of social utopias of Zamiatin, Huxley, Orwell and others could have become a daily reality of our time. The ruling top of the state power, formed by the alliance of the party and ideological fanatics, armed with all means and achievements of contemporary science, would have become invincible, and would have left no possibility for protests, no social forces able to question its might. In a certain sense, hierarchical syndrome balances ideological and party fanaticism, restrains its appetites, impedes its boundless expansion, and sets some borders to it.

Thus, the greatest probability of getting promoted into the leadership is enjoyed by those functionaries who strive for power as an end in itself or a means, an in whom all three psychic deformations are balanced (the political pragmatism being the domineering one, as to a certain degree it connects the two spheres of outlook and thus impedes their complete separation, i.e., the development of sociophrenia). Thanks to this equilibrium, all they have advantages over their rivals in the struggle for power. For them both party and ideology are a mere means to achieve their political goals. And as it is well known, these means are used by them artistically. They are actors to the same degree to which they are free from the ideological snare. These outstanding commandocrats perform as arbiters in deadly skirmishes between fanatics of party and fanatics of ideology in the crucial moments of capturing or re-capturing power, and after that they often assist them in their destroying each other. This is what happened in Bolshevism.

CONCLUSION

The twentieth century is the age of totalitarianism. Opposing its two varieties - fascism on the verge of the 1940s, and communism in the second half of the centennial - brought the world to the brink of nuclear catastrophe. Only recently, a gradual stepping away from the abyss has taken shape. Will this tendency become irreversible? One cannot be completely sure of it, because the origins of totalitarianism, its roots and its "culture medium" are poorly known in many respects.

Three common misconceptions contribute to this poor knowledge. One of them is the exaggeration of the role of totalitarian ideologies. Ascribing to them a self-contained meaning which allegedly defines expansionism as an ugly practice of totalitarian regimes, endless disputes about the meaning of individual ideological dogmas as well as unending attempts to tie ideology in with economics - all these factors divert attention from the investigation of the real causes of totalitarianism. The causes lie in the character of organization, in its universality. Also, it is often underestimated that it is supporters of totalitarianism themselves who most often stimulate, aggravate, and unleash all ideological disputes.

To this a second widely spread mistake is linked - the underestimation of the role of organization, its character and, what is most important, its universality. All varieties of contemporary totalitarianism have a common root - Bolshevism. The principle of organization of the Bolshevik party proclaimed at the Sixth "unifying" Congress in 1906 and substantiated theoretically by Lenin several years before that, is known under the name of "democratic centralism". But in reality, it contains four interconnected elements: hierarchy, centralization, political professionalism, and conspiracy. Any political organization constructed on the basis of this combination will inevitably - and very rapidly - force out all elements of democracy which were allowed at its formation. Moreover, they are forced out under the pressure of inner causes of its evolution, which has been confirmed by the eighty-year-long history of Bolshevism. Further, the first three elements define, as is known, the structure and character of the functioning of any bureaucratic apparatus, while conspiracy is a pivotal element of a plot-making terrorist organization. Thus, the organizational roots of Bolshevism were born as a result of "crossbreeding" bureaucracy and mafia. This is why a true essence of "democratic centralism" can be expressed by the term "bureaucratic mafia" (or shorter - "bureaumafia").

The greatest portion of Lenin's *What Is To Be Done?* and some other pre-revolutionary works are devoted to the substantiation of the necessity for such a "crossbreeding"; explaining it by specific conditions of fighting tsarism. Nevertheless, later on neither the Bolshevik Party, nor its numerous "replicas" in other countries refused conspiracy. They could not do it though, as the combination of the above elements proved to be a very stable political "virus": it provided Bolshevism with a number of features of so-called self-organized systems, and it is these features which account for Bolshevism's universality. Such systems are very stable, conservative, and at the same time prone to expand in all possible directions. They possess an expansionist character.

Bureaucracy has accompanied humanity since the origination of states and at the same time, it is one of the most widely spread vices of contemporary states due to the advancement and complicity of problems of organization and management. Its most characteristic features are a lack of evolution, conservatism, "buoyancy", and unrestrained inward expansion (growth of a numerical value). On the other hand, hierarchically centralized and conspiratorial mafia type organizations are characterized by high mobility, flexibility, dynamism, and a high degree of the organizational gain, i.e., high effectiveness at a small numerical value. It is not difficult to imagine the result of the "crossbreeding", when dynamism and flexibility are complemented by stability and expansionism. Indeed, Bolshevism, after having consumed Russia, and finished off its totalitarian rival, has spread all over the world with the speed of fire in a number of varieties, from Trotskyism and Maoism to the Bathist regime of Saddam Hussein. The latter not only borrowed the organizational structure of Bolshevism, but its external attributes as well, putting Islam in the palace of Marxism-Leninism (Islamic Bolshevism!). Is it not a good illustration of the organization's supremacy over ideology?!

Commandocracy described in Chapter 5 is bureaumafia. It inherited from the mafia not only a conspiratorial character, but a vertical structure as well: a dome, functionaries, and buttons. Correspondingly, commandocracy has a ruling top (the command element), apparatus (headed by nomenclatura) and rank-and-file executors. A characteristic autonomy of those making decisions from those executing them is also taken from the mafia, as well as a lack of direct contact between them (separated from each other by the apparatus). The expansionism of bureaucracy is revealed in a coercive, directed from above, implanting of standard departments with the same typical structure, and in their complex hierarchical co-subordination. Its consequence is a hierarchical construction of the whole society: an individual, an elementary productive unit (crew or shops), institution, department, the state. All this is complemented by a sophisticated system aimed at disguising the special bureaucracy and, especially, the ruling top, the origins of which can be traced in Lenin's works of the beginning of the century in his idea to combine legal and illegal work. But if according to Lenin, an illegal core of professional revolutionaries was disguised inside the broad professional organization of workers (see Chapter 2), in a mature commandocracy the special bureaucracy and its top, together with their special privileges, are hiding in a special socium, which in its turn is isolated from the society (see Chapter 5, section 5).

The third widely spread misconception is the overestimation of the role of leaders as applied to the stationary stage of commandocracy, when the formation processes are completed. At this stage it is not the charismatic qualities of leaders that play the key and defining role in the functioning of commandocracy as a self-organized system, rather it is interconnections, as well as interconnections and interrelations of its sub-bystems. Personal qualities of functionaries are completely subordinated to the interrelations of office positions of the system, or, figuratively speaking, of the chairs. And if personal qualities and a chair, for whatever reason, do not correspond to each other, then one functionary is simply replaced by another. This is the essence of the laws for the system's functioning. In other words, in the process of hierarchical selection an organization forms whatever composition which it needs. Even the Secretary General is a symbol of a ruler, a specific point in a system or its symbolic center rather than a real manager. The phenomenon that can be called "leaderism", with all its attributes (size ordering, position on the tribune, positions of banners and so on), is to a great degree one of the elements called on to disguise real powers. Universality of the uniting goal, that of self-preservation by way of parasitizing the society, is also linked to the properties of self-organization. In particular, this is why all commandocratic regimes are so outrageously ineffective in social and economic fields. A blooming economy and high civil spirit have never been among the priorities of commandccracy for the very reason that rank-and-file citizens do not belong to the system, but to the outer or inner environment of commandocracy. An indefinite and mobile border of the commandocracy proper is defined by the social discrimination between "us" and "them", and citizens are always "them", and are always dealt with on the basis of the "leftover" principle.

What is the role of ideology then? First of all, ideology is a socio-political outlook of a bureaucratic organization adjusted to its tasks and goals. Of its many functions the following should be highlighted: excusatory (mainly intended for the special bureaucracy), disguising, isolating (blocks out undesired information) and subjugative (for lower levels of the apparatus and regular citizens). Besides, ideology creates the basis of the party ritual, and forms a specific language for party functionaries to communicate with each other and thus serves as a means to identify their own people in the process of hierarchical selection. This latter function changes, gradually, the composition of the ruling top, the special bureaucracy, and all of the apparatus. Together with this, a deliberate formation of the inner and outer environment of commandocracy (i.e., the whole population) is taking place. Evolution towards a totalitarian dead end becomes irreversible.

In all varieties of totalitarian regimes, ideology is worked out by a special ideological apparatus under the leadership of special bureaucracy and is thrown down on the middle and lower levels of the pyramid of power and on all citizens in the conditions of informational isolation, alienation, and repression, thus becoming an ideocracy. The sphere of regular outlook of individuals is deformed and forced out by the ideological sphere, which can even become autonomous and give rise to paralogisms in the mental processes. Ideocracy, complemented by an omnipresent and all-penetrating cobweb of power, leads to deformatities in psyche, and to the origination of characteristic psychopathies, which often take the shape of sociophrenia. Investigation of this characteristic companion of totalitarian regimes is still in store for medical science.

The work of a typical functionary of commandocracy - commandocrat - usually goes behind the scenes of public life (one of the consequences of conspiracy). Together with collective irresponsibility, which is characteristic of any isolated centralized hierarchy, it puts him beyond the control of the society. Co-existence of the two spheres in his world outlook does not only make him double-faced, but also double-languaged (Orwell), immune to criticism. The majority of functionaries have the psychology of an "insolent slave", i.e., servility before superiors (power) and at the same time cruelty and intolerance to subordinates and public in general. The two-faced nature of a commandocrat is demonstrated in the typical combination of corruptness and self-interest with the propaganda of altruistic (communist) morality. Two spheres of his outlook - personal and ideological - make possible a double standard in evaluating deeds. And as ideology is worked out and implanted by an organization, its pressure is enormous, Consequently, enormous is the amorality and inhumanity of a commandocrat.

The problem of overcoming the aftermaths of totalitarianism and preventing its relapses becomes an international one in our days due to the proliferation of nuclear weapons. And usually two ways of solving it are discussed: a permanent or a periodical tribunal of the Nuremberg type, and lustrations, i.e., a special quarantine for the members of communist parties, security officers and other active participants of totalitarian crimes. Without discussing all their "pro's " and "con's" (they are well-known) let us consider some further deductions from this analysis of totalitarianism as a self-organized social system.

One of the most evident is the decisive role of the influence from outside, as self-organized systems are not reformable from inside.   "Brown" totalitarianism was destroyed from the outside as a result of the Second World War. Red totalitarianism (communism) was also undermined and thwarted from the outside as a result of the exhausting Cold War. However, the Nuremberg process turned out to be possible and effective only as a result of the collective will of the world community, and was accompanied by the Marshall Plan and many other measures. At present, as regards communist totalitarianism, such a single will is lacking, it was lacking in the past and does not seem too likely in the future, as was demonstrated by the vain attempts to set up similar tribunals over Saddam Hussein and the Serbs of the former Yugoslavia. In short a new Nuremberg is infeasible, criminal prosecutions of the former communists are impossible and ineffective, and the decay stage of the totalitarian monster will last for a very lengthy period of time, until the sprouts of new life and new self-orgnaization start to reappear.

Criminal prosecution of participants and their accomplices is impossible for the reason that it would be difficult to specify their crimes because of the collective and conspiratorial character of the activity in all totalitarian organizations. Further, besides the psychic anomalies discussed above, members of such organizations usually do not have the freedom of choosing whether to implement or not to implement a criminal order.   Therefore, they can be considered only partially competent citizens.   Finally, there are so many participants, their accomplices and victims, that no trials are able to ensure an objective and unbiased approach. Also, added to it, is a lack of universal moral condemnation without which no prosecutions, and no quarantine lustrations can be effective. Such a condemnation is possible only in a mature civil society, but is lacking here, as the personal sphere of "citizens" is far too deformed and narrowed. In such a society, forgiving without acquitting and rehabilitation (which is sometimes suggested as a solution) will not be effective either.

All of this creates an impression of a deadlock. However, the reality is not so hopeless. Human society long ago worked out a straight road to a more humane existence, and a considerable number of states and peoples have long ago entered this road. What is not to be done is to try to invent a special road, a separate direction, justifying it by one's singular savageness, or ignorance, or, oppositely, grandeur and exclusiveness (which is all the same).

Only a democracy, even an imperfect one, under favorable outer conditions (this is where they are really needed!), is able to uncover the major and minor criminals and reveal all their accomplices. Each of them can be approached on an individual basis, though their numbers are legion; but the numbers of jurymen (voters) are not in the least small either. Each of the "former" ones can be put on the equal for all conditions of competition in his social and political fields, as his connections and hidden material means will be balanced to a certain degree by mistrust, suspiciousness, and condemnation. Gradually, a moral atmosphere favorable for such a competition will be formed. Only democracy, free press, free elections, and a parliament or other truly representative system are able to prevent a sinister alliance of the red and the brown "ones", which have already shown their horrible teeth before the Second World War, and are now threatening a new variety of scientific totalitarianism; this time that of the twenty-first century.

APPENDIX
HOMO HIERARCHICAL

1. Systems Approach to the Self-Organized Hierarchy

The word hierarchy is usually associated with a laminated pyramid with a broad base and a steep apex. However, this is a very elementary and static image. There exists another one, dynamic: a hierarchy of generations from a common ancestor. The army is a typical example of the first image, and radioactive decay an example of the second one. In the first case, the number of levels is usually described by a geometric progression:

$$N = N_0 q^{n-1} \qquad (1)$$

where N_0 is the numerical value of the zero level, q is the term of the progression. In the second case, the number of levels is usually described by an exponent:

$$N = N_0 e^{-\lambda n} \qquad (2)$$

where n is a generation's number (time), and λ is a coefficient of radioactive decay which is connected with half-life ($\lambda = 1/T$). From a mathematical viewpoint, both formulae are identical[101] and are deduced from the assumption that the rate of change of the numerical value is proportional (or inversely proportional) to the numerical value itself.

However, such an approach to the notion of hierarchy does not take into account one more aspect, which is the most important: it is that hierarchy is the principle of organization[102] of all complex systems of any nature, and it accounts

---

[101]Both formulae coincide if in the second one we put $\lambda = (1\text{-}n/n)lnq$ and take into account that for the increasing progression $q > 0$ and $\lambda < 0$ and for the decreasing one - vice versa.
[102]The complete definition runs as follows: "Hierarchy (from the Greek *hieros* - sacred and *arche* - power) is the arrangement of elements of the whole, in order from the highest to the lowest. The term is used in sociology to denote social structure of an antagonistic society, especially that of bureaucracy; in the general theory of systems - to describe any systems objects; in the theory of organization - to denote principle of management; in linguistics, a hierarchy of levels (tiers) of languages is distinguished; in the theory of graphs - a hierarchical graph (a so-called 'tree')" (*Big Encyclopedia Dictionary*, 1983, 2nd edition). This definition

for the inequality of elements, their subordination or superiority. Applied to social systems, this principle always contains an element of coercion, lends rigidity to the system, and at the same time simplifies its management.

In the theory of organization, a hierarchy is a system disintegrated into individual uniform (in the simplest case) layers (e.g., generations, levels). Their interconnection and interdependence are the subject of study. In this case, what does a "self-organized hierarchy" mean?

Let us consider the simplest hierarchical systems in human societies: an army and a bureaucracy. What does interconnection and interdependence mean when applied to them? First of all, it is the geometry or static of a hierarchy (the values of N_o and q in formula (1). It is important to know a number of other values defining the dynamics of the system, such as the probability of promotion from any level to the next one (P_{ik}, from the i-th to the k-th one), the average time of staying at each level (a so-called "virtue of long service" in the army), and values of immigration, emigration, and many others, depending upon the model accepted. Both the army and the bureaucracy are not self-organized systems; rather, they are systems organized from outside. Therefore, the model itself and its parameters are defined by the goals for which they are created, the conditions of their functioning, and the demands made on them. Numerous investigations of such systems are aimed mainly at searching for the optimum conditions for their functioning according to the goals set. The term "self-organized hierarchy" should mean, if it has any meaning at all, that all of the above listed parameters, the character of the model, and even the goals are set by the system itself. And it is the system itself that defines the conditions of the optimum functioning.

Self-organization is one of the pivotal problems in biology. An embryo is self-organized according to a certain program laid in the genes, the process of self-organizaton being inseparable from the complication. The unit of all life forms - a cell - is a self-organized and self-reproduced system. A live organism itself is a self-organized, self-reproducing, self-governing and self-instructing system. All of the above, as well as many other terms with the prefix "self", are in one way or another linked to the problems of morphogenesis or other sections of biology. And all processes connected with self-organization are controlled by the universal goal of all living things: self-preservation and survival. Self-

---

shows a typical tendentiousness (why antagonistic society?), as well as incompleteness (biology is omitted). Still, it correctly reflects the broadness of the term.

preservation by means of adaptation, self-instruction, and self-regulation - all of these are strategies for survival worked out in the process of evolution. This is why there cannot be sub-systems within an organism with their own autonomous goals that are not in agreement with the general goal of the survival of the whole organism, and of the preservation of its entirety. Such an organism would not be able to survive or to produce progeny, and it would ultimately be excluded by natural selection. After which, the population and the species would disappear.

Such is the biological credo connected with the notion of self-organization, and it helps to explain a vast number of facts, but not all of them however. The limitations of such an approach to self-organization are revealed as soon as societies of live organisms (socio-biology) are considered. For example, in societies of completely social insects, an individual specimen (organism) cannot always be considered as a self-organized system, since it is unable to exist outside of the society (see below, section 2). Similar difficulties arise when hierarchical societies of advanced animals are considered, who also enjoy signs of self-organized systems, but for whom the goal of self-organization is individual self-preservation and development of an individual and the species, rather than self-preservation of the society, as is the case with social insects. There are other examples of possible difficulties as well. The limitation of such a biological approach to self-organization is linked to the fact that a biologist usually deals with the utmost case of self-organized systems, when the goals of sub-systems are completely subordinated to the universal goal of all living things. In other words, biological credo is formulated for the case of an utmost integration of sub-systems into a single system. All social systems are not like that, therefore the notion of self-organization should be broadened for them.

The systems approach[103] partially helps to overcome the limitations of the biological approach to the study of self-organization. It originated relatively recently, but its success in many areas of knowledge (such as cybernetics, bionics, semiotics, the investigation of operations, information theory, and many others), where the main role is played by informational, relational or structural

---

[103]It is this term that is used below, rather than "systems investigation" or "systems analysis". This way the specifics of the study subject and the incompleteness of the method are emphasized. A systems approach means a consideration of complex objects as systems, concentrating attention on their disintegration into parts (sub-systems), on the intrinsic connection between them, and on the demonstration of the wholeness of the object upon its interaction with the environment (see, for example, *Big Soviet Encyclopedia*, 3rd edition).

links, is rather impressive. More modest is its success in biology and sociology, but even there it cannot be denied. This is why an attempt to apply this method to the investigation of a department (self-organized hierarchy) or a hierarchy of departments (commandocracy) seems natural.

The term "system" means literally "a whole consisting of parts". Such a definition, however, is too general to be useful. Several dozen more narrow definitions exist, each of them designed for an individual purpose of investigation. For a self-organized system, the problem of its purposeful interaction with the environment is the most important (see below). For this reason, for further study, let us assume the following definition of a system: a complex set, consisting of a number of interconnected and interdependent elements (sub-systems), which interacts with the environment purposefully and as a unified whole.[104]

With the systems approach, a multitude of natural systems are usually divided into simple and complex ones, open and closed ones, stochastic and deterministic ones, static and dynamic ones, self-organized and non-self-organized ones, and so on. Among these categories, complex, dynamic, purposeful, and self-organized systems are of the greatest interest. In such systems a part of the system can only serve as a sub-system if such a part is sufficiently independent, and yet is at the same time integrated functionally into the system, and it performs a portion of the system's general or specialized functions. Further, it should be big enough to smooth out any display of individual properties of discreet elements. But this is not all: separation into sub-systems is defined by the goal of the study and is assessed by the ultimate result.

Now, a few words about the environment - it is essential that it does not directly affect the functioning of the system. Indirect influence, however, is not only admissible, but in such systems as cybernetic ones[105] it is imperative,

---

[104]This definition is broader than the one commonly used in biology. For example, in P.K. Anokhin's work, the following definition of a system is given: "Only such complex of selectively involved components can be called a system, whose interactions and inter-relationships acquire the character of mutual co-assistance of components in obtaining a focused useful result" (See collection *Cybernetic Aspects of Brain Functioning*, Moscow, 1970, p. 25).

[105]A cybernetic system is such a complex system that includes at least two sub-systems: a managing one and a managed one. It also includes sensory, effector, deciding, and other elements.

because the system learns about the state of the environment by way of the feedback mechanism, which introduces all necessary corrections into its behavior. It may or may not introduce them, though. The incoming information does not affect the behavior of the system directly; only after a corresponding analysis and processing in the decisive elements, which are concentrated in its managing sub-system. This is about information. As for energy and matter, they must be received and even extracted from the environment, without which a self-organized system is unable to exist. Interaction with the environment is so important to it that in the case of live organisms, a part of outer the medium transforms into the inner one; it becomes totally controlled.

Broadly speaking, the process of organization means growing order in the system; for a physicist it is decrease of entropy; for a biologist it is a purposeful complication. In this respect, the only difference of self-organization is that the purpose of this complication is not brought from outside, but is defined and set by the system itself. For live organisms, it is always universal: self-preservation of an individual, a genus, a group. How is self-organization defined with the systems approach? This is one of the generally accepted definitions:

A process in the course of which an organization of a complex dynamic system is created, reproduced or refined. Processes of self-organization are possible only in systems possessing a high order of complicity and a great number of elements, links among which have a probable rather than a fixed character. Properties of self-organization are displayed by objects of a very different nature: a live cell, an organism, a biological population, biogeocenosis, and human collectives. The self-organization processes take place at the expense of restructuring the links that already exist, and building new ones between the elements of the system. The distinguishing feature of the self-organization processes is their purposeful, and at the same time natural, spontaneous character; these processes which proceed at the interaction of the system with the environment, are to a certain degree autonomous, and relatively independent from it. (*Big Soviet Encyclopedia*, 3rd edition, 1975).

Let us pay attention to the fact that all of the examples listed in this definition are related to biology, to live organisms. This is not accidental. Man has learned how to create self-regulated systems, as well as self-tuning, self-learning, self-adjusting, and many others with the prefix "self", but he did not succeed in creating self-organized ones. In all systems created by man, the two most important properties inherent in all living things are lacking: self-complication and self-reproduction. Goals are set from the outside for them. This is why the physical theory of self-organization is still making its first steps.

With the systems approach to social self-organization and, in particular, to human collectives, it would be natural to accept the above broad definition as a basis, and then introduce some corrections and limitations to it. Besides, it is necessary to introduce the notion of the degree of self-organization, which would permit the consideration of systems with low self-organization, since all social systems belong to this type.

Let us start with the clarification of the notions of a goal and a goal integration. For a live organism, a characteristic direction of activity at any given moment of time is traditionally connected with concrete goals, and the behavior conditioned by it is called purposeful behavior. Daily goals that constantly change are connected with the universal goal of survival with the help of the inborn strategy of self-preservation, which determines the dominant direction of activity of an organism. It is often asserted that the working out of an optimum strategy for survival is the essence of the evolution of species. So, if we consider a live organism as a self-organized system, and its organs as sub-systems, then a purposeful integration has the meaning of a "strategic integration", this integration being the utmost, as all poorly integrated systems are eliminated by natural selection. In cybernetics, the notion of a goal is somewhat generalized: the state of a system achieved by means of feedback. This notion agrees with the biological one, though, as each organism possesses a complex system of feedbacks.[106]

As applied to a man as a member of a socium, the notion of goal needs one more specification. A man as an individual enjoys freedom of choice and can react to influences from outside in an unpredictable manner. The larger and better organized the socium to which a person belongs, the lesser the freedom of

---

[106]"It is very comforting for a biologist-theoretician to know that any system with feedback is automatically purposeful and that the difference between an automatically directed system and a system that pursues a goal in the result of a willful effort, is purely 'intrinsic'; it cannot be confirmed reliably with the help of any control from outside" (G. Kastler, "General Principles of Analysis of Systems", see *Theoretical and Mathematical Biology*, Moscow, 1968, p. 345).

choice. Also, a man does not have a single, innate strategy for social survival inherent in all animals. This is why in social systems a purposeful integration always contains an element of coercion and is achieved in a different manner, which will be discussed later.

The interaction of a self-organized system with the environment in its most general form is considered by G. Foerster in his work "On Self-Organized Systems and Their Surrounding" (found in *Self-Organized Systems*, Moscow, 1964, p. 113). Let us reconstruct his reasoning abridging the mathematical part. To characterize self-organized systems, the parameter "degree of self-organization" is used (it was introduced earlier by Shennon under the name "excessiveness of structure"):

$$R = 1 - S / S_m \tag{3}$$

where S is the entropy of a system at a given moment in time, and S_m a maximum possible entropy of the system without its radical restructuring. Thus, at $S \ll S_m$ we obtain $R \sim 1$, and the degree of self-organization is maximized whereas at $S \sim S_m$ the degree of self-organization equals zero.

The condition of self-organization of a system in a general forms is:

$$\delta R / \delta t > 0 \tag{4}$$

or, taking into account formula (3):

$$S(\delta S_m / \delta t) - S_m(\delta S_m / \delta t) > 0 \tag{5}$$

from where two particular cases follow:

$$S_m = \text{const} \ \text{ and } \ \delta S_m / \delta t = 0$$

and consequently,   (6)

$$\delta S / \delta t < 0$$

and

$$S = \text{const}, \quad \delta S / \delta t = 0$$

and then the condition of self-organization is   (7)

$$\delta S_m / \delta t > 0$$

In the general case, the condition of self-organization contains a sum of two members, containing products $S(\delta S_m / \delta t)$ and $S_m(\delta S / \delta t)$, i.e., a complex dependence on the change of entropy.

Let us discuss the results using the example of a live organism. The stage of an embryo is the stage of creation of a self-organized system: the number of cells is growing, the sub-systems of the future organism are constructed, and the process of their purposeful integration is going on according to the plan recorded in the genes. At this stage, the entropy of the system can grow, but the determining process is the growth of S_m and R, i.e., the creation of the "excessiveness of structure". This stage corresponds to the second particular case (7). The maternal organism serves as an outer environment in this case ("an outer demon", according to Foerster) and its influence is dominant. With the transition to the stage of a mature organism, the growth of S_m gradually slows down, and S continues to grow and approaches S_m (the activity of an "inner demon"). Now the state of self-organization is supported by the release of the excess entropy, and its outflow into the environment.[107] As a result, a stationary state is established in the system, at which the difference between the inner production of entropy S_i and its outflow into the environment S_e remains approximately the same and negative: $S = S_i - S_e < 0$, and the state of self-organization is again close to the utmost one ($R \leq 1$). Only at the aging stage is the production of entropy not balanced by its outflow into the environment any longer, and the system approaches equilibrium (death): $S \rightarrow S_m$ and $R \rightarrow 0$

---

[107]According to a well-known saying by E. Schrodinger, an organism escapes an equilibrium state (i.e., death) "by way of the constant extraction of negative entropy from the environment... negative entropy is what it feeds on." (*What is Life?* Moscow, 1947, p. 101). Of course, some inner energy is needed to be spent in order to get rid of the excess entropy.

Such an approach to self-organization is more general than the traditional approach of a biologist, as it not only includes "good" self-organizaed systems, with the utmost degree of self-organization ($S \ll S_m$, $R \sim 1$), but also "bad" ones ($S \sim S_m$, $R \ll 1$), like human societies. This is not its only advantage, though: it sheds some additional light on "good" self-organized systems, such as live organisms. With such an approach, the freedom of sub-systems as one of the conditions of self-organization is explained by the existence of the two interconnected factors ("demons", according to Foerster), and at the same time by their relative independence.

For an explanation, let us look more closely at biological self-organization. In the biosphere, usually several layers of self-organization are distinguished: a molecular genetic one, an organism one, a population one, a biocenosis one and a biosphere one. For each of them, the main structure is distinguished, as well as the main process of the corresponding self-organized system - its interaction with the environment takes place within structures of a higher order. This is why it interacts with the environment "as a whole". The interdependence of outer and inner factors is a mere consequence of the indissoluble connection of all biospheric levels which themselves originated as a result of a single process of evolution of life on Earth. It is more difficult to explain the relative independence of these factors. However, it can also be comprehended if we take into account the influence of accidental factors upon the process of a co-variant reduplication, which forms the basis of the whole evolution. Mistakes (accidents) in genetic structure, their inheritance as a result of reduplication with subsequent selection of phenotypes for survival - this is what makes this basis (see Timofeev-Ressovsky in *Systems Studies*, 1970, pp. 80-83).

The state of self-organization is a stationary but unbalanced and very complicated interaction of two systems: a small one (self-organized) and a very big one (environment). The efforts of two "demons", and correspondingly two wills - an outer and an inner one - this is a conditional but a very convenient way to describe the two main strategies of survival of the small system: expansion and adaptation. The first is used at a strong inner will and a weak outer will, and the second - at the opposite ratio between them.

The above reasoning is applicable to both physical and biological self-organized systems. Strictly speaking, the terminology used above and the conclusions are applicable only to such systems. Now, what about social systems, such as departments or commandocracy? Evidently, for them no means has been found so far to attach a strict meaning and quantitative characteristics to the terms used. This is why all further considerations cannot lay claim to conclusiveness, and are nothing but a way to reason about properties of social systems.

It is natural to start this reasoning with terminology. The most difficult term is of course "entropy", and for this reason its application to social systems can give rise to the greatest number of ambiguities. Even for open physical and biological systems entropy means both a measure of the probability of a system's staying in a given state, and a reverse measure of the ability of an isolated system to change, and also a degree of degradation (dissipation) of a system's energy (loss of ability to convert into work), and many other shades too. Therefore, in respect to social systems, it is better to use the term "information", which is connected with it, rather than the term "entropy" itself.

In natural sciences, the term "information" is used in two meanings. One of them characterizes the inner structure of a system; more exactly, our knowledge about the structure. This is a so-called structural or bound information (information "in itself"), which is connected unambiguously with the entropy of the system by a thermodynamic equation. However, in any system that changes with time there also circulates "free" information, which connects different events inside the system, its different sub-sytems, as well as the whole system with its environment. In cybernetics and communication theory, this second meaning of the term is used, which, unlike the first one (the structural information) connects the source of information with its receiver (i.e., it possesses some vector properties) and directly affects the latter's behavior. That is why free information is connected with the system's goal.[108] By changing S and S_m in the above formulae to the corresponding values for information, we can considerably simplify the interpretation of individual cases and make them more understandable. Now the result of the system's functioning is the accumulated structural information, and as for the efforts of the "demons", they should be connected with the free information.

---

[108]The value of information for the receiver is defined by the following formula:

$$v = log_2 \, P_1/P_0$$

where P_1 and P_0 are probabilities of the achievement of the goal before and after and before the information is received. This ratio directly connects information with the system's goal.

In this connection the mechanism of the complex interconnection of the two factors as applied to biological self-organized systems and, in particular, to live organisms, becomes more clear.   For it, outer information, was accumulating in phylogenesis, and it also accumulates in onthogenesis.   But in the second case, it takes place only through dissemination of inner free information (efforts of the inner "demon").   Besides, free information that flows in (constantly) from outside (efforts of the outer "demon") influences the behavior of the organism only after it interacts with the inner free information, whose source is the <u>whole</u> accumulated structure.   Thus, the past meets the future in the organism, as its pre-history and history, by accumulating in the increasingly complicated structure, influence the further evolution of the system (organism-environment), i.e., the future.   For each of the self-organized levels of biosphere named above, the future is born from the efforts of the accumulated past (inner will) and efforts of higher levels of self-organization (outer will), which perform as the environment.

Also, the interpretation of the results of the systems approach to social self-organized systems becomes more natural.   For example, in a totalitarian society, the sequence of the self-organized structures is the following: an individual, a family, a production unit, a department, commandocracy, the state. Any of these systems accumulates outer information in its increasingly complicated structure as long as it retains the ability to process and utilize it, after which its slow degeneration begins, which is inevitable because of the accumulating mistakes,[109] Another advantage of using the notion "information" instead of "entropy" is connected with the definition of a system's boundary, by a means of studying flows of information, their limitation, and blockade.

2. Hierarchical Societies in the World of Animals
   (A Brief Review of Sociobiology)

The most general properties of human hierarchical societies and, in particular, the filtering properties of a hierarchy (hierarchical selection) can be illustrated by looking at examples of similar properties of societies in the world of animals.

---

[109]Brezhnev's commandocracy was exactly at this stage, at which the most important information was distorted and blockaded on its way to the decisive organs, and these organs were losing the ability to understand, process and use it.

Animals cluster into societies because this way they have more advantages: better protection against predators, better access to food, more effective protection of their territory, better conditions for breeding and protecting offspring, more effective resistance to unfavorable climatic and weather conditions and some others.   Taken together, these advantages considerably outweigh the disadvantages of big groups, such as epidemics and limitedness of food resources.   What advantage does the hierarchical character of such a society bring?   In other words, what natural demands of animals are better satisfied in a hierarchical society than in any other?

What makes hierarchical societies different is that in them all of the above listed advantages of group life are distributed among their members according to their individual qualities.   Besides, in such a society the hierarchy itself is established as a result of aggressive acts, and a hierarchical position thus won has to be constantly defended. This is why such individual qualities as physical strength, adroitness, aggressiveness, and psychic stability have to be constantly trained, and are fastened in a series of hereditary behavioral stereotypes in the process of evolution.

Encouraging individuality and aggressiveness turns out to be useful for the whole society and even the whole species, which explains why hierarchical societies are so widely spread, especially among higher animals. This advantage is provided by the fact that physically strong, adroit and psychically stable individuals make the whole society stronger and more viable thanks to their relatively greater input in the gene fund of their population. Further, as the advantages of group life grow with the growth of the hierarchical level, and disadvantages (the degree of "beating") grow in the opposite direction, then every member tries as best as it can to climb higher on the hierarchical ladder. The lifting and pulling "forces" that originate with that make the whole group dynamic.   All this leads to the accumulation of select individuals with outstanding personality and aggressiveness at the upper levels, i.e., a hierarchy works as a filter of individuals.

So, if looking at it from a certain angle, a hierarchical society works as a "factory" of outstanding and aggressive individuals. What role do weak and ordinary, i.e. "commonplace" (from a human point of view) members play in such a society?   Are they mere material for the training of the strong and aggressive ones? No, not only that, although this role is also allotted to them. If the weak ones were included in society for the sole purpose of being beaten, they would constantly have been leaving it. Such an emigration does exist, and it serves as one of the ways of spreading the population,[110] but its role is relatively small. On the other hand, not a single species has worked out a means of forcefully keeping their weak ones in a hierarchical society as humans do. No doubt the process of emigration from the society is kept within certain limits by the advantages of joint living for the weak and non aggressive ones.

What are these advantages and how are they defined? First, it is the norm to curtail aggressiveness in general and that of dominant individuals in particular. Aggressiveness is usually confined to the periods when the hierarchy is being established or restructured. But even in this case, fights rarely result in serious wounds or injuries. In quiet periods, fights give way to ritual acts.[111] Further, in many animal groups, ranks are established not only according to the principle of strength and aggressiveness. Age and life experience is also taken into account, females with cubs are made exception of, as well as the close associates of a leader. Some cases are known of stronger members defending the weaker ones. In some societies, a leader plays an important role in curtailing aggressiveness.[112] On the one hand, it reminds us of the rudiments of human morale, on the other, it imparts to a hierarchical society some elements of "democracy" including freedom to join and leave the society, and freedom of vertical movements.

Curtailed aggressiveness and the stability of the hierarchical structure over lengthy periods of time decrease the dynamism of the society, but at the same time they allow animals to do their business peacefully. Once achieved, the hierarchical position does not take much effort other than fighting to defend it.

---

[110]"In the majority of societies animals at the lowest layer of hierarchy are able to emigrate. This possibility gives them a chance to survive, especially in the conditions of over-population... The higher the numerical value the stronger is the pressure upon the subordinate members, which ultimately forces them to emigrate. They are ousted by the dominant individuals as a result of direct conflicts. The emigrant's chances to survive are small, but some of them manage to find a new habitat with favorable conditions and to occupy a dominant position there." (O. Solbrig and D. Solbrig, *Population Biology and Evolution*, Moscow, 1982, p. 439.)

[111]It was pointed out first by K. Lorenz. Examples of ritual acts are given, for instance, in R. Chauvin's *Behavior of Animals*, Moscow, 1972, pp. 97-98.

[112]For example, baboons solve their major conflicts, if not with the participation of the leader, then at least in his presence (Ibid., p. 92).

This is why it is in fact a "payment" for the previous effort of ascension.[113] This character of hierarchical "privileges" is best demonstrated in cases when the hierarchical organization of a society is combined with the territorial one.[114] As a rule, the right of an owner to a certain territory which has once been gained is not disputed any longer. To defend this territory it is usually sufficient to demonstrate a "ritual of aggression".

To better offset the distinctive quality of this "hierarchical way of adaptation" of species that live in societies, let us compare it with the way characteristic of social insects. The society of bees has one member who can be compared to the dominant member of a hierarchical society. It is the queen, the pregenitor of the whole family. However, her exclusive (at least the key one) "profession" is laying eggs. In all other respects, the queen is absolutely defenseless, and working bees kill her in cold blood as soon as she becomes unable to perform this duty satisfactorily. Who sentences her to death and and how this verdict is carried out is, as yet, unknown, but it is done promptly, with no right of appeal. The only function of another specialized caste - drones - is to make a single attempt to fertilize the queen in the air during their short life (about two months). Out of a multi-thousand population only a few (and not always) succeed in doing this. They are not armed with any means of defense and are even more helpless than the queen. Finally, the last part of the population is the working bees. Each of them goes through consecutive stages of development during its short life (no more than two months in summer), and carries out various "public" work for the family, different at each stage. These stages do not make a hierarchy of the society, however, as they are defined by the physiological stages of the organism's development.[115] Unlike hierarchical

---

[113]Especially if we take into account that the hierarchical position itself often depends on the "history of previous victories and defeats" (O. Solbrig and D. Solbrig, *Population Biology and Evolution*, Moscow, 1982, p. 438).

[114]Territorial societies are often considered as a variety of hierarchical ones, which originate with a low population density. Their characteristic feature is that it is an owner who always dominates on "his" territory. Hierarchical society can at the same time be a territorial one (Ibid., p. 440).

[115]The first three days of life a working bee cleans cells and the hive, then it feeds the larvae with honey and bee-bread. From the sixth to the fourteenth days it develops milk glands and feeds larvae in a different manner. Beginning from the tenth day, its wax glands start to function and it can begin constructing honey-comb. It does not fly out of the hive to collect

societies, this sequence of stages does not contribute to individual development, they are mere stages of specialization. Therefore, the evolution of all social insects goes along the lines of specialization rather than individualization.

If the statement that the "social way of existence turned out to be an effective means to maximize individual adaptability" (see Dewsbury, *Behavior of Animals*, Moscow, 1981, p. 108) is true, then hierarchical societies and societies of social insects can be considered as two alternative ways of such a maximization. In the case of social insects, it is reduced to the utmost specialization and de-individualization of an individual specimen, utmost to such an extent that the specimen blends with the society, becomes like its cell and is unable to exist outside the society.[116] Oppositely, in hierarchical societies the specialization of a member is minimal, and many individual features are developed to their utmost. Such societies are changeable because of their inner dynamism. They are inherent in all higher animals including man, whereas societies of social insects are very conservative and their species changed very little over millions of years.[117]

These two directions of evolution can be compared with two types of social psyche, alternative in many respects. One of them, typical of hierarchical societies, is for the most part based on the rivalry among individuals within the society, and the other, typical of social insects, is based on their on-going cooperation, and at the same time, on the irreconcilable hostility to the specimens of the same species but from another society. If to use human notions, the motto of the first one is subordinated to the stronger one and chasing the weaker one (without killing him) while the motto of the second could be subordinate to the ritual, or law of being, set once and forever, according to which an individual family enjoys complete equity and brotherhood within its borders and mercilessly destroys any outside intruders who attempt to

---

nectar until the age of fourteen to eighteen days, and it ends its life as a guard at the entrance to the bee-hive.

[116]"In essence, what we speak about are not societies, rather, as I will explain later, they are true organisms. And if it is so, then only a bee-hive, only an ant-hill makes a definite reality, as for a single bee, or a single ant - they become kind of an abstraction... In the world of insects an individual is consumed by the society with remarkable consistency." (P. Chauvin, *From Bee to Gorilla*, Moscow, 1965, pp. 19-20).

[117]Origination of social insects is considered to have taken place in the second half of the Mesozoic epoch (100-150 million years ago). There are about 500 species of completely social bees and they have not changed for about forty million years.

violate its wholeness.[118]   Here the main division is between "us" and "them": individuals of the same kind but from a different group.   In the hierarchical psyche, the division is between "me" and "him", as for "us" and "them", this division is pretty vague.   This is why freedom to leave the society or to join it, as well as freedom ("right") of vertical movements, are unalienable elements of hierarchical democracy.

3. Distinguishing Features of Human Hierarchies

It is assumed that what makes humans different from animals is their well-developed brain and, consequently, more advanced intellect and psyche.   In its turn it means that humans represent a much broader spectrum of individualities. The diversity of human mental and psychic characteristics is remarkably greater than that of sizes, heights, physical strength, and other similar features.   This is why one may expect that the hierarchical societies of our ancestors were more complicated and numerous among the Primates.   The possession of articulate speech promoted the creation of amore sophisticated and advanced system of communication and thus made possible even further growth of societies.

However, humans possess one more distinguishing feature alien to animals ,which does not follow from their more advanced brain and more complicated psyche: it is their unprecedented aggressiveness towards their own species.   No other animal victimizes and destroys representatives of its own kind with such a persistence and fanaticism as humans do.   This feature of *Homo Sapiens* leaves its indelible mark on the character of human hierarchical societies.

Hierarchy in the societies of animals is always established as a result of aggressive acts and therefore it is unalienable from aggression.   However, only those species survived in the process of evolution which, together with a hierarchical form of societies, worked out an effective means to curtail intra-species aggressiveness.   The main of them is the inborn prohibition to kill representatives of one's own species no matter whether they belong to the same

---

[118]The wholeness of a bee family and its unity are established in the on-going process of sharing food, a special sound background and gas composition in the hive, as well as extraction of specific volatile substances - pheromones (several dozens of them!). A singular odor of the nest is an "ID" which helps discriminate between "insiders" and "outsiders". When a strong family attacks a weak one, the effective defense of the nest usually lasts for about one half hour, until the queen who symbolizes the wholeness of the family is killed.

society or not. This prohibition also decreases isolation of societies and, consequently, the harmful influence of inbreeding. The ways of keeping under control intra-species aggression which were considered above, are typical of the whole family of Primates except *Homo Sapiens*. Humans had evidently inherited them from their ancestors as well, but then they lost them for so far unknown reasons.

The hypothesis that this unconditional reflex was lost in the "time of unrest" in the group relationships, when the species was formed and when several close forms of *Homo* existed simultaneously and had to ferociously fight among themselves for existence, seems to be most probable. The epoch of *Pleistocene* with its four periods of glacial invasions created very specific and very difficult conditions for survival, especially for such a relatively weak creature as *Homo Sapiens*, deprived even of the cover of hair to protect him against the cold. However, such an assumption cannot be considered separately from the whole of the survival strategy. After all, *Homo Sapiens* differed from other *hominids* not only by his escalated aggressiveness, but also by higher sexuality, walking in the upright position and many other features. Besides, he has to be classified as a territorial predator, which is also an exception among Primates. It is the acquisition of such qualities that makes up the survival strategy.

The time sequence of all these new acquisitions and their inter-connection have not been studied well so far. However, for the study of hierarchical societies the most important and even crucial point is that *Homo Sapiens* survived the struggle for existence as a social creature, which is evidenced by the excavations of their most ancient settlings. According to these excavations, these societies had really been more complex and comprised more members than what had been established for their relatives and ancestors. And this is in spite of their elevated intra-species aggressiveness! This means that the new survival strategy was aimed at the survival of a society, most probably, of a big isolated group - a genus.[119] In its turn it means that his new survival strategy was really

---

[119]The family is believed to have been the main social group at the earlier stages of human history (O. Solbrig and D. Solbrig, *Population Biology and Evolution*, Moscow, 1982, p. 268). A book by D. Johanson and M. Edey, *Lucy* (Moscow, 1984, pp. 237-52) provides a detailed discussion of a hypothesis according to which it is a twosome family that lies at the origins of *Homo*, and that its origination is connected with the erect-walking and the change of the reproduction strategy at the earliest period of the species formation.

forced out in the field of inter-group relations at the very beginning of human social evolution. This is where the unconditioned reflex forbidding to kill those of one's own species could have been lost. This fact had tragic consequences for the whole social evolution of the species.

Let us look at some of these consequences more intently and pay special attention to the changes in psyche. Any live organism accumulates the records of its ancestors' "experimenting" and stores them in its genes, its subconscious, instincts, behavioral stereotypes, psyche, and so on. Man is not an exception in this respect. Therefore the hierarchical (individualist) psyche considered earlier, behind which stands millions of years of evolution, could not be completely forced out by an alternative (collectivist) psyche accumulated over a considerably shorter evolution of the species. If at the first stage of evolution an individual was the unit of selection, and at the second one - a society, then one would expect that elements of both types of psyche superimpose, intertwine and penetrate each other.

As it was stressed earlier, the division into "us" and "them" is one of the bases on which the collectivist psyche rests, and "us" can be defined not only by appearance, but also by odor, as is the case, for example, with social insects (see footnote 117). In spite of such a distinct separation, a single isolated family cannot exist for any lengthy period of time: mating with "outsiders" is needed for the sake of the inflow of fresh genes. This is why the isolation of a bee family is never total, and fights with "outsiders" almost never stop at the entrance to the hive. On the contrary, in the hierarchical psyche, the division into "us" and "them" does not play as important a role as a "me" (an individual) and "him" (a rival) squeezed in between them. Relationships with a rival and a competitor become a defining factor of social life. If we assume that intra-group aggression was forced out into the field of inter-group (later on - inter-tribal, inter-racial, and so on) relations when the initial social cells were formed, then inside the groups it could only be suppressed. "They" simply hid and got new faces. The psychology of subordination to the stronger and persecution of the weaker did not disappear, and could not disappear, as it was already inborn; tied to innate acts of behavior. The unconditioned reflex "do not kill" anyone of your own type did not disappear, but was only weakened, or split. The prohibition now encompassed members of one's own society only, and excluded an enemy. And if at the beginning of the transition period a Neanderthal man, for example, was an enemy, then later on it was some closer "dissident", very little different from a typical representative of a society, but who was still an alien.

At that point the psychology of suspiciousness and distrust was added to the original psychology of inequality and persecution, complemented with the psychology of equality and obedience. It was supported and aggravated, on the one hand, by permanent inter-group wars, and on the other - by this very similarity of one's own folk and the aliens; by their belonging to the same species and even to the same population. It is because an "alien" can always pretend that he is not an alien, and join the society, while such a thing would be impossible for a bee. Little by little and at an increasing rate the unconditioned reflex " do not kill" started to be violated in the intra-group relations as well and was replaced by various "taboos". Since then distrust, suspiciousness, instability, and oscillations have become permanent satellites of *Homo Sapiens* throughout his social history.

The superposition of other elements of alternative types of psyche turned out to be as peculiar as, and no less contradictory than, the above. Strict subordination to the pre-set ritual, equality, and the brotherhood of "professionals" of the collectivist psyche overlapped with the freedom and democracy of the hierarchical one. It gave rise to the dream about freedom, equality and brotherhood in a society filled with rivalry, suspicion, and distrust. The inevitable overpopulation of the lower levels in isolated hierarchical societies left, in its turn, its mark on this combined psyche. Intelligence, boldness, resourcefulness, initiative and foresight - all of these individual qualities were trained and practiced less and less. The field in which they could be applied, narrowed. Hierarchy as a means to "produce" strong individuals transformed itself into a "factory" of the weak ones. Accordingly, the inner dynamism of societies went gradually down, since it was sacrificed to the outer dynamism which was important for inter-group, inter-tribal and inter-racial wars. Now societies with greater membership and better unity became more viable than those with better inner dynamism: the great "editor" of nature - natural selection - started to work at a societal, rather than an individual level. All these processes lead to the destruction of the social hierarchy, to the alteration of the role of the leader, to the restructuring of all inter-group relations and, finally, to the establishment of an anti-hierarchical system, which is usually called "primitive communal" or "primitive tribal" communism.

However, an inborn hierarchical (individualist) psyche backed by millions of generations of human evolution, did not disappear, but rather was temporarily suppressed, and driven into the subconscious, creating intrinsic contradictions in the political, and economic, social structures of any society, in any human organization and even in any individual.   The accumulating intrinsic contradictions were released in a fierce explosion, which laid the foundations for the creation of states and civilizations. This contradictory dichotomy of psyche is also revealed in the case of an isolated hierarchical society (a department and commandocracy which is of interest to us. First,this contradiction is revealed in the fact that such a society inevitably splits along the vertical into two isolated parts as soon as its numerical value exceeds a certain critical level, with one of the alternative types of psyche dominant in each of them.   The character of hierarchical selection changes too: on the one hand, it acquires some features of the group selection inside the society, and on the other - it enhances individual rivalry by channeling individual wills, often almost exclusively, in an upward movement along one of the many social hierarchies. The vector of hierarchical selection and the will of the individual (as well as his psyche) became split.

4. Informational Theory of the Will[120]

Disputes about the notion of "will" have already been on the surge for two centuries. The most narrow definition of the term is: "Power to choose activity and to exercise an inner effort needed to implement it" (Big Soviet Encyclopedia). Straight after these words an addition is made: "It is a specific act which cannot be reduced to the consciousness and activity as such" (Ibid., which evidently invites a reader to make generalizations. As for the broadest definition of the term, it is given in voluntarism: "The highest principle of existence and consciousness" (Schopenhauer: "World as will and presentation"), i.e., will is deeper than reason and goes before it.   The narrow definition is related to man and to the "conscious" will, and the broad one - to nature as a whole.

Let us not go deeply into the discussion of terminology;   instead, let us focus on the rational elements of voluntarism. Self-organization is a "continuous adjustability to the continually changing inner and outer conditions of existence,

---

[120]This section was added as a response to some questions discussed by V. Chalidze in his book Hierarchical Man.

and a <u>continuous perfection of behavior</u> under the unchanging conditions with the <u>previous experience taken into account</u>."[121] (underlined by the author). As applied to any self-organized system, the will can be defined as an element of the self-preservation strategy, i.e., an element of the homeostasis mechanism in the broadest meaning of this term. Let us use this broad definition as a starting point, and later on we will clarify and specify it, first for biosphere and then for the sociosphere, and, in particular, for a man.

Levels of self-organization of biosphere listed above (p. 222) are hierarchically connected among themselves by a common origin, and by the exchange processes (of information, matter, and energy), and, therefore they cannot be considered separately. For each level it is mainly the previous level which serves as a source of inner information, and the levels above it - as a source of outer information. In this manner, for an organism that occupies a central place in this sequence, a genotype and the experience, accumulated in ontogenesis, will be the source of inner information, and population, biocenosis and biosphere - the source of the outer one. Accordingly, it is necessary to differentiate between the reactions to these two types of information (for a man it will be emotions).

Here it is important to underline two significant circumstances: not all signals mean information, but only those that are perceived by the system, i.e., connected with its demands (needs). The second circumstance is linked to the vector character of information: its affect on the organism depends not only on the receiver, but on the source as well. Free information accumulated in genotypes, over the whole phylogenesis, becomes structural information.

Information accumulated in the ontogenesis (experience of the organism transforms into the structural one in the consciousness (memory) and in the subconscious sphere (the super-conscious, the over-conscious, intuition, and so on).

According to the informational theory of emotions (G. Simonov, D. Price, J. Barrell) "emotions are defined by an actual demand and the possibility of its satisfaction, characterized by the probability of the goal achievement. Assessment of this probability is performed by an individual on the basis of both, individual inborn experience, and that acquired earlier in life, by automatically comparing information about the means, time, and resources presumably needed

---

[121]It is one of the broadest definitions of self-organization belonging to G. Foerster (*Self-Organized Systems*, Moscow, 1964, p. 6).

to satisfy the demand with the information incoming at a given moment." ("Psychology", Dictionary, Moscow, 1990, p. 462). In this process, growth of the probability leads to positive emotions, and vice versa. The sequence from demands to actions (demands → interests → goals → emotions → actions) does not contain a notion of will; the latter is exposed only if there is resistance. And this is not normal, since the role of will is not taken into account at the actualization of demands, selection of a goal and means of achieving it.

Let us enhance the scheme as applied to an organism, using the definition of will given above. The demands, abilities, and possibilities of an organism can be considered as three discrete spaces. Demands and abilities are products of emotional development of the system "organism - environment", while possibilities are for the most part defined by incoming information at a specific moment of time. Structural information accumulated in phylogenesis and ontogenesis is a source of an inner free information which, in its turn, influences formation of demands and, what is more important, abilities. The will of an organism to self-preservation as an element of the homeostasis mechanism, is revealed in the comparison of outer and inner free information, with the subsequent inclusion of psyche and the transformation of potential abilities and possibilities into real ones, i.e., into actions.

Such is a rough scheme. Let us consider it in more detail, highlighting the role of the will. Discrete space of demands is, as known, hierarchical. On the top of the hierarchy one or several most important, i.e., actualized, demands are located at any given moment of time. Under the influence of inner and outer free information actualization can change. The first and the most important act of the will, is the choice of a top priority demand. After that, its satisfaction becomes a dominant goal, and inner and outer signals transform into information. This act can be either conscious, when information is analyzed by the brain, or unconscious.

The second act of will is the assessment of the probability of a goal's implementation. To do that, additional energy (effort) is needed for comparing the spaces of potential abilities and possibilities. It is evidently achieved by conscious or unconscious sorting out and comparing of individual members of these spaces and separating those of them that coincide, and, taken together, they form a sub-space of possible realizations. The third and the last act of will is the inclusion of the emotional sphere and, consequently, all energy of the organism, after which an action follows.

Turning on psyche is a threshold effect which demands relatively little energy just like sorting out the alternatives (struggle of motives). Consumption of energy on a willful act grows only when there is an outer resistance or when difficult alternatives are considered.   Usually, only this is considered a demonstration of will.

This is how matters stand as applied to a live organism and, in particular, to a man when one of the varieties of will (conscious will) coincides with the conventional (mundane) understanding of the term. How to deal with other self-organized systems, for which the clarity of the notion is lost?

The homeostasis mechanism of any self-organized system is aimed at preserving the main structure (structural information), by maximizing the suppression of the uncontrolled influence of the environment.   The main preserved structures are known and studied for all levels of biosphere: it is genom for the cell, genotype (and the constancy of the inner environment) for an organism, gene fund for population, and species composition of organisms for biocenosis. The ability of this structure to change slowly in response to the changes in the environment (adaptation) means the birth of the inner free information. Its comparison with the outer one can be considered as the first and main function of the system's generalized will. This links the demand of the system to preserve structural and functional organization with its demand to adapt in the conditions of the constantly changing outer environment. Since any self-organized system is stationary but unbalanced, there is a necessity for some sensitive mechanism that registers all departures from the stationary state and returns the system to a new state of stationary functioning at all dangerous deviations. Estimation of such a deviation and turning on this mechanism can be considered as two other functions of the system's generalized will for self-preservation.

Let us go back to man; what additions are needed in order to consider a socium?   A regular biologic sequence of self-organized structures is complemented by two more members, as it is shown on the following scheme:

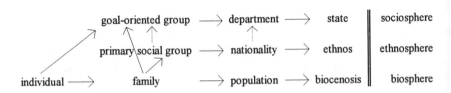

It means first of all, that the number of channels of outer information increases, and the accumulated inner structural information makes two additional layers and forms two additional types of demands: social-ethnic and social. The homeostasis mechanism becomes considerably more complicated, and interpretation of the notion of will as one of its elements becomes more complicated too.

First, let us consider an idealized case of minimal interference of the state with the private life of its citizens (a free democratic society), when each structure of the upper row of the diagram can be considered self-organized, i.e., it possesses self-government, and keeps under full control influences of the environment and is able to adapt to them. Then, for each of these structures we could construct a mechanism of the social homeostasis, introduce the notion of the collective will, find out its role in the mechanism, and so on. It does not seem to be of practical interest or perceptional value though. In a free democratic society all such structures are too changeable, and participation of an individual in each of them can be very brief and therefore may not leave traces neither in the heredity nor in the subconscious, or behavioral stereotypes. Therefore, the corresponding flow of inner information is lacking, and all outer information influences only the space of possibilities, but not the space of abilities and demands (needs). One might conclude from this that the upper social sequence by itself has very little influence on will, psyche and human behavior.

However, this is not true, because the influence of the intermediate social-ethnic sequence is not taken into account. The role of this sequence turns out to be crucial for understanding human nature and human social history. Formation of two alternative types of psyche at the first stage of the social evolution (before the origination of states) considerably complicated the relationship between biologic and social factors and at the same time enhanced the influence of the latter on human behavior and human will.

Separation of a single psyche into two alternative ones is directly linked to the division of demands into individual and collective (social-ethnic) ones, which means the split of the primary goal. "Everything for an individual" is the motto of the first of them. "Everything for the society" is the motto of the other. They both are combined in one person, but one of them dominates when the person's dependence from the social surrounding is minimized, and the other dominates when it is maximized, as is always the case in a rigid, highly centralized totalitarian system. According to it, two types of will should be distinguished: an individualist and a collectivist (conditionally outer) ones. Now when the space of potential abilities and possibilities is compared, one of the two alternative types of psyche switches on, and the mechanism of the will is complicated by the problem of a choice between the two, by their inter-connection and interaction. This is what makes the influence of the upper social sequence of structures stronger. Now the collective will of the goal-oriented social system (a goal-oriented group, a department, the state) is fortified by the collective will of the corresponding social-ethnic structure (see dotted-line arrows in the scheme). The bigger the society, the better it is organized and the more definite its goals are, the greater this influence is.

Such a duality is characteristic of any self-organized system, not only of man, as in each of them the past joins the future (see above, p. 229). Every individual is an element of biosphere, ethnosphere and sociosphere, therefore for any individual the future is born out of all the accumulated past (inner will) and efforts of higher biologic, ethnic and social levels of self-organization (outer will), which often perform merely as the environment. In a man this duality is demonstrated in the duality of the accumulated structural information, in individualist and collectivist demands, in the duality of the self-pereservation goals, in the duality of the will and psyche, and in many other things.

Social hierarchy can be considered as a means of the maximum realization of this duality. A hierarchical society makes it possible to combine both alternative types of psyche in each of its members in the best possible manner, and by so doing, satisfies in the best possible manner both the individualist and collectivist demands simultaneously. Also, the problem of choice, which often paralyzes a man as a member of society, is made easier. The role of hierarchy also grows because it ties up all three sequences of structures: a hierarchy of generations is created by the family (biosphere), every primary social-ethnic commonality (ethnosphere) is hierarchical, and finally, any goal-oriented social organization (sociosphere) is hierarchical too. Therefore, the hierarchical nature of man is rooted not only in his subconscious, but in his heredity as well. All this makes a man not only *Homo "Sapiens"* but also *Homo "Hierarchical"*.

BIBLIOGRAPHY

Albrow, M., *Bureaucracy*, London, 1970.

Anokhin, P., *Cybernetic Aspects of the Brain Operation*, 1970.

Arendt, H., *Origins of Totalitarianism*, 1951.

Avtorkhanov, A., *Origins of Partocracy*, 1974.

Burlatsky, F., *Maoism and Marxism*, Moscow, 1967.

Chalidze, V., Hierarchical Man, Terra Publishers, 1991.

Chaplin, Ch., *Inostrannaya Literatura*, 1976, #7.

Chauvin, R., *Behavior of Animals*, Moscow, 1972.

Chauvin, R., *From Bee to Gorilla*, Moscow, 1965.

Dewsbury, D., *Behavior of Animals*, Moscow, 1981.

Dostoyevsky, F., Diary of the Writer

Foerster, G., "On Self-Organized Systems and their Environment" in *Self-Organized Systems*, Moscow, 1964.

Galbraith, J., *Industrial Society*, Moscow, 1969.

Galbraith, J., *Economic Theories and Goals of the Society*, Moscow, 1976.

Galkin, A. A., *German Fascism*, Moscow, 1967.

Gannushkin, P., *Clinical Picture of Minor Psychiatry*, Moscow, 1964.

Go Mojo, *Philosophers of Ancient China*, Moscow, 1961.

Grant, W., *Evolution of Organisms*, Moscow, 1980.

Johanson and Edey, *Lucy*, Moscow, 1984.

Johnson, R., Cast, F., and Rosenzweig, D., *Systems and Management*, Moscow, 1971.

Kafka, F., *Process*

Kafka, F., *Castle*

Kardin, V., *Ogoniok* Weekly, 1990, No. 19.

Kastler, G., "General Principles of Analysis of Systems" in *Theoretical and Mathematical Biology*, Moscow, 1968.

Khruschev, N., Memoirs, in *Ogoniok* Weekly, 1989, No. 27.

Kuhn, T., *Structure of Scientific Revolutions*, Moscow, 1962.

Kontinent, 1975, No. 2.

Lenin, V., *Complete Work*, 4th and 5th editions.

Makarenko, V. P., *Faith, Power, and Bureaucracy*, Moscow, 1988.

Manhaim, K., *Ideology and Utopia*, Frankfurt on Main, 1969.

Marx, K. and Engels, F., *Complete Work*

Montesquieu, Ch., *Spirit of Laws*, Moscow, 1955.

Neizvestny, E., "Lik, Litso, Litchina", *Znamya* Monthly, 1990, No. 12.

Perelomov, L., in *China, Society and State*, Moscow, 1973.

Pierls, R., *Construction of Physical Models*, UFN, 1983, Vol. 140.

Porshnev, B., "'Us' and 'Them' as a Constructive Feature of Psychic Commonality" in *Materials of the Third All-Union Congress of the Psychologists Society*, Vol. 3, 1968.

Porshnev, B., "Function of Choice as a Personality Foundation", in *Problems of Personality*, Moscow, 1969, Vol. 1.

Rostow, *Stages of Economic Growth*, Moscow, 1954.

Schrodinger, *What is Life?*, Moscow, 1947.

Sent-Deaurdi, in *Principles of Self-Organization*, Moscow, 1966.

Shanyang, *Book of the Ruler of District Shan*, Moscow, 1968.

Shepanski, Ja., *Major Concepts of Sociology*, Novosibirsk, 1967.

Shuhb, D., *Political Activists of Russia*, 1969.

Soddy, F., *History of Nuclear Energy*, Moscow, 1979.

Sokolnikov, G., A Letter to N. Krestinski, *Izvestia*, March 11, 1989 (article by Sirotkin, F.).

Solbrig, D., *Population Biology and Evolution*, Moscow, 1982.

Solzhenitsyn, A., *Kontinent*, 1975, No. 2.

Spencer, G., *Foundation of Sociology*, 1898, Vol. 11.

Timofeev-Ressovsky, N., in *Systems Studies*, 1970.

Tkachev, P., *Collected Work* in 2 volumes, 1976, Vol. 2.

Vlasov, Ju., *Junost* Monthly, 1988, No. 10.

Volkenstain, M., *Entropy and Information*, Moscow, 1986.

Voslensky, M., *Nomenklatura*, 1984.

World History in 10 volumes, 1955-60.

Zaionchakovsky, P. A., *Government Apparatus of the Autocratic Russia in the 19th Century*, Moscow, 1978.

With the exception of Albrow, all other sources are Russian publications, in Russian.

English translations of Marx, Engels, and Lenin used:

The Essentials of Lenin in 2 volumes, Hyperion Press, Inc., Westport, Connecticut.

Lenin, V. I., *Selected Works*, International Publishers, New York.

Marx, K. and Engels, F., *Selected Work* in 2 volumes, Foreign Languages Publishing House, Moscow, 1962.

Tucker, R., ed., *The Marx-Engels Reader*, Princeton University, W. W. Norton & Company, Inc., New York.

INDEX